7 Deadly Sins of CORPORATE MISMANAGEMENT

What they don't teach in business schools

SEVEN SINS OF MISMANAGEMENT

Of the numerous sins of mismanagement committed by senior managers and entrepreneurs on a daily basis, the following ones occupy the first seven positions.

1. Mismanagement of Human Resources
2. Mismanagement of Financial Resources
3. Mismanagement and Decision-making
4. Mismanagement of Talent and Technology
5. Mismanagement of Markets and Customers
6. Mismanagement of Communication
7. Mismanagement of a Crisis.

When a reader travels through the pages of this work, he or she is bound to alter and/or extend the above list.

AUTHOR'S NOTE

This is to certify that the contents of this book are primarily based upon factual corporate work-life situations, through which the author has passed, during his over 40 years corporate career. No part of this work rests upon any imagination or fiction. It mirrors the reality of the corporate work environment, in factual form, as a first-hand experience.

7 Deadly Sins of CORPORATE MISMANAGEMENT

What they don't teach in business schools

DR. UDAI VIR SINGH

PENTAGON PRESS

7 Deadly Sins of Corporate Mismanagement / *Dr. Udai Vir Singh*
Includes preface and index

ISBN 978-81-8274-409-7

First Published in 2009

Published by
PENTAGON PRESS
206, Peacock Lane, Shahpur Jat,
New Delhi-110049
Phones: 011-64706243, 26491568
Telefax: 011-26490600
email: rajan@pentagon-press.com
website: www.pentagon-press.com

Printed at
New Elegant Printers
Mayapuri Phase I, New Delhi-110064

Preface

The idea of this book germinated because the author, during his long and intense exposure to the corporate world, closely witnessed a multitude of mismanagement situations;

- damaging corporate outputs, competitiveness, and bottom-lines,
- creating varied levels of work environment related stresses,
- cutting short or damaging several bright careers,
- unrighteous distribution of performance-related credit and discredit, and
- numerous other negativity-bred performance depressing manifestations.

The study of mismanagement on wider scale led to the unveiling of the extent of damage that this anti-productivity monstrosity is capable of inflicting upon a corporate work environment, its competitiveness and, in some cases, its very survival in a productive mode.

Any intention or effort of freeing the corporate work environment from the ill-effects of mismanagement had to be backed up with a thorough understanding—particularly its genesis, spread, containment and/or control: Its eradication, as per its very nature, is not possible. The evil of mismanagement seems to have been endowed with energies of omnipotence and omnipresence. Yet, it seems possible to contain it within harmless levels, with suitable handling and training of the human resources of the victim corporate.

While handling situations of mismanagement, or avoidable failures, in practical corporate environment, as per some management experts, consumes a major part of management time and energy, modern management literature, Indian as well as Western, is fully devoid of any helpful details in this regard. While management gurus and teachers seem to have forgotten to deal with the phenomenon of mismanagement, **Lord Krishna**—the master manager of humanity—had dwelt upon its manifestation, wherever and whenever unrighteous and evil forces gained dominance upon the virtuous. He discoursed to **Arjuna**, in relevant detail, how the ***tamsic*** forces of anger, greed, selfishness, attachment, unrighteousness, and lust could lead to delusion of thought as well as action, which without fail caused fertile conditions for mismanagement.

Since a task should never be left incomplete, the malaise of mismanagement had to be given a fitting treatment, so that management practitioners, teachers and students could have recourse to dependable means of dealing with it, in all possible effectiveness. The present work had to be taken to its logical conclusion.

Beyond Business Schools

Business schools do not teach anything about mismanagement. It is not part of their curriculum: AICTE, the central authority that governs and approves curriculum for management schools, does not specify it as one of the inclusions for its MBA and other courses. They do not probably like to scare the young minds engaged in the study of management with this malaise of the corporate world. However, being aware, even of an undesirable eventuality, is not bad: Being forewarned is like being fore-armed.

It is, however, more difficult to comprehend why the executive training and retraining programmes too do not touch the crucial aspect of mismanagement.

A study of this work, in the view of the author, will help practitioners of management, young and old, professionals and otherwise, to be in a better position to face this evil manifestation of the corporate world when they encounter it in any form.

Even a preliminary ability to understand and appreciate the measures described herein for containing the malaise of mismanagement, as and when encountered, will be of immense utility. In all possibility, what is said and detailed in this work is likely to act as a performance acceleration recipe for the mismanagement victimized sections of the corporate world.

Corporate Mismanagement—Impact on Common Man's Life

The September 2008 crash of the US financial markets, the most serious since 1929, sent over half a dozen of its leading financial institutions and corporates running for cover and—begging for relief and protection from the Federal Reserve and the US Government, amounting to US $700 billion, affected almost all aspects of the common man's life in USA.

Also, it sent a chilling impulse down the spines of almost all the major world markets, including those of the emerging economies of Asia, India and China. It was not difficult to assess how the investment active public of the major economies of the world suffered.

The US economic meltdown was undoubtedly an accumulated impact of corporate mismanagement practised for a long time by the financial giants of the capitalistic economies.

The smell of mismanagement was emerging for some time in the form of the phenomenon of foreclosures in the housing finance market and several other symptoms and signals in the form of choked credit lines, massively leveraged firms, sinking mortgages, assets gone bad, panicked consumers, and paralyzed companies were visible to all those who wanted to see.

The US government and the Federal Reserve for long did almost all things wrong—which now they are attempting to correct.

In the process, the general public suffered massively a classic impact of corporate mismanagement. Its residual effect shall continue to adversely impact the life of the common people for a long time, much beyond the boundaries of the US and other Western economies.

The present work on this topic of vital economic interest shall serve, in the view of the author, a great common human interest.

Corporate Mismanagement Reduction—A Potential Magic Wand

India's GDP has recently touched the $1 trillion mark, with which the country has joined the elite group of about a dozen countries enjoying its level of productivity.

In terms of the Indian rupee it works out to over Rs. 45,00,000 crore. Business and industry or the corporate sector contribute over 70 per cent of it. A reduction of a mere 10 per cent in the current levels of mismanagement in various sectors of the Indian corporate world, offers potential for a very large addition to the nation's income—as well as towards significantly larger collection of additional taxes and levies. It can, indeed, throw up large additional resources for growth, including implementation of programmes for social justice and inclusion.

It can be a true magic wand for the nation's rapid growth.

International competitiveness of the Indian industry, production and supply of goods as well as services, could see a significant surge if a reduction of a mere 10 per cent is achieved in the current levels of mismanagement prevailing therein.

Management practitioners, professionally trained and/or otherwise, and teachers and the vast populace of students of management are offered, through this work, an opportunity to effectively understand the malaise of mismanagement—and equip themselves for the desired reduction of its interplay in the corporate world, for the greater benefit of mankind.

Dr. Udai Vir Singh

Contents

to prove oneself right, exhibiting work stress on your face, tolerating inadequate written communication, expecting others to read your mind, deprecating your own knowledge workers, talking of unpleasant past, encouraging motivated feedback from juniors, being bullheaded in your expressions, jumping to offer wagers on slight provocation, exhibiting directional confusion, and passing sweeping remarks.

Acknowledgements

Credit for my thought intensification that led to the punching of this work goes to the key mis-managers with whom I had opportunities for intense interaction in my long and varied corporate work-life. Observations on the numerous acts of mismanagement perpetrated by these champion mis-managers, namely GRV, KNS, RNS, KRD, SM and KSC, leaving aside a larger number of actors of lesser consequence, led to repeated re-stressing of the need, to my mind, to record the same for the benefit of the corporate fraternity. Observing KSC intensely multitasking in the field of voluntary and/or involuntary mismanagement, served the purpose of a detonator for the already heated up mass of observations that were straining to escape.

Brief information on these and some other personalities of massive mismanagement is provided in Attachment-II. And a lot more are to be found scattered all over this work. Their contribution towards the genesis and completion of this work is deeply acknowledged in light of the fact that the acts of mismanagement, especially those effected with design, need employment of substantial energies and ingenuity.

Dr. Udai Vir Singh

Abbreviations

ABA	Avoidable Brusque Attitude.
ADAs	Actively Damaging Assets—part of HR resources.
ADM	Autocratic Decision Making.
AEL	Avoidable Ear Lending—eagerly listening to such information inputs that tend to damage corporate work environment.
AEMs	Avoidable Ego Manifestations.
AICTE	All India Council for Technical Education.
AOD	Accumulation of Disaffection—amongst corporate workers.
AOFR	Absence of Formal Reporting—a symptom as well as a cause of mismanagement.
ASP	Ajeet Singh Pratap (a mis-manager) .
ATD	Active Thought Deficiency.
BAB	Bread-and-butter Business—that earns the basic revenues of a corporate.
BMC	Business Management Committee.
BMTs	Boss Management Techniques.
BOL	Bay Organics Ltd.
BOLT	Break-up of Logical Thinking—process which often precedes mismanagement.
CAL	Coromandal Agro Limited.
CBNP	Critical But Not Persuasive—one of the key deficiencies of mis-managers.
CCEs	Collective Creative Energies.

CDA	Credit and Discredit Apportioning—a very important activity in corporate work environments.
CDM	Clear Decision-Making.
CFF	Constant Fault Finding—habit of some mis-managers.
CMD	Chairman and Managing Director.
COI	Conflict of Interest.
CRA	Clear Responsibility Assignment—a requirement for effective corporate action.
CRI	Cost Return Illiteracy.
CSIR	Council of Scientific and Industrial Research.
CWE	Collective Work Environment—commercial establishments where a large number of people work for common purpose.
DBS	Dog-Bone Syndrome.
DDA	Deliberate Decision Avoidance.
DDM	Double Directional Mismanagement—often seen in departmental or in-house promotees.
DKs	Decision Killers.
DOA	Duplicity of Approach—practices wherein two sets of rules are applied.
DS	Deficiency Syndrome.
FGE	First Generation Entrepreneurs.
FL	Financial Looping.
FO	Flat Organization—where a mismanager attempts to control a large number of employees of various levels.
GBPP	Gaps Between Preaching and Performance.
GTG	Germination of Trust Gaps.
HB	Hurried Branding—an erroneous management practice of totally undesirable consequences.
HEC	High Ego Concentration—a symptom of excessive negativity.
HWE	Harmony of Work Environment.

IA	Inclusive Approach.
IAG	Individual Axe Grinding—an intense expression of negativity interplay.
IARI	Indian Agricultural Research Institute.
ICU	Intensive Care Unit—when a business is in a delicate condition.
IE&I	Impulses of Energy and Information—it is the scientific expression for thought.
IIMs	Indian Institutes of Management—located at Ahmedabad, Bangalore, Kolkata, Lucknow, Indore and Guwahati.
ION	Interplay of Negativity—constituents of a collective work environment.
ITP	Inner Thought Process—the voice of the soul.
JIT	Just In Time—a timely supply oriented concept in management that disallows build up of inventories—yet the process of production delivers.
KAA	Know-All Approach.
KCG	K.C. Gulati—the author's guide for doctoral research.
KIL	Krishi Industries Ltd.—an agro-inputs company located in Northern India, and having its operations in the northern, central and western parts of the country.
KNS	Krishna Narayan Sharma—a great expert in practice of mismanagement.
KRD	Kirti Raju Damodaran—a technocrat-turned-entrepreneur.
KSC	Karam Singh Chaudhri—a mis-manager of multilateral deficiencies.
L&R	Langoti (loin-cloth) and Ramayana (a long Indian epic).
LP	Loss Perpetuation.
LSB	Law of Stress Balance.
LSC	Large Span of Contact—a symptom of some mismanaged organizations.
LTP	Logical Thought Process—which gets disturbed in case of negativity manifestations in active or silent form.

LTP	Long-term Planning or LRP—long range planning.
MAC	Mutual Appreciation Club.
Marwaris	A traditional business community of India.
MAUC	Misplaced and Unproductive Criticism.
MBA	Master of Business Administration.
MCR	Multiple Capacity Reality.
MDS	Multiple Diversionary Stresses—operative on some mis-managers.
MIS	Management Information System.
MNCs	Multinational Corporations.
MOPs	Measures of Performance.
MPD	Maturity Perception Deficit.
NAE	Nepotism and Extravegence—often resorted to by mis-managers.
NDP	No Draft Please.
NEOP	Negative Energies of Power—they help in mismanagement.
NLR	Non-line Reporting.
NPAs	Non-performing Assets.
NPP	Non-Performing Performance.
NRDC	National Research and Development Corporation.
NT	Niraj Tiwari—a manager who cared for dues and rights of his subordinates.
NTP	Negative Thought Process: It is one of the basic causes of mismanagement.
PCAs	Power Concentrate Attributes.
PCEs	Productive Corporate Energies.
PD	Performance Dysfunction.
PG	Parveen Gandhi—a coworker of the author who had a high level of negativity. But he was able to learn the job well.
PN	Primary Negativity.

PP	Peer Pressure—a work environment attribute.
PPF	Past Performance Failures—some managers attempt not to stop carrying out the same in the present context.
PPP	Perception of Power Performance.
PSV	Preferentially Selected Vision.
RCD	Ram Chand Dewan.
RCT	Ramesh Chand Tyagi—an egoistic engineer of doubtful integrity—turned general manager. He was a master mismanager.
RNS	Ram Naresh Saroff—a mis-manager of significant manipulations.
RPA	Righteous Performance Appreciation.
RTI	Right to Information Act—recently implemented in India; under it, all citizens are entitled to seek and obtain information on matters of their interest, from any department of the Central or State governments.
SC	Samir Chauhan—quick decision maker.
SDR	System of Defused Responsibilities—an erroneous method of work practised by some mis-managers.
SM	Sayad Miraj—an incompetent second generation businessman.
SMPs	Self-motivated Performers.
SN	Secondary Negativity.
SSD	Supervised System of Delegation.
STPA	Stringency Towards Performance Appreciation.
SWOT	Strength, Weaknesses, Opportunities and Threats—a widely employed management tool.
TAAD	Thought and Action Deficiencies.
TC	Toxic Communication.
TDL	Time-decision Linkage.
TPPC	Target Person Pleasing Capacity.
TRAR	Talent Recognition and Rewarding.

U/A	Understanding and Acceptance—a requirement for effective management.
UCDA	Unrighteous Credit and Discredit Apportioning—an important activity of a good management.
UKBM	United Krishi Business Models.
ULOI	Ultimate Level of Incompetence.
UMBC	Unnaturally Modified Business Cycle.
UN	Unhealthy Nexuses—that damage corporate interests.
VKM	Vijai Kumar Murthy—a MNC, mis-manager.
VSM	Visual Stress Manifestation.
WAAS	Wide Arena of Action Spectrum.
WLB	Work Life Balance—vital for an executive to be effective in the long-term.

Directions of Mismanagement

The consequences of mismanagement in a corporate work environment normally take four specific directions.

OR

A mis-manager may inflict four-directional damages.

- His/her own business interests/performance may be damaged;
- May damage employer's/corporate business performance;
- May damage his/her own career;

AND

- May damage careers of others working for or with him/her.

Introduction

A lot has been said and written about management, particularly in the twentieth century—and the process continues as an ever-growing self-energized stream of words and sounds. For induction of new recruits to this human engagement, new management institutions continue to proliferate with epidemic vitality, particularly in developing countries. And the already existing multitude of management practitioners—professionals or otherwise, too engage precious corporate time and resources for in-house as well as outsourced training and retraining programmes. Besides, a variety of management gurus, consultants, and advisors are busy contributing their expertise in this field.

Despite best intentions, efforts, and resources allocation, the corporate function of management is nowhere near to achieving even a fraction of its stated objectivity. A little scratching of its surface veneer promptly exhibits a massive deficit in its processes as well as performance. Lost opportunities, missed targets, bleeding bottom lines, bruised egos, and avoidable burnouts, and even disasters and devastations become visible without any magnifying glass or searching efforts. For almost all corporate bodies, a long list of management deficits—persistent and/or transitory, could be drawn up with amazing effortlessness.

Mismanagement: Meaning and Scope

As per ***Lord Krishna's*** philosophy, mismanagement encompasses all human deeds that have collective a impact and smell of unrighteousness. Several leading characters of the ***Mahabharata*** (one of the two ancient Indian epics), particularly Dhritarashtra, Duryodhana, Karna, Bhishma and, in a way, even Yudhishthar, (the upholder of righteousness) committed acts of mismanagement—some by design and others by default. And, individually and collectively, they had to face the consequences of their unrighteous acts of omission and commission.

Modern management gurus and experts, for certain reasons that do not seem fully explainable, have not attended to this vital aspect of corporate work environment. Most of the time, they have been busy telling how to do things in a better and more productive manner. Since the scope of the present work does not permit an in-depth analysis of this puzzle of modern management, it is left to be dealt with separately at some future date.

Mismanagement always leads to unpleasant and undesirable consequences. The Bhopal gas tragedy, India's 1962 defeat at the hands of China, East Pakistan emerging as Bangladesh in 1971, Russian occupation of Afghanistan towards the end of the last century, Pakistan's misadventure in *Kargil*, and the 21st century's first American Vietnam in Iraq, are some of the disastrous instances of mismanagement of recent occurrence. A list of disastrous mismanagements, even for recent times, could indeed be never-ending.

State bureaucracies often operate through mismanagement—generating consequences of such magnitude that even the combined army of the world's economists, small or big, known or unknown, will find itself utterly incapable of assessment of the losses or damages so caused. And it is not specific to India alone: No human activity, anywhere in this world, fully escapes manifestations of mismanagement.

On the corporate front, mismanagement occurs every minute, in every individual entity, often by default—and equally frequently by design. The impact of mismanagement on the corporate bottomline becomes visible only in its final phases of accumulated manifestations. In less visible or in partly or fully hidden forms, mismanagement continues to gnaw at the vitals of the diseased corporate bodies. Corporate losses or economic failures are often man-made.

MISMANAGEMENT—MIS-GOVERNANCE AND MISDIRECTION

As per the Oxford dictionary, **"mismanagement"** is a noun arising from the verb 'mismanage' which means managing wrongly or badly—or to mismanage one's business affairs, finances, accounts, etc. The New Penguin Thesaurus includes verbs such as mal-administer, misgovern, misdirect, misconduct, mishandle, botch, bungle, mess up, foul up, cook up, screw up, etc., while explaining the term 'mismanage'.

In the practical corporate world, it tends to encompass terms/verbs such as misconduct, misconstrue, misguide, misjudge, mislead, misrepresent, misinterpret, mismatch, misrule, misuse, and many more. At places, mismanagement is simply meant as being careless or inefficient—and misgovern is seen as equated to mismanage.

Mismanagement, when looked through the lens of corporate practicality, seems to be more central to deficiencies of implementation and output—while mis-governance tilts towards implementation and control failures. Misdirection happens to be an important component of both. But, neither mis-governance nor misdirection, singly or collectively equal mismanagement: It seems to have a much wider meaning, depth, and applicability.

Mismanagement, as per the author, encompasses all actions of commission and omission that are:

- taken the way they should not have been;
- the ones not taken the way they should have been;
- those representing active or passive deviations from accepted plans;
- for which your inner-self or the soul did not fully support you;
- the actions that continue to scratch your conscience;
- the ones that have potential to damage the corporate work environment, its productivity and output or the potential for the same;
- those smelling of selfishness and negativity;
- the ones that gave you pleasure at the cost of someone else,
- and/or the actions that you would not like someone else to take.

Whenever an act of mismanagement is undertaken or planned to be undertaken, the ***inner thought process*** (ITP) of the doer always activates itself to tell the potential mis-manager, howsoever mildly, that what was planned to be done or being done is not right from the point of view of the larger corporate interest or the interest of society. No act of mismanagement, when taken by design, occurs without some internal conflict or warning which the mis-manager normally suppresses. Only such acts of mismanagement that occur by default, without prior knowledge or assessment of consequences, or in absence of skills and or experience, are free of internal conflict or warning. As soon as one comes to know that an act—avoidable or undesirable is done, a conscientious doer should accept the mistake and/or take corrective action. If and when such an action is avoided, the element of participation or design creeps in. Only people with strong elements of righteousness are capable of such a corrective behaviour.

Mismanagement—An Emphasis Deficit

Management literature, from a large number of authors and gurus, seems to be devoid of attention to mismanagement, mis-governance, misdirection, and/or other terms, which go to express actions and consequences of this nature. Since management or modern management, as taught and practised today, originated in the Western world—where the negative forces of mismanagement were very weak or non-consequential, the subject of mismanagement easily escaped specific attention. Mismanagement primarily or say, more dominantly, is a problem of developing and underdeveloped countries—and hence, it is they who should pay attention to its study and develop ways and means to manage this malaise of long-term consequences. Economic growth, which is very central to the well-being of the third world, faces an enormous threat at the hands of a large number of mis-managers who infest the corporate world, as well as the state apparatus of governance in this vast segment of the world population.

In view of the mismanagement's enormous capacity to bleed corporate bottom-lines—and divert scarce developmental resources of state agencies and/or corporates towards personal gain of those involved with their handling, it is truly surprising to see that little or no emphasis is placed today on this malady by modern management training institutions in India and/or in other major countries, which suffer a great deal at the hands of a multitude of mis-managers. An examination of the training courses composition of major IIMs and other leading institutions in this field tends to confirm the author's apprehension in this regard.

If the present-day students of management, at graduate and/or post-graduate level, are not made aware of this widespread anti-performance phenomenon, then how are they going to face the same when they enter the corporate world with all their idealism and expectations? Are they not likely to suffer disillusion on the one hand —and, by default, end up becoming a part of the mismanagement apparatus, which invariably operates in varying proportions, in almost all the corporate bodies—particularly those active in the third world countries? In the author's opinion, they need to be trained:

- To anticipate and identify the forces of mismanagement in any corporate work environment that they might end up joining.
- To assess and measure, in a discrete manner, the extent of damage that the negative forces of mismanagement are exerting on the bottomline of the companies of their work.
- To know how to avoid becoming part of the apparatus of mismanagement.
- To exert such care and precautions that the vicious forces of mismanagement do not scare the new additions to the white collar corporate work force.
- And last, but not the least, to be able to assess whether the senior management of the corporate of their choice has any active interest in limiting or controlling the operations of these result-limiting forces.

Often, MBAs and other products of modern management institutions have been blamed of a theoretical bias in their training—which, to a considerable extent, is being presently corrected through employment of case studies and business/corporate related work assignments. But, the attention to mismanagement and its devastating effects on corporate performance is conspicuous by its almost total absence. The reasons for such a situation could be numerous—but the following ones seem to be having a decisive influence.

1. The major part of the current faculty of these institutions enjoys only a limited exposure to practical corporate work environments. They are not adequately equipped to appreciate the malaise of mismanagement.
2. The management and the faculty of these training institutions, probably do not like to expose the young minds to the dark elements of mismanagement: In their view, the new entrants to the arena of practical corporate work should learn it the difficult way.

3. And further, since the subject of mismanagement has not been a part of the curriculum approved by the controlling agencies such as AICTE, the need for extra efforts has not been felt actively.

Like all other chronic diseases, the disease of mismanagement is not easily visible and/or measurable—and its symptoms, as well as consequences are mixed up with various other positive and/or negative signals that might emerge from victimized corporate bodies. The hue and cry against corruption in the Indian state bureaucracy or the apparatus of governance—and the consequent need for good governance and transparency has led to implementation of the RTI Act, which is beginning to bear preliminary results. There is, thus, an active need for good governance or minimization of mismanagement in the corporate work environment too—and until and unless some effective measures are initiated, a situation might arise where the need for extension of the RTI Act to the corporate world, or a modified version of the same, becomes unavoidable. Hence, the corporate world should start getting ready to effectively face and minimize the impact of the forces of mismanagement. There can be no better way of making a beginning in this direction than educating our future managers, the BBAs and MBAs, in this regard.

Managers and Damagers

Managers can be classified in various ways:

- those trained formally through management institutions,
- others who learn the trade through in-house grounding,
- generalists with no specific technical skills,
- technocrats moving into managerial positions,
- those who delegate work,
- others who accumulate work or monopolize over it,
- some who righteously distribute credit amongst performing juniors,
- those who steal credit creating widespread disaffection,
- on the other hand, there are those who build performing teams,
- and others who destroy even performing groups,
- some managers are ***thought warriors*** who always come up

with new ideas but never attempt to convert them into actions,
- others who are ***action warriors***,
- a minority that possesses a good mix of thought as well as action warriorism,
- some being good leaders of people—along with being performing managers,
- some are endowed with ***Sattavic nature***,
- others with dominant ***Rajjasic prakriti***,

The managerial population landscape, more often than not, is dominated by pseudo-professionals endowed with a high degree of ***Tamsic nature***—they being the ones full of negative tendencies always attempt to keep their self-interest ahead of corporate objectivity. They misuse authority, and promote inefficiency and corruption. They understand the meaning of management only when it is coloured with their self-interest, in one or the other way. They are the damagers—their number, in fact, is much larger than the rest. They contribute to a major part of mismanagement in the corporate as well as the non-corporate work environments.

The author experienced close encounters with a number of mis-managers or damagers, in his over 40 years strong corporate work exposure; most of these find mention in this work at appropriate places (please see Attachment-I).

Notwithstanding, it is difficult to refrain from mentioning a specimen of this species who happened to be a senior manager in a renowned MNC—and the author, by default, had to deal with him. He was a cunning and scheming boss, an Olympian in thought warriorism—but fully devoid of action. He did not want to admit that anyone in his department ever did anything right. He was mortally scared of assigning any credit to any of his subordinates—fearing that their good work coming to the notice of the senior management might cause danger to his own position.

He had refined ways to grab total credit for whatsoever good work emerged from his department. He always rued, in front of his bosses, that he was burdened with a group of incompetent subordinates—that they were good for nothing. Amongst his juniors, he often attempted to cultivate a feeling of inadequacy, and fear of senior management. But, he often loved their company in evening sessions of booze, during which he attempted to create a false hold on their mental faculties. He was a devil amongst mis-managers. He had four subordinates, all well-qualified and competent in their individual specialties, but all of them were on the virtual verge of desperation. They did not know what to do or how to deal successfully with their uncommon boss or the tormentor. A few years down thc line, all of them performed well under a new boss. Attachment-I gives details of the several mis-managers encountered by the author in his own corporate work life.

Professionals and Non-professionals

Corporate professionals with or without formal training, tend to turn into mis-manager/damagers, by default or design—and their formal qualifications and training seems to bear only a very little relevance

Mismanagement by default	*Mismanagement by design*
May occur due to incompetence.	Is a product of negative competence:
Innocence may contribute to it.	There is no trace of innocence in it.
Lack of attention may allow it to creep in.	It is a consequence of intense attention and reflection.
Its impact emerges without warning.	Manager, or more precisely the damager, has planned the negative outputs.
The contributor will normally be receptive to suggestions.	Its contributor may deliberately display innocence.
It is easily correctable.	It is not easily correctable as the perpetrator resists correction.
Ego and negativity do not come much into play.	His ego and negativity comes into display.
Not likely to spoil corporate working environment in the long-term.	It spoils the team spirit.
Not likely to demoralize a productive team.	Consultants are often not welcome for its remediation.
Consultants can easily help in its remediation.	It normally exerts a long-term negative impact on corporate bottom-line.
Its impact on corporate bottom-line may normally be transitional or temporary.	

to the exhibition of this trait. True professionals, in principle, should be totally free from the malady of mismanagement; they are indeed hard to come by. To be a good manager does not really make un-humanly huge demands on the skills and energies of subject individuals: What really counts is possession of the rare commodity known as ***common sense***, and a capacity or willingness to employ the same with the necessary input of impartiality and righteousness.

Situations of mismanagement that occur by default are easier to handle through information input, training and guidance. But, what is inflicted by design is difficult to cure. The two types of mismanagements exhibit the following peculiarities.

As said earlier, the major part of mismanagement that occurs by default is preventable through suitably designed information inputs, training and guidance—and most of it can definitely be cured or corrected. The other variety of mismanagement, the one that is foisted through design, is difficult to avoid as well as cure. In both cases, it requires tougher measures, and greater skills and commitment on the part of senior management to handle the situation effectively. Diagrammatically, the two forms of mismanagement are depictable as under:

Omnipresence of Mismanagement

Mismanagement is a widely prevalent disease of the ***corporate*** world. Whether small or big, public or private—no business organization is truly or totally free from this malady. To be more realistic, no part

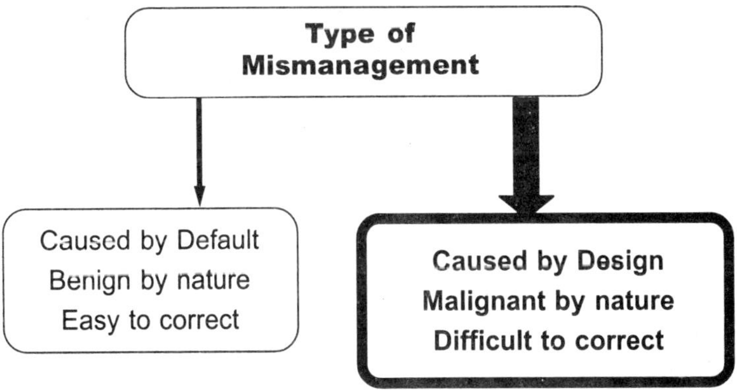

Note. The size differential of the two arrows and blocks depicts their existential relationship in an actual corporate work environment.

of human activity—particularly the collective ones, can ever be fully free from this deficiency. It is a consequence of operations of the negative energies in human beings that propel them into action, which go against the concept of common or collective good.

Mismanagement, in fact, is of a parasitic nature: It is incapable of survival or growth in an environment that is free of human beings. No other part of the animal world suffers from the vagaries of mismanagement.

In a sense, mismanagement is time and space independent—it has been part of human civilization all through the times—right from its inception. In fact, several great civilizations were lost due to mismanagement of one or the other type. And it shall always show up or germinate wherever human beings would attempt to live and work in a collective manner. There is no need to spend excessive human energies towards attempting to eliminate it—since it cannot be totally eliminated. It will change forms and intensities—but will always give company to collective human working. Timely prevention or suppression of mismanagement, even to a partial extent, is good enough: It should not be allowed to assume limiting or severely damaging proportions.

Cause and Effect of Mismanagement

Mismanagement is elusive in its perceptions as well as manifestations. Its perpetrators as well as victims remain substantially deluded about its causes and effects. In practice, there is only a thin line that separates its cause and effect, which always tend to exist in an equilibrium. But despite that, its impact is very easily felt as compared to identification and/or isolation of its causes. It is akin to the relationship of light and sound in a thunderstorm—wherein light manifests itself before the sound is heard, though the latter is more near to the causes of the whole phenomenon and its effects—the intense friction of water-bearing clouds.

The primary causes of mismanagement are concentrated in the ***negative thought process*** (NTP) of human beings—their active desire for self-aggrandizement, in order to gain dominance over others—through actions of omission and commission that agitate against the common or collective good. Such efforts could be overt as well as covert—and often, the same are actively hidden by the mis-managers under the garments of common good.

The mis-managers' ardent faith in their capabilities to keep their actions and also intentions wrapped beyond detection prompts them to indulge into activities causative to mismanagement. Inadequate or total non-appreciation of the consequences of their unrighteous actions, or faith in their capability to come out with adequate justifications, further emboldens them. Collective working of mis-managers as a group, i.e., involvement of seniors and/or juniors, further adds to the perpetuation of their actions, and the boldness with which they often operate.

The impact of mismanagement, mild or disastrous, is easily felt as irritating bites to the corporate body—which subsequently tend to develop into festering wounds. It is essential to quickly sniff the presence of mismanagement in a corporate work environment, identify and isolate its causes, and limit resultant damages as early as possible. The present work, based entirely on factual experiences of the author and his intense interactions with some classic mis-managers, is designed for this express purpose.

Equilibrium of Forces of Management and Mismanagement

In any collective work environment, the forces of management and mismanagement tend to gain equilibrium—when one grows, the other retreats or adjusts—and then recovers to gain ground. The up and down movements of the two opposing sets of forces continue to be interactive—until and unless one type of forces do gain overpowering influence.

Any disturbance in the mutually balancing forces of management and mismanagement should be slow, otherwise normal working could be disturbed—causing long-term damage to the already not-so-healthy work environment.

Most managements– professional and otherwise, fail to differentiate between or appreciate the impact of these forces. Recognition of mismanagement, more especially its acceptance is a difficult exercise for most managers, if they are not fully righteous and deeply interested in the corporate good. It is not a job for time markers or boss pleasers: Corrective action against the forces of mismanagement demand a lot of guts—and commitment for righteous actions.

Negative forces or the forces of mismanagement	*Positive forces or the forces of productive management*
They originate as negative thoughts—the desires for self-benefit.	These are the positive forces or the forces of productive work for collective good.
They assume the form of actions of mismanagement—by routing the inputs or outputs of productivity for personal gain.	The positive forces take the form of productive actions—enhancing outputs at acceptable or lower costs.
In such situations, evil and wickedness might raise their heads—to perpetuate the gain.	Here, righteousness and virtue might out-perform the forces of mismanagement.
Credit and discredit distribution becomes faulty.	Credit and discredit distribution becomes balanced or less biased.
Here, team functioning is disturbed.	Team functioning gathers momentum.
Bottom line tends to bleed under influence of such forces.	Resources for future growth are generated.

Management and Mismanagement—Two Sides of a Coin

The concept and practice of management—and its deviant form namely mismanagement are intensely related—like the two sides of a coin. All actions of management enjoy only a very thin dividing line that prevents them from assuming the undesirable form—and hence, only righteous and experienced professionals can be significantly safe from the eventuality of attracting the tag of mismanagement, for their acts of commission and omission.

The theory of sets suggests that things, material as well as non-material, tend to occur and interplay in sets of one and its reverse: Very rarely do they exist in perfect isolation. Numerous instances, inclusive of the ones listed on the next page, form part of this concept.

The origin of management and mismanagement is similar to that of gold and lead—the component particles of which, at the micro level, are non-differentiating or the same.

As explained by Deepak Chopra,[1] the subatomic particles such as protons, electrons, quarks and bosons that make up an atom of gold

Matter and antimatter	Right and wrong
Negative and positive	I, we, and you and they
Action and inaction	Thought and non-thought
Performance and non-performance	Cooperation and non-cooperation
Friend and enemy	Individual and team
Credit and discredit	Righteous and unrighteous credit apportioning
Persuasion and imposition	Expectation and surprise
Suggestion and order	Collective and individual
Full and empty	Personal and non-personal
Profit and loss	Active and laggard
Service and dis-service	Known and unknown
Public and private	Good and bad
Clarity and confusion	....
Sweet and bitter	

or lead are exactly the same. In fact, what we call particles are not material entities; they are impulses of energy and information. It is only the arrangement and quantity of these impulses of energy and information that differentiates gold from lead. Very much like the material stuff (the goods and products), the non-stuff of the universe, the thoughts—good as well as bad, are nothing but the ***impulses of energy and* information** (IEIs). Thus, management and mismanagement at the IEI level are not at all different—it is only the difference in their packaging and intensity that converts them into two different sides of the same coin.

In our head, the crucible of thought genesis and concentration, IEIs convert into thoughts, very much like atoms assemble into molecules and then take the form of matter. Their flow, retention and concentration, compounds them into the need for action—and the build-up of critical concentration of the latter spurts into action. The energy and information stress, i.e., the compacting of IEIs operative during the process determines their nature—the goodness or non-goodness of the same.

It is possible to influence, i.e., alter and/or modify the thought process: Thus, through proper intervention, with the help of righteous dialogue, the occurrence of mismanagement could be stopped right at its germinating stage—and its alteration into positive action of productive management should also be possible. Energies of thought, i.e., the IEIs are the true instruments of productive management—

the management of the crucial human factor, for the meeting of our stated or planned objectivity.

Lord Krishna[2] was the first known authority to explain the relationship between matter and non-matter, thought and action, righteous and non-righteous, action and inaction, and many more, during his intense dialogue with ***Arjuna***—the Pandava warrior, prior to the battle of Kurukshetra, the final lap of the epic struggle between the forces of evil and wicked, on the one hand, and the good and virtuous on the other.

Mismanagement—Its General Impact Flow

The general flow of the impacts of the forces and processes of mismanagement is depicted by the following diagram.

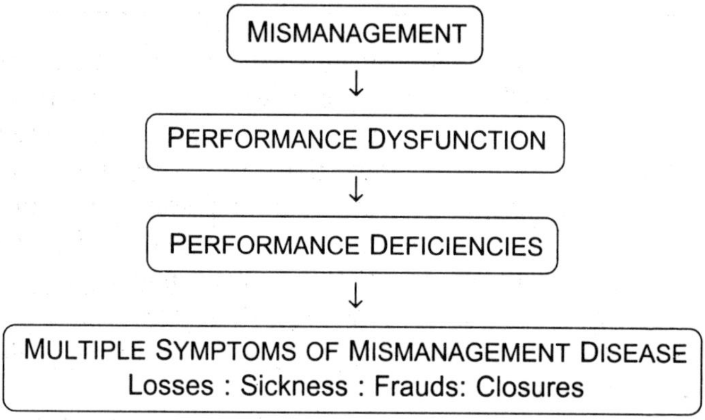

Various negative energies arising out of actions and interactions of mismanagement progressively tell on the functional health of a victim corporate—leading to performance dysfunction (output and quality both)—and, in due course, deficiencies of performance begin to manifest. Depending upon the intensity of causative forces and response of the management—and the resultant balance, the final symptoms and consequences in—form of losses, sickness and closure —do follow a pattern of flow.

Corporate Mismanagement Reduction—A Potential Magic Wand

India's GDP has recently touched the $1 trillion mark, with which the country has joined the elite group of about a dozen countries enjoying this level of productivity.

In terms of the Indian rupee it works out to over Rs. 45,00,000 crore. Business and industry or the corporate sector contributes over 70 per cent of it. A reduction of a mere 10 per cent in the current levels of mismanagement in various sectors of the Indian corporate world, offers potential for a very large addition to the nation's income—as well as towards the resultant collection of taxes and levies. It can, indeed, throw up large additional resources for growth, including implementation of programmes for social justice and inclusion.

It can be a true magic wand for the nation's rapid growth.

International competitiveness of the Indian industry, production of goods as well as services, could see a significant surge if a reduction of a mere 10 percent is achieved in the current levels of prevailing mismanagement.

CHAPTER 1

Mismanagement and Human Resources

Human resources are the prime movers of the corporate work process. Their handling, deployment, and motivation determine the quality of movements in a collective work process. Since all inputs of production and service outputs are governed only by the human element, management or mismanagement remains entirely dependent on manipulation of this most critical determinant and/or the action force.

Money does not manage itself; land does not develop by itself; materials don't move themselves; machines don't turn themselves; plans don't come up automatically; and goods don't sell by themselves. In fact, very little happens without human effort—more so in the corporate work environment.

Mismanagement of human resources leads to de-motivation of the work force, irrespective of the colour of its collar. Mis-managers resort to numerous tricks, by default or design, which de-motivate and/or inactivate the productive human element, thus defeating the very fundamental reason of existence of the corporate activity. Described herein are some of the techniques/actions, which mis-managers often resort to for movements in this direction. Corrective measures that could neutralize such impacts too are detailed herein.

NON-DIFFERENTIATION BETWEEN TALKERS AND DOERS

There are two types of white-collar workers in a corporate work environment—one who talk a lot and work very little, and the second, who work a lot and talk little. The first category comprises the ***thought warriors*** for whom talking—or the use of words and expressions—not only comes easy, it becomes an end in itself. Once they have talked, they come to the conclusion that work or their job has been done; it is, in their view, some one else's job to see that actions are initiated. They are skilled with words and expressions and employ them with the specific purpose of influencing the boss, and to the extent possible, escape with credit without really doing anything. They are the, ***I told you types.*** They hardly contribute anything substantial or measurable to the corporate bottom-line, except bleeding it to the extent possible.

The second category of workers, who work more and talk less, are the ***action warriors***; they act as per the demands of the situation, with or without adequate supervision. Work or say work-output is important for them—they don't even like to advertise it. They feel, and rightly so, that it is the job of the boss to see and evaluate the work-output. They are the true soldiers of the corporate and their contributions feed the bottom-line, keeping it healthy and green. They are practitioners of the ***Principle of Karma*** as postulated so brilliantly by ***Lord Krishna.***[2] An efficient professional manager or a proficient CEO should be able to identify and differentiate between the two categories of workers, in the interest of the health of the corporate that he or she might head. When they fail to do it, by design or default, the tag of mismanagement becomes difficult to avoid.

Practice of Requisite Transparency

Total transparency is not feasible to be observed—as all the corporate operations cannot be open to one and all. Hence, the practice of transparency has to be observed in a relative manner, i.e., in relation to the people involved with the activity or decision concerned—leaving no room for speculation.

At the senior level, the practice of non-transparency is a sure recipe for mismanagement. Lack of information creates doubts of intention as well as objectivity. Cumulatively, it leads to loss of speed as well as direction of work. Energies of thought as well as action, which should have taken a predetermined creative direction, are lost in the dark alleys of non-transparency.

Hence, initiative, innovation, and co-operation—and consequently, team work suffers from inaction and diversion of energies of thought as well as action. Firstly, the thought warriorism is replaced by a confused state of mind—and then action warriorism refuses to start with energy insufficient for productive action.

In the constructive equilibrium of productive thought energy, nontransparent practices by senior managers tend to poison the vital work processes. There is no dearth of senior professionals, especially the owner CEOs, who themselves do practise active non-transparency and then, as a defence mechanism for incorrect blame apportioning, accuse juniors for practising inadequate transparency.

Shared information generates co-operation need not be forgotten in the interest of efficient management. In brief, the following two areas of corporate function are most crucial from the angle of transparency.

1. **Human Resources: Credit and discredit apportioning.**
2. **Financial Management: Purchases, payments, expenses, collections, and accounting.**

Wherever, in a corporate work environment, transparency is ensured in the above two crucial areas, efficiency and bright results don't take much time to emerge.

Practice of Excessive Turf Protection

Wherever human beings engage into any group activity—particularly in corporate activities, areas of specific interest or turfs tend to emerge. For initiators of such activities, it is an exercise of defence, i.e., not allowing others to enter or interfere in areas of specific interest or influence. It is an extension of animal instinct of territory or beat marking and defence. Self-aggrandizement too, often, is the cause of such efforts. Turf occurrence automatically leads to turf protection, which results in acts of omission and commission, creating fertile grounds for growth of mismanagement. Managers, professional or otherwise, attempt to preserve and grow their areas of influence—and for the purpose they often assemble teams of yes-men, who will do their bidding for righteous as well as unrighteous activities.

Such emergence of turfs of interest and their active protection by seniors plants the seeds of non-transparency, under protection of which numerous acts of mismanagement tend to germinate and flourish without hindrance. The consequences for the subject corporate bodies, in terms of spoilage of work environment, are invariably substantial.

In an MNC, the author witnessed turf genesis and protection being actively practised, in a manner, that the key functions of finance and production were cornered, respectively by Bengalis and South Indian groups. Entry of any other person into these areas, meritorious or otherwise, was totally incidental and/or peripheral.

At KIL, a first generation entrepreneurship, the CMD and his cousin had taken hold of the key department of materials and purchases—assisted by a nondescript assistant. After years of mismanagement within their specific turf—and facilitated by an incompetent group of workers in the finance department, the company ran into a serious financial crisis—owing huge sums to suppliers, on one hand, and their customers in the market, on the other. Interest accumulation on advances from customers and borrowings from banks was on the verge of negating the total assets of the company. Part of the working capital was diverted towards creation of fixed assets at two new project locations.

When this group of two was not able to face the cumulative pressures from suppliers, customers, and bankers, it was decided to form a ***business management committee*** (BMC) through induction of some outside experts. And after sustained deliberations spread over months to analyze the situation, it was decided to create a purchase committee. In this decision, the duo saw a threat to their long established turf. The necessary notification for creation of the said committee was not issued despite repetitive discussions on this lapse in the BMC on more than one occasion.

It was a typical case of creating an injurious turf and protecting the same despite continued injuries to corporate performance. It adversely affected the morale of senior functionaries of the company who were being pressurized to improve working of the same. Here, the non-transparency and turf protection assumed a damaging proportion—and, as such, represented a serious form of mismanagement.

Development of Trust Deficit

When ***trust deficit*** develops in a working relationship, whether between a customer and a supplier or between an employee and his/her boss or employer, the basic foundations of a mutually satisfying work relationship are shaken for ever. They cannot be easily repaired or regenerated. Even with persistent and genuine efforts, recovery of trust and confidence in such a situation is never complete and sustainable; doubts are likely to continue to offer resistance on a long-term basis. Situations of trust deficit often arise by default, as no one normally attempts to plan or design the same. In a ***corporate work environment*** (CWE), actions as the ones enumerated below, always end up generating the undesirable trust deficit.

- Not sustaining a promise of payment, irrespective of the size or pendency of the amount.
- Failure to honour a financial instrument.
- Accepting an order from a valued customer and not honouring it.
- Not maintaining promised or expected quality of supplies.
- Failure to service a complaint with an expected promptness.
- Altering contents of a delivery without the consent of a client.
- Promising certain incentives and not providing the same.
- Promising certain facilities to a performing employee—and management reneging on the same.
- Deviating from a written agreement without attempting its renegotiation.
- Leaking a confidential information/document despite an understanding to the contrary.
- Treating ordinary matters as confidential
- Non-inclusive or non-participatory decisions.

The list of such instances and causes of ***trust deficit genesis*** (TDG) could virtually be endless—and enumerating more of the same here shall not serve any great purpose.

Trust deficit, in most cases, can lead to ***performance deficit*** (PD) via the route of ***confidence deficit*** (CD) and ***initiative deficit*** (ID) developments. Its repeated occurrence has the potential to damage the corporate bottom-line to a substantial extent, as well as its competitiveness. Trust deficit acts as a deadly poison in all components of the corporate action spectrum. Actions of omission and commission from the upper pyramid of management are the biggest causatives of this effect.

Sometimes, in family-run enterprises, it is caused by autocratic or irresponsible actions of promoters and/or their juniors who are attempting to learn the ropes of the business. In such situations, the undesirable impacts can be truly distressful. Manifestation of the negative impacts of trust deficit commences from damage to the ***logical thought process*** (LTP) of the affected persons. The stressed and/or dislocated thought process often fails to sustain righteous actions, especially the timings and magnitudes—and the consequences of such an imbalance do not take time to manifest in damaging formations.

Duplicity of Approach

To have ***duplicity of approach*** (DP), or two sets of rules, is a manifestation of negative intentions or a form of emerging mismanagement. It sets subordinates to doubt sincerity and integrity—which finally prompts deterioration of moral authority to lead and/or manage effectively. With this type of thought genesis in the minds of junior staff—their desire to co-operate, take initiative, and perform beyond the minimum required, starts diminishing in an exponential manner. Duplicity of approach may relate both to financial and/or non-financial matters. It is undesirable in all its forms and manifestations.

Credit and discredit apportioning (CDA) or reward and punishment, among others, forms a major part of duplicity of approach. Moral behaviour and ethicality are other areas where duplicity of approach is not tolerated by the junior staff. A good leader, in fact, should not do or appear to be doing what he or she does not like in others. A simple deviation on the part of a leader or manager and also those close to him, like the observance of office arrival time, is observed as setting deviant reactions. Leading by example, or managing by example, has a lot of merit for discipline and productivity management.

Lord Krishna[2] was a great proponent of this principle throughout his long and arduous fight against unrighteous forces. He asserted that the very purpose of his taking birth on this earth was to extend protection to the virtuous and righteous against the unreasonability of the wicked and unscrupulous. The corporate fraternity has to learn a lot from the distilled wisdom that he so graciously left for mankind in the form of the 'Song of Wisdom' or the 'Bhagavad-Gita.'

Tolerance of Deadwood

In the corporate context, the term ***deedwood*** refers to unproductive manpower—the human NPA or non-performing assets. It consists of people who, for various reasons, are either unwilling to contribute or are incapable of doing so in positions where they are presently placed.

Such people, irrespective of their positions or the number of years that they have put in, exert an unhealthy influence on the rest of the corporate work force. It conveys the message that the productivity or contribution of a person has no relevance to the benefits which he or she is drawing from the company. Often, such people also become a hindrance in the progress of performing people, as they block the steps of the corporate ladder. Their unproductive or unoccupied presence becomes a source of avoidable gossip in the affected organization.

Deadwood invariably accumulates due to deficiencies or weaknesses in the management decision-making process—its actions of omission and commission that convey messages of unprofessional practices. As such, it is a serious manifestation of corporate mismanagement.

Putting the Cart before the Horse

Unreasonable conditions, when put forth in business processes, act like putting a cart before the horse. Even if the horse attempts to pull it, no movement is likely to emerge. Some senior managers were noticed by the author engaging in putting such unreasonable conditions that discerning line managers either did not accept, or if acceptance was somehow pushed through, little or no performing movement could occur.

Once in a project evaluation meeting in a large family-based group located at Kolkata, a senior director of the group asked whether I (the author) could give a written personal guarantee in regard to the projected profits of the project that was drawn up. He made this point to impress his masters who were present in the meeting. It was a totally unprofessional approach on the part of a senior director who had spent, at that time, over 40 years with the group. When he insisted on the point, I agreed to do the needful provided the company agreed to give me a good share of the profit. He did not relish my counter remark but I proceeded to elaborate that normally it was the job of the entrepreneur to bear the risks related to a new project, as the profits were to accrue to him. The proprietor CEO appreciated my point and chided the director for putting the cart before the horse.

During another assignment with a company that had fallen on bad times, the author witnessed its CEO demanding that the sales staff should first underwrite payments to suppliers through DDs or at par checques, for raw material purchases for the products that they needed to service their respective markets. To the sales staff it looked as if the horse was being put behind the cart—and some of them did not hesitate in saying so. Since, due to the precarious finances of the company, there was no other way out, the proposal was grudgingly accepted—but, as expected, no acceptable results came out of this approach.

Both the instances, despite their merits and demerits, represented a degree of mismanagement.

Emergence of a Cat-and-Rat Work Environment

When boss is around, every person is on his or her workstation or is attempting to draw the attention of the boss either to his work-related problems and/or related achievements. Everybody attempts to look busy or concerned. But as soon as the boss leaves the office, the majority of the workers normally falls back to gossiping or attend to personal work. Some are busy having long conversations on the phone at the cost of the company.

That rats make merry when the cat is away, is an appropriate expression for perfectly summarizing such situations—which are not of rare occurrence in corporate work environments—wherein mismanagement has taken active roots. It is often more prevalent in single-owner enterprises or in organizations where mis-managers do not allow, by default or design, a departmental structure to develop.

More often than not, the boss comes to know when such a situation develops. This development by itself is a consequence of some mismanagement. And a more serious act of mismanagement is perpetrated the moment such a boss decides not to do something substantial to remedy the situation.

KIL, during the financial crisis that it encountered, in its 36th year of existence, through numerous acts of mismanagement inflicted on it, exhibited a classic situation of the cat-and-rat syndrome. When its CMD was not in his cabin, a majority of work stations were deserted. Telephones continued to scream for attention while groups of gossiping staff were seen in various corners.

Unrighteous Credit and Discredit Apportioning

Credit and discredit apportioning is a critical area of human resources management. Only managers of righteous mental balance or those with ***sattavic prakriti*** are capable of right distribution of performance credit or discredit. Most of them tend to grab as much credit as possible, while righteously it might belong to a junior. Discredit distribution is much easier for them as spotting a junior for this purpose happens almost effortlessly. They prefer to totally dissociate from an activity gone astray than be part of it and undertake a job of explaining the circumstances that contributed a situation of failure and or non-performance.

The practice of ***unrighteous credit or discredit apportioning*** (UCDA) inflicts long-term damages on an organization. Unrighteous discredit distribution encourages the wrongdoers to repeat such activities with impunity. In another situation, unrighteous credit apportioning acts as a severe discouragement to performing people who might end up being blamed as non-performers. In both the cases the subject corporate bears an impact of long-term significance: The human capital of the company suffers incalculable damage for no fault of itself.

The author witnessed a CEO of a nearly 40-year-old company openly blame incompetencies in its finance and marketing departments for the corporate's failings—while an impartial analysis pointed in a different direction. The persistent drag of the blame pushed the said departments to truly nonperforming depths.

BEHAVING LIKE DHRISTRASHTRA

In corporate management, there is no scope to act as a blind king—blind to the misdeeds of one's junior, a protégé or a relation. Dhristrashtra,[2] from the epic, the Mahabharata, was the king of Hastinapura—and his unbridled love for his evil son became the major cause of the destruction of the *Kaurava* clan, along with their friends and supporters. Non-punishment for wrong doings on the part of persons close to authority is a very dangerous development: It often invites ruinous consequences.

In a corporate closely watched by the author, wrongdoings by a younger cousin of the CEO were ignored for long—and finally, they landed the company in a serious financial soup. In another case, a business partner of the author did not like to know the deficiencies/failings and indiscipline of his son, which in the long run saw to the ending of a long association. Unrighteous acts, particularly on the part of those near the centre of power, serve as irreversible poison to discipline and output in a collective work environment.

In the interest of active flow of energies of innovation and superior output in a corporate work environment, a CEO should be totally intolerant of unrighteous activities of people who are near to him or who may so claim.

In the absence of such an approach, the consequences of mismanagement do not take time to manifest with their all-out disabling results. Like the Kaurava clan, innumerable corporate entities are destroyed or turned sick by unrighteous CEOs or owner-entrepreneurs, for their uncontrolled love for their progeny or relations—through endless masking of their wrongdoings.

Prevalence of Extra-buck Syndrome

Once, the author had an opportunity to work as a consultant with a 40-year-old organization, with three plant locations and engaging approximately 150 people. A large section of its white-collar workers had put in over 20 years of service—and almost all of them seemed actively dissatisfied with how things were managed in the company.

Deterioration of the finances of the company due to some unwise investments and defective planning, led to delay in salary payments and clearance of other dues of the employees. Delayed increments and growth opportunities diminution had activated negative talk/gossip tendencies amongst its people. There frequent talk as to how some people made some extra money and how some were prospering through this type of anti-corporate activities. Even the managing director of the company was not spared of this malicious gossip.

On a deeper look, the main cause for this tendency emerged from the top functionary of the company, who had not taken precautionary measures to prevent the emergence of such tendencies. He and a cousin of his were directly controlling all purchases, procurements, and finances—and all efforts to introduce a system of competitive quotations and evaluation committee-based purchases were frustrated, in order to keep the defective practice alive. Hence, the gossip syndrome was unavoidable in these circumstances.

With the lapse of time, it led people to firmly believe that the practice of making an extra buck commenced from the top —and that its tentacles touched all corners of the pie. Further, whosoever was associated with any type of purchase or procurement (even remotely) was viewed to be making an extra buck. People on the top too contributed to talk and comments that promoted such an unhealthy gossip syndrome.

It affected the efficiency as well as the morale of most of the key employees of the company. The preaching from the top to have more transparency in different activities of the company was not viewed seriously at all. It was, indeed, a situation of grave perceptions and moral mismanagement.

Allowing Emotions to Cloud One's Mind

Emotions are a double-edged instrument with positive and negative manifestations. They have to be employed with great care and objectivity. Management professionals/CEOs are often found wanting in effective and judicious application of this vital tool. They allow the cloud of emotions to blunt their own judgements. Imbalance or bias in selection of people, responsibility assignments, credit and discredit apportioning, reward distribution, and in several similar motivational and de-motivational activities, emotions are found to cloud actions and reactions of senior management professionals and/ or entrepreneurs. Such clouding of decision-making, if repetitive and intense, ends up adding up to mismanagement. Misplaced brotherhood (caste, creed, and kinship bias), not so uncommonly, has been found superseding qualifications, experience and performance potentialities.

Emotions such as attachment, hope, fear, greed, enmity, hate, revenge and many other positive and negative ones are consequences of imbalanced/clouded thought warriorism. They come in the way of righteous decision-making—and finally effective management actions get distorted under its influence.

Unbiased and unclouded mind is the best insurance against such situations of mismanagement.

Encouraging Generalists over Technocrats

Most CEOs tend to exhibit a degree of incompetence in balancing relationships that is necessary for them in their dealings with generalists and technocrats operating in key positions of the company. Technocrats are often limited by their own specialization—and, even when they exhibit capabilities to quickly imbibe skills of generalists they encounter resistance from seniors, by design or default.

Over certain levels, all corporate positions become generalist in a major part of their content: They become positions for management of people and resources. Despite this fact, arguments are often used to deny technocrats a fair opportunity to move into wider areas of responsibilities. It leads to accumulation of discontent—the negative energies of thought. Initiative and performance suffer for this simple act of mismanagement: The righteousness of growth opportunity distribution is missed.

In an American MNC, with which the author spent eleven long years, one manager code-named SC, and well known for efficient decision making, exhibited an active bias against well-qualified managers—particularly those holding doctorates in technical specialties. Some loose remarks, particularly about those holding doctorates, often escaped from his otherwise well-restrained tongue. He was particularly non-tolerant towards one of his colleague named KNS, and it could be understood in view of the latter's innumerable incompetencies. But, this peculiar habit or inconsistency of his, often extended to other persons holding deserving doctorates—and performing well in their assigned positions.

He was himself a generalist—and not too well qualified, though the convent school background had given him good communication capabilities. He, possibly, had missed opportunities for securing better qualifications at an early stage of his life, and this lost opportunity created in him a tendency for non-tolerance or non-appreciation of those who happened to be better qualified. Consciously or unconsciously, he had to fight the emergence of an inferiority complex — and hence the unrighteous utterances in favour of the highly qualified people, escaped from his otherwise well disciplined managerial self. His numerous management decisions, appreciations, and associations emitted sparks of bias as indicated earlier—but, except on a few occasions, he managed to escape the resultant ugly manifestations of this personality discrepancy.

Damage to Workplace Harmony

Workplace harmony represents the flow of positive energy in a particular work environment. It is the energy of a work team, the energy of co-operation or the energy of "let us do it."

In a collective work environment that has the benefit of harmony, work flows like a silent but energetic stream, progressing towards its goal—overcoming all resistance and obstructions. Here, team participants share the joy of output—as they have no anxiety in regard to apportioning of credit—monetary or otherwise. To a considerable extent, righteousness prevails here. Some managers—who fall in the category of mis-managers or damagers, do not like harmony of a work system. For them, something working smoothly is really not working at all. They see action in chaos or disturbance—they love to create crises. They like to make a place for themselves in it—as their negative personality thrives on conflict. Their misconceived self-interest propels them to disturb the harmony of a smoothly operative system.

Mis-managers, professional or otherwise, when they come to occupy senior positions such as location head or CEO, invariably end up damaging the ***harmony of a work environment*** (HWE). It may occur by default or may be pushed in by design—normally the latter being of more frequent occurrence. A good percentage of ***first generation entrepreneurs*** (FGE) who fail to make the grade as successful businessmen, end up exhibiting destructive tendencies of mismanagement. Various acts of mismanagement that contribute towards damage of the harmony of a work environment are described at appropriate places in this work—and hence, it is unnecessary to enumerate the same here, so as to avoid repetition.

Operation of Unhealthy Nexus

Unhealthy nexus (UN) development in corporate work environments is not very uncommon. It sprouts in numerous forms through un-professional practices that take roots as manifestation of selfishness fuelled by lack of systems and controls. The lack of transparency, under the guise of confidentiality, effectively irrigates the unhealthy nexus that often eats into the foundations of efficiency and profitability.

Concentration of power in a select few hands is a cause as well as effect of unhealthy nexuses. The author witnessed the operation of the following nexuses of varied intensities in diverse corporate work environments.

- Between purchase manager and suppliers,
- Between purchase manager and his boss,
- Between project management and contractors,
- Between sales manager and dealers,
- Between logistics manager and transporters,
- Between quality control and suppliers—and so on.

The list tends to grow almost endlessly.

Any unhealthy nexus, irrespective of the people involved, is an obnoxious form of mismanagement—and the latter, in numerous circumstances, serves as cause as well as effect of this malady.

Weak and inefficient professionals—and also those having their own axe to grind are often seen to tolerate this unethical practice.

More than the direct economic loss that such practices cause to corporate interests, they damage the moral fabric of a society; people start losing faith in the governing apparatus of the afflicted corporate and its fairness. All types of nexuses, small or big—and irrespective of their level of occurrence—give out some warning and identity smells and it is up to the senior management to pick up the same, go to their roots —and finally eliminate their cause as well as their effect.

Dysfunctional Peer Pressure

Peer pressure (PP) is a highly useful tool for accelerating superior performance in competitive work environments. An intelligent CEO will make his key people work effectively through pressure of one on the other—to let ***standards of performance*** and evaluation come into active operation. Managers, senior or junior, among themselves, should be allowed and encouraged to ask for and offer information, assistance, suggestions, and constructive criticism. It sharpens the competitive edge of an organization.

A mis-manager CEO might, on the other hand, strive to limit meaningful peer interaction. if he suffered from a concentration of negative energies and/or a tamsic prakriti.

His attention normally centres on power concentration and dividing people for maximizing meaningless controls. He, in fact, suffers from lack of productive interpersonal skills—and, as such, promotes mismanagement.

Disinclination Towards Performance Appreciation

People with inherent insecurity or those suffering from some ***deficiency syndrome*** (DS) are scared of appreciating the good work done by a junior or a colleague. They behave as if they stand to lose something by so doing or the recipient of appreciation might ask for some raise or benefits. They are not people managers—don't have skills for non-material motivation. They are, in fact, deficient managers or mis-managers, and do a lot of harm to the organization that they belong to. They inactivate the performance energies of initiative and innovation of willing workers.

The writer had direct exposure to one known as KNS who was terribly scared of appreciating any good work done by any of his juniors or coworkers. Senior management came to know of this deficiency and, in the final analysis, he paid for it—but, in the process the careers of several of his juniors were damaged. Some of them suffered permanent scars to their personalities.

There are KNSs in every corporate work environment. Organizations operating in competitive environments, or those attempting for faster growth, should expeditiously isolate such managers into non-crucial areas and let them operate alone with only a secretary to assist them.

Insensitivity to Personal Situations of Employees

It is a situation that manifests itself in major sections of the business world in varying intensities. Some employees do run into problems related to health, finance, transfers, and other related inconveniences. When such situations are beyond the capability of the concerned individuals, the need for an empathic approach arises—and if appropriate assistance and/or guidance is not provided in such times, interactive negative signals start spreading in the corporate body—undermining its intrinsic bonds of co-operation and productivity.

Here, the author would like to cite an example of a junior colleague of his who was working with him in the early 1980s in a MNC. He was a highly amicable and widely liked person in the corporate family. He developed a coronary heart problem and needed open heart surgery. In those days, for this kind of treatment people normally went to the USA, which for his honest means and dealings looked unmanageable. Interactions within the employees' corporate body soon led to the emergence of opinion that the company should offer to assist him in this time of unexpected ordeal. This thought interaction had a positive impact and the needed assistance was extended to him by the company. It earned a lot of positive feelings in favour of the company—sparing it from development of a situation of human resources mismanagement.

Pulverization of Organizational Structure

Some proprietors and CEOs, being unprofessional and autocratic—suffering from insecurity or negativism, don't allow organizations to develop any meaningful structures. Often, structures might exist on paper or in charts, but they are rendered non-functional due to autocratic efforts aimed at power concentration.

Such mis-managers want to deal directly with every one and for every thing—they want every single slip of expense to be pre-signed and pre-approved by them. Every order is to be processed and placed by them. They believe in unipolar management. They want department heads/section heads, technocrats, and experts to be totally subservient rubber stamps, and yes men—always standing in attention. They either do not know what delegation is or, due to their insecurity, do not know how to delegate. They want one exclusive centre of power—which is against the basic concept of a corporate or creation of a ***collective work environment*** (CWE).

Some of them operate as single broom sweepers—using the same stick to handle everyone. In practice, they operate a 180 degree flat organization, dealing with peons, drivers, and senior most department heads, in the same manner and breath. Their language usage or variation skills too are insufficient, or so they behave, to create an unnecessary impression of their omnipotence. They are all mis-managers or damagers.

This disease of ***unipolarism*** is seen strongly in first-generation entrepreneurs, who are not trained in the intricacies and benefits of management professionalism.

They may initially grow an organization to a certain level due to a certain favourable combination of circumstances—but finally they end up destroying it or making it static and unviable for competitive growth. Some of them also end up destroying what was created by their previous generation.

The author was a witness to two such events—one at Hyderabad in the middle 1990s, and another in the NCR region, a few years later. In the first case, he was a technocrat turned into a first generation entrepreneur. Initially, he was very successful and the enterprise grew well for the first 6-7 years; but his non-delegation and consequent non-development of the organization over-burdened him. He hired several qualified senior people but never loosened the strings of authority enough, to permit organizational structure take any roots. Any senior person who seemed to become effective was not tolerated. It led to frequent senior staff turnover giving him a bad name in the industry, on the one hand, and further burdening him with work, on the other. Finally, overburden and lack of physical activity killed him.

When just around 50, he succumbed to a heart attack while distributing cards for the wedding of his only daughter.

The second one almost killed a well developed and profitable business in a rush to create multi-location production facilities, without keeping track of diversion of working capital, mounting establishment expenditure, and inability to secure business to fruitfully engage the facilities that were created.

Appointing Senior Professionals and then Ignoring them

For new cash-rich companies or start-ups, it is easy to hire senior professionals. The lure of prestige for the employer entrepreneurs and the smell of cash for the professionals lead to this often short-lived phenomenon. Some old family-run companies too suffered from this malaise, particularly prior to the liberalization of the Indian economy.

It is a serious form of mismanagement in the vital sphere of thought as well as action management, since both the parties suffer from incapability to deal with the complications that often arise from such attempts. Both the parties might lack experience to deal with each other and have expectations that are difficult to be met. The professionals expect to be treated (consulted, trusted and respected) in accordance with their professional standing, while the employer looks to be treated as an all-powerful boss—and the final authority in all matters. In principle, both sides are immature to handle complicated communications and human resources situations.

The author personally witnessed KRD, who was a successful first-generation entrepreneur with a king-size ego, engaging in the process of hiring professionals of standing in the fields of R&D, engineering, and marketing, and soon getting dissatisfied with.... Subsequently, when overtaken by righteous thought processes, he admitted to the author his own inexperience and incapability to deal with people of capabilities equivalent or superior to those possessed by him. He promised to make a conscious effort to scale up his capabilities in this field, but did not live long enough to give a practical shape to his amended thought process.

Practice of Senior-Bashing in Public

Highlighting performance, or lack of it, in relation to a corporate worker—senior or junior, is one of the essential functions of management. But, this crucial function requires extreme care and delicacy; it needs experience too—as the judgement of how and how much emerges from the same, is essential. Juniors should invariably be handled, for this purpose, through the channel of their reporting and supervision. More care is necessary when seniors have to be handled in this regard. On no occasion should a senior be berated publicly as it breaks the morale of all those who witness such spectacles, or come to hear about it afterwards. Appreciation, however, can always be administered openly.

A good section of corporate managers, in multinationals and others, are seen as deficient in the art of administration of appreciation or depreciation in terms of selection of time, place, and methodology. Hence, the intended results are not achieved.

Particularly, seniors-bashing in public, in the presence or absence of the persons concerned, always becomes an act of mismanagement. Undesirable results, visible or otherwise, always follow such avoidable activities.

Events of bashing of seniors and/or subordinates arise out of a combination of incapabilities and/or insecurity syndromes that cause communication deficiencies. The destructive love for authority exhibition too sometimes incapacitates righteous thought processes. All of it ultimately manifests into situations of performance damaging mismanagement.

TOLERATING INCOMPETENCE AND INDISCIPLINE

With the concentration of power in one or few selected hands, incompetence and inefficiencies tend to proliferate in an uncontrolled manner. In the absence of adequate departmental structure, selection of staff, their training, placement, and work assignment becomes an uneven and irregular process; suppliers and customer selection suffers—resulting into inefficient purchases, sluggish supplies, and dissatisfied consumers. Lack of supervision leads to unrighteous practices that push work ethics through the window.

Work output and efficiency take a back seat, as the employees are able to offer a variety of excuses; reasons for not doing a good job and getting away from its consequences multiply. It breeds a difficult-to-stop process of incompetence and indiscipline genesis.

Soon dissatisfaction starts accumulating—growing to the extent that the whole process of corporate productivity looks lifeless and nonrevivable. Hence, tolerating the existence of incompetence and indiscipline, and the causes that contribute towards the same, add up to a matter of gross mismanagement.

To say that one is surrounded by incompetent subordinates and still not do something to remedy the situation amounts to compounding the folly of mismanagement. RNS and KSC both exhibited this uncommon characteristic of mismanagement. Those suffering from indecisiveness and fear of action, in addition to other incapabilities, tend to exhibit such traits of mismanagement.

For effecting improvements, such mis-managers, in view of the author who had direct work experience with the two personalities cited herein, have to improve from within if they can summon enough righteous energies in a decisive and persistent manner.

Looking for Your Own Reflection in Senior Professionals

Several entrepreneurs and business proprietors expect to see their own reflection in their senior employees; they would like them to sit late hours in office, not take holidays, and have the same concern for business matters as they do themselves. It is a very unwise expectation—and whenever it is not met, they start feeling let down. Some even turn expressive about it. KSC was seen being particularly expressive in this regard: he tended to regard this as one of the major causes of his enterprise's multilateral failures.

Such mis-managers forget that these employees, irrespective of their seniority, do have their personal and family responsibilities. They also disregard the basic elements of human psychology—how human beings react to avoidable and unnecessary stresses. Also, they do not attempt to put themselves in place of the subject employees, even for a second. These are, in fact, manifestations of ***deficits of professionalism*** (DP) on their part—a serious form of mismanagement, at least, at the thought level. Minimization of this deficient thinking is the best way of avoiding, at subsequent times, its serious manifestations.

Not Giving-in in Time—Behaving Like an Unwilling Goat

Some senior managers do not know the art of giving, whether it is a promotion, an increment or even a change of designation. They think, though erroneously, that a delay or deferment by itself is a solution. In fact, they behave like an unwilling goat being milked: She gives in but after putting in a few of her droppings in the receptacle of milk—losing an opportunity of creating a feeling of gratitude. It becomes—giving without grace or under compulsion.

Some of them do not like even giving a compliment when it is due—thinking that the recipient might start expecting some monetary benefits too. They do not know that money is not the sole necessity for effective motivation of workers, particularly the white-collar ones.

That time and timing are of crucial significance in motivation of people to greater heights of action is not part of their thought and expression apparatus. It is a serious management deficit stemming out of the negative thought concentrations and confidence deficits on the part of such mis-managers.

This tendency was often seen with KSC who quickly gave in to those becoming loud and insistent in their demands or expectations. His manufacturing and quality control people felt that the marketing department, the head of which—short-named as NT, was more insistent and loud about his peoples' interests and that he got away with whatsoever he wanted. It is not a good feeling to create in long-term corporate interests.

Allowing Untimely Burnout

Work life balance (WLB) is essential for long-term productive utility of human resources. Some people, either as per forces of circumstances or due to non-appreciation of the vital WLB, fall prey to the all-work-and-no-play situations. Excessive work pressure application, by default or design, is not an attractive proposition from any angle. It can put the ***body, mind and intellect*** (BMI) combine of a corporate worker under destructive stresses—and soon the person might get physically and/or emotionally drained. A variety of sicknesses too can set in. Such burnouts, when related to key personnel, prove immensely costly for the corporate.

The author had an opportunity of seeing two CEOs, both first-generation entrepreneurs who were committed to prove themselves as super successes or achievers, burning out much before time. One lost his life to a heart attack at the inopportune time of the wedding of his only daughter. He was a highly self-conscious and egoistic person—and strongly believed in intense multitasking. My advice that he should allot some of his precious time for the care and management of his own physical body was ignored—continuing with his heavy smoking and over 18 hours of daily multitasking. It was difficult for him to effectively delegate any important work—as he suffered from significant trust deficit. Soon after, his diligently built and highly profitable business collapsed due to non-existence of a supporting second line of managers, and a total absence of succession planning.

The second person too had most of the characteristics of the first one: He too was in the same type of business—and almost of the same age and ambitions. While the first one was a technocrat, the second one happened to be a commercial person without adequate professional work environment experience. Though not a smoker, he too had the dream of making it big in a short time. He had an unsustainable taste for association with MNCs, primarily for prestige—and profits expectations only in the long range.

He invested borrowed funds to create multi-location manufacturing capacities, for which adequate work could not be secured—thus landing the organization in a severe financial crisis. Losses mounted in an uncontrolled manner. And he too suffered a burnout—forcing his inexperienced wife to step-in and take part of the load. Both were the classic cases of mismanagement of work-life-balance, with disastrous consequences.

Presence of an Undisciplined Corporate Prince

Princes are an unavoidable part of kingdoms. Their disciplined presence is an asset to the ruler as well as the ruled. Quality attributes of a prince can make or break the future of a kingdom. Prince Paras of Nepal is a recent case in point—through him emerged the ruins of the Royal Nepalese household. Much before, Duryodhana[2] of Hastinapura, from the great Indian epic Mahabharata, became the sole cause of elimination of the renowned Kaurava dynasty, through the great battle that took place between the forces of righteousness on the one hand, and the accumulated evil and wicked on the other, on the battlefields of Kurukshetra.

In the corporate world too, emergence of pampered princes is not totally avoidable. Almost all family owned/controlled industrial houses do suffer from the presence of one or more favoured youngsters who waste resources and become the cause of growth of indiscipline, favouritism, and intra-corporate politics. They create multiple situations of serious mismanagement.

In cases of diffused ownership or public limited companies, some employees who happen to be near the top management, tend to assume the role of princes, breeding favouritism and, often, even corruption. Corporate efficiency and discipline takes an obvious beating in all such cases.

Irrespective of the form that it might assume, the malady of the presence and/or operation of an unduly favoured person in a corporate work environment is a form of mismanagement—and such cases must be resisted at all costs.

Allowing Growth of Hangers-on

It is very pleasant to hear 'Yes Sir' from one's subordinates and/or co-workers; and still more pleasant to lend an ear to information carriers and hangers-on. These people have the capacity to poison management perceptions, its reactions, and finally its judgements and actions in a negative and unproductive direction.

Undoubtedly, it requires a character of righteousness, and superior management skills to resist this category of people. For such a situation—where people simply hang around to unload unnecessary or designed information, the responsibility lies squarely on the subject target or the management. These people are not only unproductive—they set a chain reaction of unproductive interactions in the collective work environment.

Firstly to encourage them—and then to tolerate their presence in an organization by avoiding active effort to weed them out is an act of gross mismanagement: A large number of senior professionals and even CEOs are guilty of these acts of mismanagement.

Expecting Beyond Capabilities

Normally, people tend to scale up their output or performance as per demand of a situation—but there are limitations for performance beyond capabilities. Whenever supervisors or managers make demands on subordinates much beyond their capabilities, and if the latter do not highlight their inability, situations of mismanagement might arise—leading to non-performance and/or delay of the planned work. In such a situation, blame apportioning is normally attempted downwards, while in reality it should be otherwise.

Essentially, it is the job of seniors to assess capability requirements for implementation of a project—and adequate POLC, in this regard, need to be undertaken by them. There is no point in blaming juniors, if the results or progress deviate substantially from plans or expectations. At KIL several situations of this nature were cropping up. Its accounts department exhibited several capability gaps in financial planning and management—and the senior-most executive continued to live with it. Yet, he did not hesitate to blame the department for lack of transparency in the company's financial affairs. It was, indeed, a case of expecting beyond competence.

Expecting People to Work without Facilities

It is also not uncommon in small and medium companies, particularly those having little or no input of professionalism, to expect people to work without the requisite facilities. Mis-managers such as KNS, RNS, SM, ASP, and KSC, among others, were seen often expecting their juniors to work and produce results without facilities—or with only rudimentary ones. Some of them also expected that the juniors should employ their contacts and resources to do the job at hand. In a way, it is a symptom of mismanagement: It reflects the lack of POLC efforts on the part of seniors.

Lord Krishna[2] expected a lot of battle performance output from his warrior disciple Arjuna against the better equipped and better endowed Kauravas: The latter had, in their ranks, over half a dozen invincible warriors. Hence, prior to attempting a battle with the formidable opponents, Lord Krishna had advised/enabled Arjuna to gather some ***Brahmastras***, in order to take care of the invincibility of the opponents. Complete POLC were attempted in this regard—and results too followed the expected course.

Hiring People without Preparation

In some companies, hiring of new hands does not follow an organized system leading to, among others, the following deficiencies.

- Preparations are not made to provide a workstation and associated facilities.
- New additions are not received enthusiastically—are not suitably introduced to people with whom they are supposed to work.
- They are cold-shouldered by default or design.

- Initial training and guidance is not adequate.
- They are not briefed about the corporate culture—its presence and absence.
- Not warned about possible non-cooperation from disgruntled coworkers.
- The initial problems of relocation are not looked into.

Several business entities are found deficient in regard to the above and associated factors—primarily for lack of attention on the part of HR-functionaries and the subject department. While only minor situations of mismanagement may develop from negligence in this regard, corporate image becomes the biggest sufferer.

Frequent Utterance of "You are Wrong"

In corporate work environments, especially in collective interactions, there is very frequent usage of the two words—namely ***right and wrong,*** which mostly takes place with utter carelessness. Senior managers and CEOs tend to exhibit their superiority through usage of these tools of communication—and more often than not, the usage is inappropriate or wrong.

Right usage of ***right and wrong*** from the higher echelons of management can signal an employee's motivation, performance graph (including the resultant promotability), attachment to the organization, and most significantly his or her image as a knowledge worker. Misplaced motivation or de-motivation could occur in a fraction of a second—with a substantially lingering effect.

Often, the perceptions of right and wrong are influenced by personal considerations—the judgements are, more often than not, erroneous and unrighteous—coloured with personal considerations.

On deeper analysis, it looks surprising how such perceptions and utterances tend to brand an employee—and point fingers on his/her performance and personality—with long-term impacts. This approach smells of immaturity as well as negativity (at least in part of the cases) on the part of the seniors who attempt this type of branding of people: It might amount to closing the scope for in-depth evaluation and/or re-evaluation—and giving a go-by to the feasibility of effective employment of his/her strengths.

Such corporate perceptions of right and wrong, or what is acceptable or non-acceptable, are relative and contextual in nature:

They ignore the personal sensitivities of employees involved. By so doing, the senior management also seem to be attempting to absolve itself of the responsibility in regard to an employee being viewed in this manner—forgetting that he or she is being affected by the corporate work environment and inputs emerging from the seniors: The two are not dissociated—and hence, the responsibility of an employee's performance is never single directional.

The senior managers have often been seen by the author as being in a hurry in branding people—as good or bad—performers and/or non-performers. They seem to prefer the ease of such an approach as it allows them a lot of leeway in their interactions with the subordinates; the in-depth analysis and evaluation is never easy.

This hurried branding (HB) is a serious form of mismanagement—its impacts on the career and psychology of the employees involved are long-term and debilitating. It must be avoided under all circumstances.

The author witnessed several senior managers and also some CEOs employing the erroneous technique of HB while dealing with their subordinates. KNS was never so explicit—he preferred to de-motivate and un-nerve his juniors through inaction and non-appreciation. GRV often used the HB terminology to push up the people of his own clan—and attempt to browbeat those who did not agree with him—but, he often effectively mismanaged in this effort: He was never successful and paid through his nose for all his acts of mismanagement.

KSC was often seen as being in a hurry in employment of the word ***wrong***: He succeeded well in de-motivating his own key people through this unwise usage of words—and several other acts of mismanagement. KRD's fat ego too tempted him in application of the ***wrong*** word, but he was careful in not damaging the motivation and productivity of his people.

Badmouthing a Departure

The tendency of job-hopping is growing in almost all types of corporate work environments. Particularly, the BPO and the IT industry in India reported growing problems in this context. As always, new business entrants or startups find it convenient to pick up staff from existing operators, instead of investing time and effort in locating and training new hands. For employers who have invested time and effort towards converting raw human materials into efficient and performing workers with productive customer contacts, it becomes substantially inconvenient, and sometimes even frustrating, to see trained employees leave for greener pastures, with or without adequately contributing to the corporate that trained them in the finer aspects of business. On the other hand, some non-performing employees or those who indulge in incompatible or ethically unsound practices need to be pushed out. Both the situations, often, result in inconvenient departures, which need to be handled carefully.

Inexperienced and/or professionally unsound HR managers, and even a number of CEOs, are often seen losing their cool or creating situations where the employee prefers to leave—leading to bad-mouthing, which tends, among others, to have the following undesirable impacts on corporate working.

- Spoils the corporate work environment,
- Adversely affects morale of other employees,
- Clients may draw unhelpful conclusions,
- There might be some loss of business,
- Corporate image in the industry might suffer,
- Demands from other employees might grow,
- Filling the gaps so created might need special attention, and
- Competition might assume an upper hand.

Such situations of mismanagement can easily be avoided through application of the ***madhura technology of communication (MTC)***, as practised by Lord Krishna[2] the most efficient manager known to mankind. As a matter of principle, staff departures should always be made smooth and pleasant: It is always better to send out a goodwill ambassador so that in his or her future references only a good word emerges from the mouth of a former employer.

CHAPTER 2

Mismanagement—An Interplay of Negativity

Negativity* is the ***black hole*** of management. It is one of the major causes of corporate mismanagement. Undercurrents of non-cooperation and intrigue in an organization are products of negativity interplay within its various constituents. It is a complex expression of the forces of selfishness and unrighteousness that prompt a human being to act and behave in a manner that its consequences and/or effects go against the larger interests of human society or the grouping with which he or she is intensely associated, or interacts with in a frequent manner. Such a grouping could be a team, a family, a caste, a village or a country as a whole. Although no part of human activity is ever free from manifestations of negativity, here we focus on its exhibition on the part of corporate workers, as an avoidable interaction of ego within a collective work environment. ***Interplay of negativity*** (ION), in a collective work environment, is essentially multi-dimensional—rendering its true and total expression, or their enumeration, beyond human skills and capabilities. Some of these are as under:

- Biased selection and placement of people.
- Unfair credit and discredit apportioning.
- Employing any criteria other than efficiency and merit as ground for credit and reward.
- Work avoidance—with or without tenable excuses.

*Interactions of negativity presented herein are part of the ***Theory of Negativity*** propounded by the author in mid 1970s.

- Inadequate or deliberately controlled output.
- Instigating coworkers for reduced output or disturbing work-flow.
- Poor quality of work output—products or services, despite being capable and trained for doing otherwise.
- Deliberate or designed damage to physical assets or production facilities of the company.
- Diversion of inputs or outputs of corporate work.
- Deficient maintenance of corporate assets.
- Excessive anti-establishment expressions.
- Personalized criticism of any coworker—junior or senior.
- Doubting others' intentions or integrity without adequate reason or proof.
- Lack of initiative or inciting others to avoid work.
- Fighting with one's tools.
- Perpetual absence of initiative and innovation.
- Hiding innovation for subsequent usage.
- Picking cuts in purchases and supplies.
- Punching holes in the plate one eats from.
- Behaving like a dog in the manger.
- Experiencing difficulty while required to appreciate others for work or merit.
- Experiencing multilateral insecurities.
- Back-biting or information carrying.
- Any practice of groupism, favouritism and nepotism.
- Hiding facts by design.
- Unwillingness to accept one's fault and say sorry.
- Repetition of the same error or mistake.
- Frequent application of I/me/mine—instead of we, us or ours.
- Practising excuses galore for inefficiency and inadequate outputs.
- Various other actions of omission and commission.

EMERGENCE OF NEGATIVE INTERACTIONS

Allowing flow of excessive negativity, or its accumulation, in a corporate body is a serious form of mismanagement. It could be a cause or effect of absence of productive team spirit in the organization. In a medium sized multi-location company (KIL), which was doing fairly well just a few years ago, development of intense pockets of negativity were witnessed by the author during a recent spell of observations. Some repetitions of wrong decisions saw its finances take a sharp tumble. Its inherent imbalances and deficits soon became starkly visible.

Here, senior management was in the habit of lending an unnecessary ear to those who indulged in information carrying for their own selfish reasons. The company's already weak systems and structure started collapsing, sending its self-conceived omnipotent CEO into a spin of delusion. The large flow of people that he had allowed, as a general practice, to come to him with small requirements, complaints, information and/or stories, became too much for him to handle; he started admitting that his office was a pocket of intense negativity. He no longer liked to spend time in the office; working from home became much more peaceful and relatively less stressful.

It was, however, not the right solution. The bull of negativity manifestations commenced to take a more sinister form—as idle hands started engaging in purposeless talk and speculation. Confidence dropped and people started exhibiting symptoms of desperation—as they were not used to working without the CEO's full time presence: No one was trained or authorized, formally or informally, to issue instructions in his absence.

The fall in the fortunes of the company continued unabated.

INNUMERABLE MANIFESTATIONS OF NEGATIVITY

Once it assumes a critical mass, the ***negativity manifestation*** can take innumerable forms. Absence of a system of grievance redressal or an active HR department can throw up unmanageable issues as they get ignored and accumulated.

Not creating a viable system for initiative appreciation, performance valuation and its rewarding, always hastens to assume a serious form of mismanagement. It can suffocate merit and hinder initiative to the disadvantage of the corporate involved.

Exhibiting intolerance towards ***honest dissent*** is a disease that easily assumes an avoidable form of mismanagement; and often, it is of common occurrence in collective work environments. On the other hand, any practice of offering excessive, misplaced, and unproductive criticism too is not free from the malady of mismanagement. Lending ear to one and all is another form of ***communication mismanagement***—as the practitioner of this nefarious habit is often over-confused and deluded—adding to his inability to take timely and righteous decisions. Its roots too are deeply embedded in the interplays of negativity or ION. Display of anger, justified or otherwise, leads to consequences akin to mismanagement—as anger by itself conveys a situation of ***break-up of logical thinking*** (BOLT) process on the part of the affected person. And, the BOLT acts as an active hormone for negativity manifestations and multiplications to sprout and accumulate.

The presence or occurrence of situations of obvious management favouritism, for any reason, does not add to corporate efficiency; it sends desperate messages to other persons in the collective work environment, and its final consequences are always undesirable.

Permitting ***individual axe grinding*** (IAG), in any manner or magnitude, resembles a management weakness, and any support to people indulging in this practice assumes a form of mismanagement.

Any collective work environment that displays a practice of ***dominant egotism*** (expressions of I or me over we and us) is never conducive for collective or co-operative work productivity—and its tolerance, in any manner, is a symptom of mismanagement.

Absence of an ***inclusive approach*** (IA) towards growth and its benefits distribution is a definite sign of interplay of negativity. It leads to genesis of active disaffection and consequent fall of productivity. The author's own management work experience strongly suggests that an active practice of IA immediately starts giving results in the desired direction.

Some senior managers and CEOs have been noticed openly branding human assets as ***incapable***, and still expecting them to perform out of the way—or as part of a perfectly motivated team. It is an attempt on the part of the management to hide its own deficiencies—in fact, a practice of ***destructive delusion***. Dhritshastra, a dominant character of the Mahabharata[2] suffered from an unusually heavy delusion of this nature. He created one of the greatest situations of mismanagement ever witnessed by mankind.

Permitting your intellect to generate negative energies of thought and action brings you near serious failures on multiple fronts with unavoidable consequences. It may end up assigning the affected person the attributes of always being ***critical but not persuasive*** (CBNP). Most of the unsuccessful or just tolerably productive senior managers or CEOs are seen by the author to possess a significant and visible content of the CBNP.

Richness of this negative attribute was specifically intense in the persona of KNS, RNS and SKC. Shooting down a good proposal, simply because of its origin not being of your liking, is another serious manifestation of negativity—an actively damaging form of mismanagement. Board meetings and conferences are full of such manifestations—consuming precious corporate time, and allowing unproductive deviation of energies.

Starting with negative thoughts and/or reactions is an expression of accumulated negativity—and it does not take much time to convert situations into mismanagement.

The author has witnessed senior professionals and CEOs persisting to see their own ***past corporate failures*** (PCFs) in the present context too: They become incapable of or unwilling to see opportunities for success in the changed environment of today. It renders the job of consultants very difficult. Some of these mis-managers make active efforts to prove others wrong based on their past failures or consequent negativity accumulations.

Also, there is no dearth of senior professionals and CEOs who behave like a dog's tail, never shedding their incompetencies and prejudices that have overtaken them due to the heavily accumulated stocks of negativity. They become blind to their own misdeeds under the unrealistic belief that others are not able to see through their activities of mismanagement.

Omnipresence and Omnipotence of Negativity

The preceding paragraphs have stressed multiple manifestations of negativity: They point towards the omnipresence of this human characteristic. To be more specific, all collective work environments (CWEs) suffer from the presence of negativity—only its form of manifestation and intensity varies. Some CWEs, depending upon the quality of their component reactants, manage it better than others—but none, in the true sense of the matter, is ever able to fully escape or negate its impact.

Negativity is omnipotent in the sense that it is capable of influencing all human beings—irrespective of their background, education and training. There is no exception to this rule—no one totally escapes its presence as well as its impact; only reactions and responses vary. Consequently—or by implication, no CWE can ever be fully free of the interactions and/or manifestations of negativity. In a way, it is non-destructible—as attempts to suppress it help change its form and virulence.

Negativity is the major cause of mismanagement—and hence, senior professionals must attempt to understand its nature, occurrence, and manifestations.

Primary and Secondary Forms of Negativity

Primary negativity (PN) is prevalent in tribal, rural, and backward societies and their component individuals: Its expressions are straight, sharp and un-camouflaged. Expressions of anger often form part of this type of negativity since those possessing it are not much experienced in usage of linguistic intricacies. Often, expressions of anger in such cases take a physical form. Hence, it is easily identifiable—which renders its management relatively more effective. Mostly, the people rich with primary negativity are devoid of capabilities to hide their real intentions: They are poor in reactions and emotions masking capabilities.

Secondary negativity (SN) manifests itself in a way that is entirely reverse to that of the PN—its practitioners tend to do a quick profit-loss analysis of any expression that they might make or engage with. They attempt to use diplomacy and sophistication of language to say what they want to say without any edges and friction. They have great capacity to misguide the management—even to push it into areas of mismanagement. They accumulate expertise to say what they mean without so doing and also its reverse manifestations. In management, one needs greater care when dealing with people of such SN expression capabilities. They are masking experts—and, as such, inflict more damage to the fabric of corporate productivity. The author, in his long and intense corporate career, often attempted to unmask such practitioners of SN; but success was only partial—and instances where such operators succeeded in inflicting targeted damages too were not infrequent.

GETTING ENTRAPPED IN ONE'S OWN NET

The author has witnessed negativity assuming numerous forms—and, almost in all of its manifestations it was found to be capable of leading to situations of mismanagement. Envy or jealousy is one of its vicious forms: It can land its practitioner in a hot spot. The person who throws the net of envy can himself get entangled (if the targeted person or executive is sharp enough to recognize the same and initiate timely prevention) in it before he or she realizes what really happened. Such situations manifest in personal and non-personal situations—including corporate and non-corporate settings.

One such encounter the author had in 1963, when he joined IARI for his doctoral studies. Since the major and minor courses, which were assigned to him by his guide, for completing the necessary credit load, were not truly challenging for his intellectual capabilities, he decided, with the express permission of his guide, to commence the research work without any waiting. It necessitated spending a lot of time in the laboratory, where he encountered a senior operator of the department—who along with being a part of the departmental faculty and research team, was engaged in completing his own doctoral research. His negativity interactions, because of the author's personality and its compounding with the grades that he obtained—and also the latter's rapport with the head of the department, irked the self-conscious senior, who for the purpose of this piece, we will call by the identification of RCD—and, the head of the department, as KCG.

By this time RCD had spent over a dozen years in the department—but had nothing substantial to his credit as a contribution. But, being a senior, he exhibited a fat ego—which with the entry of the author as a research student, was somewhat damaged. As influenced by the new entrant's personality, the support staff of the laboratory started flocking towards him for various problem resolutions. Obviously, RCD did not appreciate dilution of his established authority.

Stung as he was, RCD planned to entrap the young researcher with the help of the head of the department. He proceeded to inform the good doctor, though fully unrighteously, that the young researcher was breaking a lot of glassware in the lab. Soon, the department head called the young researcher to his office and confronted him with the feedback that he had received through RCD. The informer had not thought through the consequences of his unrighteous acts: That, it could boomerang on him, had not crossed his mind. The head of the department wanted to confront the young researcher as he wanted to know the truth. And the young researcher, as he was not in the habit of telling untruths, promptly admitted to having broken some glassware. Further, he was equally prompt in stating that not even a single test tube would get broken from tomorrow onwards. This statement startled the good doctor, who could not restrain himself from asking as to how this feat would be achieved. The young researcher blurted out that from now onwards he would not touch any equipment and, therefore, there shall be zero chances of any breakage. He proceeded to add that he too will follow the practice of RCD—and that there was a way of doing research without really doing it. It startled the good doctor into action and he promptly asked the young researcher to go out and do his work normally—and not pay any attention to such complaints.

Next day, the head of the department summoned RCD to his office and, in his characteristic low tone, told the mischief monger to everyday break some glassware and report to him at the close of each working day. RCD, the cunning mouse that he attempted to become, was entrapped in his own net: Now, he had to struggle to complete his research—and took longer time than the young researcher whom he had targeted by his manifestations of negativity.

In corporate work environments, such interactions of negativity occur almost every day—and some of them turn into situations of mismanagement—and only consciously righteous members of this breed can successfully ward off such developments.

Not Promoting Team Spirit

A corporate, by its essential nature, represents a **collective work environment** (CWE)—and all CWEs are limited by the essentiality of team formation and teamwork. Individual work or contributions do not take a corporate very far—and they could, often, be at cross-purposes and/or in opposing directions. Negativity, at the thought level, opposes the very genesis of the energies of co-operation—and hence, individuals with a high concentration of negativity do not exhibit any initiative or tend to resist initiatives for coming together to form a productive team.

The thoughts of co-operation, or collective working, do not cross the mental screen of such people. They see others as opponents or competitors—until and unless training and guidance wake them up to the benefits of collective energies and outputs. More often than not, they have to be pushed to become a part of a team under a strong and hard taskmaster team leader. Compulsion or force does mould the practitioners of PN into collective working, with some hiccups, which take a little long to disappear. The example of the armed forces illustrates the situation very clearly—as most of the recruits (lower and middle level) to such forces are from a background of rural communities rich in PN, who under strict discipline and punishing force become productively co-operative—forming performing teams even under most challenging circumstances.

Individuals with high concentrations of SN easily form into teams—but their dependability as productive components of the team, under severely challenging circumstances, is poorer than those with the PN. Not forming a team, i.e., any tendency to work as a loner or not to initiate adequate efforts to form a productive team—inclusive of training it to assume a form of a collectively performing machine, if you are a senior, amounts to mismanagement. Any efforts—and excuses or explanations, shall not help in washing away the strains of such mismanagement.

Absence of a System of Performance Assessment and Rewarding

In corporate work environments, it is essential to assess the performance of individuals as well as that of teams operating towards the stated corporate objectives—and it should be done without allowing any bias or negativity to be operative against the basic principle of righteousness and fair play. Simultaneously, there should be a non-failing system for rewarding individuals and team members who have performed beyond the basic minimum demands or levels. It is imperative to have these two systems operative in such a manner that a good majority of the white collar workers are freed from the avoidable anxiety about distribution of the fruits of good work, within the stated corporate policy. It can generate massive positive energies; and failure for doing so will, in due course, invite the stain of mismanagement.

There is no better way known to modern management (or even to the ancient sages), than the righteous apportioning of credit for performance—and discredit for non-performance. It is one of the Brahmasastras of men motivation for long-term productivity.

But, unfortunately, very few corporate entities find the way of locating and practising it—and that is why so many situations of mismanagement are encountered in the corporate world despite it being full of trained and experienced professionals. In principle it is not a difficult thought to fathom: Forces of negativity often turn it non-operative.

Exhibiting Intolerance to Honest Dissent

Tolerance of dissent is the prime symptom of good governance—and corporate management is no exception to this rule.

The possibility of dissent propels a doer or the initiator of an action or a proposal, for an in-depth analysis or study of the pros and cons—including alternatives. Often dissension also opens the path for more remunerative alternatives: More often than not, dissenters themselves open up with alternatives—the comparative cost and returns specificities of which are always open for discussion. They open the way for wider co-operation, which in a collective work environment is of deciding significance. Work environments that permit dissensions help in dissipation of accumulation of negative energies—and prevent their further accumulation. All types of energies require an escape route or safety valve—and permitting dissensions does exactly this job, in a very cost effective manner.

Any gagging of honest dissent, by design or default, leads to progressive build up of the dissenting or negative energies, which tend to burst into confusion of mismanagement, in due course of time.

Misplaced and Unproductive Criticism

The purpose of any criticism in a corporate work environment should be aimed at focusing people's energies on productive work: Hence, it has to be objective and in right dosage—misplaced and/or unproductive criticism should not be touched even with a long pole. It kills energies of initiative and innovation—which take a long time to recoup and reactivate.

The ***misplaced and unproductive criticism*** (MAUC) has capacities to replace positive energies of thought and action into the negative ones—losing good workers and laying the ground for uncooperative ones to develop.

Even genuine criticism is a very delicate exercise that corporate managers often indulge in in a reckless manner, without a strategy and/or plan for reorienting workers' energies in the right direction. A senior manager's job does not end with the rendering of criticism even when it is rightly directed: He should get it accepted and appreciated by the recipient—so that larger positive energies emerge to do more of the planned work. Any deviation from this path leads to development of situations of mismanagement.

Display of Avoidable Anger Expressions

Anger expressions, in corporate work environments, are byproducts of a manager's inability to suitably articulate his or her frustrations, genuine or designed, and effectively clothe the inherent negative load, if any, towards the person or situation involved. Inability to understand the person, or situation in question, too gives rise to such expressions.

Here, the deficiency primarily manifests on the part of the manager getting into such expressions—not on the recipient. The author, at some stages of his long and diverse work career, witnessed situations where, in some cases, he was the originator of such expressions—and, in others, a recipient. In both the situations, manifestations of mismanagement did not take much time to emerge—and invariably, the initial arrows of mismanagement were seen hurting the junior player on the scene. The heat of mismanagement always took a longer time to reach and hurt a senior, who merited the major responsibilities to avoid the same.

In addition to the parties directly involved, anger expressions severely damage the subject corporate work environment—which, in the long run, inflicts greater damages to its competitive productivity.

Though it might look otherwise, the negative impact of anger expressions—especially on the part of the recipient, never fully disappears; a lingering tinge always continues to remind the sub-conscious of the victim. On the other hand, the perpetrator of anger expressions may tend or pretend to forget such impacts. Hence, the wise and righteous always attempt to avoid such expressions: They, indeed, form the true measure of a professional's maturity.

Persisting with Ego-dominance Display

The majority of successful entrepreneurs and a variety of technocrats tend to make a giant display of ego-dominance. For them I, me and mine dominate over we, us, and ours: Negativity and perception of capability actively emerges as a persistent flow of ego. Consciously or otherwise, an excessive deposit of ego turns them into highly sensitive and touchy beings.

While at IARI, as a doctoral research worker, the author was able to closely witness the naked display of ego and negativity on the part of the scientific staff of the institute, capable and the not so capable ones. Most of them treated the scientific equipment in the laboratories of their departments or sections as their personal assets or turf—not allowing any one to make even limited use of the same, until and unless their fat ego was serviced in some right form. RCD, a member of the author's own department, had substantial concentrations of avoidable negativity: A few pieces of old and non-operative—almost useless—equipment in his room, which rarely worked, had allowed him to behave like an unwise rat with a piece of cloth—who was prompted to think of himself as a great stockist of cloth—and did not hesitate to brag about the same.

The mask of ego, in case of RCD, was blown off several times—the most striking one being when he attended a course of statistics where the author too was a co-student: His intellectual deficiencies forced RCD to copy from the author's note book for managing to pass the subject course. And this little event humbled him a lot; he lost the mask of intellectualism.

Even work environments of MNCs were found full of such characters of needlessly inflated ego—which, in many cases, the author had opportunity to deflate. Ego display on the part of the untrained and uneducated could be expected and tolerated to an extent—treating it as a case of ignorance –but in practice it emerges where, in reality, it must not—if true professionalism or scientific training has to have any meaning.

Whatsoever the situation, irrespective of its practitioner, technologist, professional or generalist, dominant display of ego or arrogance is never conducive for effective operations in collective work environments. It causes numerous situations of mismanagement and unwanted anti-productivity consequences.

Following Exclusive Approach Towards Benefit Distribution

In the majority of cases, corporate work process results in growth and profits, and the same need to be judiciously distributed every year or at an acceptable periodicity, in favour of various heads and beneficiaries. This distribution of benefits is the acid test for performance of the management: It gives the management a choice to paint itself in whatsoever colour that it might desire and decide—depending upon the relative intensities of positive and negative energies governing its actions and perceptions.

When the fruits of growth are distributed in an even manner, without discrimination—and giving due consideration to merit, commitment and performance, then we call it as the ***'inclusive approach'***. And the reverse of it—when steeped in discrimination and ignoring merit, we term it ***'non-inclusive approach'***. The two have diverse and opposing impacts, in short as well as long term: The first one activates positive action forces well catalyzed by the energies of mind and intellect—cementing commitment of employees for superior action.

The exclusive approach sows seeds of disaffection, activating negative thoughts and energies, which invariably diminish initiative, co-operation and output. Such an approach amounts to practice of mismanagement—the consequences of which adversely affect all components of the corporate structure.

BRANDING YOUR PEOPLE—IN NEGATIVE COLOUR

Branding products always helps—as assignment of values and perceptions is aimed at a certain group of consumers. But sadly, it does not work the same way with people—particularly with employees. Branding any one of them as inefficient or incompetent robs the person concerned of whatsoever intentions there existed, within the person, for any improvement. Here, the management's word is viewed as final—since it is very rare that such an ill-equipped management will try adequately to re-motivate the person thus affected. On the other hand, the positive branding does more harm than benefit—because the excluded employee shall always resent it—and the beneficiary too might slow down thinking that a long-term effect has been achieved. Unhealthy interplay of negative energies tends to become active in thus altered situations.

There exists a vital difference between rewarding, celebration, and branding: The former always motivates all involved—beneficiaries as well as non-beneficiaries, while the latter does not have such positive merits.

Generating Negative Energies through Words and Actions

Many senior managers—including CEOs—have been seen as being incapable of restraining their own negative thoughts from their emergence in the form of unhelpful or biting words and also actions that de-motivate and alienate their subordinates. Through such failures, consciously or unconsciously, they fuel negative energies in the whole work environment.

Some make prophesies of doom with the hope that these shall make the targeted persons fall in line of thinking and action deemed most suitable. But the author, during his long and diverse corporate life, has never seen this approach being effective or productive. ASP and KSC were particularly prone to utter words of doom—and both proved themselves experts of mismanagement.

Normally, actions speak louder than words—but, in management, actions do leave some scope for correction or retreat—while the toxic words once uttered are totally out of control. Toxic communication (TC) is the worst form of mismanagement.

Speaking with a controlled and/or measured tone and well weighed terminologies is one of the best tools of management—and if one desires to be verbose, then he or she should have the skills of Lord Krishna,[2] his charisma, and also his *madhura* system of communication.

Cultivating a Habit of Saying No—Needlessly

As per defective thought concentration, for some managers an opportunity for saying no resembles the flow of corporate power—or the authority that they think to have accumulated by virtue of the positions held.

They relish shooting down of any proposal if the same did not emerge with their prior consent and/or if it did not serve their interests, personal or corporate. Such an approach represents a massive flow of ego or negativity, which is highly injurious to corporate health.

Criticism of what does not originate from or belongs to them or their cronies, often, comes more as a reflex action—not that any considered thought or input so necessitates. Such nay-sayers, often, are incapable of initiating any new idea or project, primarily for the fear of criticism from their peers—and also from the likelihood of failures. Discouraging such people from their chosen path is fairly difficult—but they often tend to melt under direct confrontation.

This group of people offers a double danger to corporate health—one, they interfere with the genesis of initiative by others and two, they never themselves initiate a beneficial action until and unless it serves their personal needs and interests. They are mis-managers of a highly dangerous category.

CHAPTER 3

Mismanagement of Financial Resources

After human resources, finance is the second.most important reactant in the crucible of corporate work process. It is put in second place because of its inertness—as human element is needed to manage and manipulate it into action, as an input of productivity.

Like other elements of production, finance too is incapable of ***self-management***. On account of its critical nature as a corporate productivity input, its mishandling forms a majority fraction of the total spectrum of corporate mismanagement, irrespective of the nature and type of the corporate in reference.

Everywhere and at every stage of corporate activity, financial mismanagement remains the most significant part of what is undesirable in the corporate world. Some of the key causatives or practices of the financial mismanagement, as discussed in this work, are presented below.

OBSERVING NON-TRANSPARENCY IN PURCHASES

Purchases (raw materials, equipment, and other physical inputs of production) consume a major part of corporate funds—in some industries it represents over eighty percent of all the input side of financial transactions. Lack of transparency in purchases, practised often by design than default, is one of the most serious areas of mismanagement. In some corporate bodies nothing gets purchased without a cut for the purchase manager, his assistants, and often also for his boss. Attempts to correct it are met with dogged resistance from various levels having direct and/or indirect interest in the matter.

The author experienced some serious encounters with this problem right from his college and university days—and the more serious of the same came his way during his consulting assignments in the past two decades.

One Kolkata based corporate group had a sick unit located at Ankleswar in Gujarat. It was engaged in production of agrochemicals. Its economic viability, like any other business of this type, was dependent on its competitiveness based on process efficiency and consequent cost of production. Since the process of production, in this case, was capable of superior yield, the cost of production should have naturally come lower than its multinational competitor; but the facts were otherwise.

Further, in-depth analysis revealed that its raw materials purchases were made at a higher rate, more by design than default. Existence of vested interests was starkly visible; yet efforts to get to the depth of the matter and to stem the rot were resisted on various counts. Lack of transparency was killing the corporate body, and finally the disease had the better of it.

Additionally, in the year 2006-7, the author was associated with a multi-location corporate body with an impressive product list on one hand, and multiple MNC manufacturing contracts/associations, on the other. Yet, its finances were in disarray. It had an accumulated debt burden of over Rs. 150 million. Intense interactions led to its product costing and purchase procedures study, and in the final analysis it came out that the company did not follow standard purchase procedures; rarely took quotations, and supplies came from sources wherefrom, as per confidential sources, the purchase head's interests were duly protected. The purchase manager and his assistant openly quarrelled on rates and sources of supplies. The matter was discussed in depth in the ***business management committee*** (BMC) at several occasions, and it was decided that there should be a purchase committee to vet and decide all major purchases.

The CMD of the company was required to issue a notification on behalf of the BMC—to the effect that such a committee was appointed and its areas of operations and authorities specified. Despite reminders, the notification never got issued and the said committee never saw the light of day. Operations of the company saw a steep fall in the months that followed; suppliers' bills remained unpaid for months—and for years in some cases. Salary payments were delayed for 3-4 months, and people started leaving for alternatives. The signs and symptoms of serious financial mismanagement became starkly visible.

Permitting Revenue Leakages

Revenue leakage of any type, at any level, and whether by default or design, emerges as a serious form of mismanagement. Apart from small leakages, which are difficult to locate and plug effectively, large diversions of revenues normally occurs with design only. Under billing, supplies without bills and allowing disproportionate or unjustified business facilitation/market development expenses are some of the common modes of revenue leakages that occur with or without consent or involvement of senior management.

In both cases, it is a serious form of mismanagement. Financial mismanagement, whether through purchase cost mark-ups, designed revenue leakages or any other method, do not remain secret and hence the disease slowly spreads to the lower strata of the afflicted corporate. Finally, after long-drawn struggle it brings the business to sickness and eventual collapse.

Allowing Absence of Internal Audit to Persist

Many small and medium enterprises do not erect a regular and effective system of internal audit. While some organizations avoid it under justification of financial stringency, others either do not feel the need for it or they avoid it by design, as a convenient way to conceal diversion of costs, expenses and revenues. In all of its manifestations, absence of effective audit in a commercial organization amounts to serious financial deficiency.

In all situations, shareholders' interest suffers. In a way, it amounts to officially sanctioning the practice of financial mismanagement. Its absence becomes truly mystifying when the chief shareholder or the proprietor himself exhibits interest in its non-presence: Such situations become truly testing for outside consultants when they are engaged to find and suggest ways and means for correcting inefficiencies accumulated in such a corporate.

Sacrificing Returns for Relationships

Some small companies tie-up with large companies or MNCs as manufacturer/supplier, and if they are not good at negotiations or exhibit eagerness for association, they end up pushing themselves into losses. Smart and experienced MNCs are able to negotiate ***bone-dry terms*** (BDTs) of supplies wherein the small supplier ties up its limited financial resources in such tie-up supplies. Payment terms, more often than not, get deviated; thirty days become ninety, and as a consequence the financial cycle comes under strain. The smaller party ends up meeting the statutory liabilities (central excise, etc.) too on behalf of the large partner. Its own business, i.e., the supplies to its own trade channels that formed the bread and butter, too get starved. Financial crisis starts developing: and often the MNC partner, on some pretext, changes the supplier—leaving the smaller partner totally bruised and disoriented.

The author recently witnessed a disastrous operation of such a tie-up business—how a management's misplaced eagerness to remain linked to MNCs/large companies, for the sake of false market image, totally crippled it financially. Firstly, the transfer rates negotiated for supplies left hardly a margin of two percent or so with the manufacturer/supplier, while the factual cost of servicing the order added up to equivalent or more of the margin so allowed. Secondly, a large part of management time and energy was spent in servicing this large order—often there were frayed tempers from the beneficiary side. The manufacturer supplier's own market got starved; its customers from whom large advances were collected earlier with promise of supplies got disappointed. The whole sales force was demoralized; collections dipped with reduced billings—and a crisis situation developed. Payment of salaries, travelling expenses and other dues became a nightmare. It became a classic case of financial mismanagement.

Unremunerative Product-Supply Relationships

A product-supply relationship can be sustained only if it is mutually beneficial. As and when such a relationship starts tipping in one direction, the symptoms of its eventual discontinuation become visible.

The author once had a first-hand experience of this financial eventuality. As head of a small-scale production unit, he had entered into a supply contract for an agrochemical formulation with another much larger and well-established company. It was made amply clear by the author, right in the beginning, that his small company was not to bear the working capital load for this operation; all production inputs were to be supplied or promptly paid for by the other party. After a few months of operation, the latter started to stretch the matter by delaying payments and, the limited working capital resources of the producer/supplier started getting blocked in this operation. It started affecting the small partner's core business—and consequently its profitability. Reminders and discussions across the table brought inadequate improvements. As dictated by the common management wisdom, the smaller partner promptly discontinued the arrangement, saving himself from a situation of financial mismanagement.

On another occasion, the author closely watched another much larger multi-location company failing to extricate itself from unremunerative supply relationships; they had tied up its scarce working capital resources to supplies to an MNC—and it led its own ***bread and butter*** (BAB) business to dry up in the face of inefficient supplies. Employees suffered in absence of in-time payments of salaries and other basic dues. Statutory dues accumulations and other unmet demands created a situation of severe financial mismanagement, with all its associated ill-effects.

Creating an Excessive Load of NPAs

An organization can accumulate a variety of non-performing assets and all of them, in one way or the other, contribute as a drag on its performance. Physical NPA may include production sites, buildings and offices, and plant and machinery. Apart from those having strong feasibilities of long-term appreciation, all other such facilities should be looked with an emotion-free lens—for the purpose of converting them into liquid assets that could be put to better usage for efficient management.

Loans, advances and investments that are not yielding return commensurate to market conditions need to be looked upon very critically. Unutilized, inadequately utilized human resources or the people who have turned into deadwood, for one or the other reason and, as such, are not likely to improve despite reasonable stimulation, need to be looked upon from the angle of possible disengagement.

Normally, in any organization it is the twenty percent active human element that contributes eighty percent or more of the output—and the rest eighty percent, the inactive or the less active segment just drags on: They are the human NPAs or the deadwood. This drag, visible or otherwise, reflects the degree of mismanagement operative in the subject organization.

Each person's performance—as well as his or her potential for the same must be analyzed. Reduction of such NPA load is a measure of

management performance evaluation (MPE)—and must be indulged in at all costs. High performance and superior competitiveness does not come easily. But in most cases, incompetent seniors always tend to oppose such measures.

Thin Spread of Resources

Stretch your feet as per the size of your cover-sheet, is an old Indian saying. It has its own truth and rationality. It is wiser to increase the size of the sheet before attempting to over-stretch your feet.

In the commercial world this simple old wisdom has a wide utility. Expanding too fast, beyond your resources, can leave you repenting; and spreading resources too thin in several activities or on multiple locations often brings more headaches than returns. The author had several opportunities to witness this thin spread of resources—bringing established businesses to their knees—or suffer a substantial slowdown. SM, a second-generation entrepreneur in Chennai, was one such businessman who stretched his feet much beyond his financial provisions. First, he put up a greenfield agrochemical unit based on RRL-Hyderabad technology and, even before it became functional work on establishment of a unit for textile dyes was commenced. The working capital funds secured for the first unit were diverted to the second one. And as bad luck would have it, the international dyes market collapsed under competition from China and the international restrictions/awareness in regard to usage of non-organic dyes. The whole operation ran to the ground. The effect of over-stretching of financial resources became clearly visible as mismanagement. In due course, both the units closed down—and were subsequently attached for recovery by financial institutions.

Securing a Cut in Everything

Some senior mis-managers have been noted indulging in a sort of an advance tax collection: They secure a cut in everything that they buy or sell. In an Ankleswar based agrochemicals company, its general manager and the two Joshis who assisted him, ensured an efficient collection of advance tax for whatsoever was done or got done. As a consequence, massive inefficiencies were built in; and they had explanations/excuses for everything.

As a chance happening, the author had accepted the responsibility of setting things right for the subject corporate. They were, however, able to frustrate most of the initial moves that were designed to improve the situation. After sustained efforts of 5-6 months and a lot of plain speaking, the situation started to improve. Once, out of frustration, the author stated that, between the two stones, profits of the company were being pulverized, and that the company could not be resuscitated until and unless one of the stones was removed. And, as a result, one of the two mis-managers was put out of the way—despite the visible resistance from both the parties involved in the long shared mismanagement. Thence onward, the pace of improvement became brusque.

Securing a cut in everything that comes in or goes out is a dangerous form of mismanagement—that too when effected by design. Also, it is difficult to correct this kind of situation as it amounts to snatching a meal from the mouth of a habitual carnivore.

Very rarely, peers and/or juniors of such managers are able to gather enough courage and resources to confront the mis-managers: The danger to their own careers, and sometimes even to their physical selves, is indeed great. The job of ***whistle blowers*** is never easy: it needs courage despite the uncertainty of results.

The late Peter F. Drucker [3] often considered as the father of modern management, dealt with the subject of weaknesses of executives: In regard to corruption, he said:

> "There is nothing more corrupting and more destructive in an organization than a forceful but basically corrupt executive. Such a person might well operate effectively on his own; even within an organization, he might be tolerable if denied all powers over others. But in a position of power within an organization, he destroys. Here, therefore, is the one area in which weakness in itself is of importance and relevance."
>
> ***He proceeded to add, 'By themselves character and integrity do not accomplish anything. But their absence faults everything else.'***

The great guru fully realized the disabling influence of corrupt practices in corporate work environment, but he did not employ the term "mismanagement" to describe it or its disastrous impacts.

PRACTISING EXCESSIVE DIVERSION OF FUNDS

Corporates normally have two types of funds—fixed capital and working capital. Often, mis-managers indulge in diversion of both of these funds, without concern whether the same came from promoters and/or financial institutions.

More often than not, funds diversion commences as soon as a project starts taking roots; it becomes active in the building construction and equipment purchase phase. As a result, some projects commence suffering from the strains of mismanagement right in their initial construction/establishment phase. Many others run into problem within a few months of commencing production. Wherever such diversions occur, the consequences of mismanagement cannot be dissuaded from appearance—only delay is feasible when the mis-managers are very skilled in this nefarious art.

Some smoothly running companies too divert funds into unproductive assets and diversifications—ailing divisions and/or sister concerns employing terms such as inter-corporate transfers—mostly being of short-term nature. In more cases than not, the symptoms of mismanagement soon become visible. The author, in his long corporate work life, witnessed numerous instances where working capital funds were put to other applications—and disastrous consequences did not take much time to emerge. SM and KSC actively engaged themselves in this kind of activity—the former under the misguided approach of his two senior executives mismanaged his current as well as future business. Under intense desire to create multi-location production facilities in quick succession, KSC effected a massive diversion of funds—leading his corporate into a long-term sticky situation.

Functioning Without Contribution Analysis

Return is the most sanctimonious objective of business. Each product, service, technology, investment, location, and person should, in principle, make a positive contribution. The level of contribution should be more than the total cost of production of a product or service, its marketing and servicing, and also the overhead costs that the subject business necessitates, if it is to be viewed as profitable. The author has seen several organizations as being partly or fully blind to this fundamental requirement of the business. They continue to carry loss-making products and/or services, along with the profitable ones, without any commercial logic. On questioning about the wisdom of such a practice, the first response normally is that of disbelief and, in some cases, efforts are made to justify the same by saying that they were needed by the market or were part of our old ***core-business***. Marketing and/or commercial experts, in most of the erring companies do not even understand the difference between ***supplying and selling*** activities—leave apart marketing which has substantially intense and elaborate connotations. They strongly put up to the management what is demanded by the market and forget to know or stress that the products are needed to be sold with the sole objective of keeping the company's ***bottom line*** green. Losses are inevitable if this basic principle is ignored even to a minor extent.

Here, the ***information deficit*** or ***capability deficit*** plays the dominant role in emergence of mismanagement and its consequences. Sometimes, cunning and smart purchase or business managers are able to push in products and services in which they have secured interests of cuts and kick-backs. The author has witnessed, isolated and even highlighted such situations, in the course his diverse corporate engagements.

Sometimes even marketing people of dubious intentions are able to develop undesirable links with dealers/distributors, and insist on supplying such products in which the producing company has little or no contributions but the recipients continue to benefit.

This situation was starkly apparent in KIL wherein, out of its 47 products a dozen actively lost money for every kg or litre of sale—another two dozen just touched the break even point and the rest—the profitable ones were paid only scant attention. The company lacked a dependable product costing system, and product cost inquiries did not elicit very pleasant response. Its purchase department was busy purchasing—what was convenient and serviced established interests. It suited marketing too but the company lost money, and soon ran into inconvenient situations of mismanagement.

Similarly, it is necessary to develop a ***contribution analysis*** of the key people involved in a business; no one should be allowed to become a drag on the company's resources. Technologies involved, physical locations, and investments too should not escape an unbiased contribution analysis.

Perpetuation of absence of a cost-return consciousness, in any manner, amounts to laying foundations of mismanagement.

PREVALENCE OF *LAISSEZ-FAIRE* ATTITUDE

Many people, in corporate or otherwise, lack the attitude or inbuilt desire for improvement and/or proficiency in relation to work output. For them 'what is happening' is good enough, until and unless, a superior strongly points out the need for improvement, lines up a road map, and insists that the desired change be effected within an accepted time frame.

This '***laissez-faire***' or '***chalta hai***' attitude has a contagious effect in collective work environment, especially in India and in several other developing countries. It primarily sprouts from the ***tamsic nature*** of people for whom the concept of improvement, refinement, and service touch only through its total absence.

It is also seen as the residual continuation of the non-competitive tribal past of the people involved. In a competitive work environment, it should not be allowed to occur and/or flourish in any manner. Its tolerance, in any manner, sows seeds of mismanagement the unpleasant fruits of which are sure to emerge at a later date.

Normally, inefficiency and work avoidance is very infectious: it tends to spread fast amongst even the better performing employees. Further, it exhibits uncomfortable connotations of negativity. The best antidote for this infectious disease is a strong organization structure with well-enabled and trained departmental heads capable of creating/exerting requisite ***performance stresses*** on everyone falling under their jurisdiction.

Having Cloudy Concepts of Profitability

The concept of profitability, in its full refinements, is not easy to be understood by untrained entrepreneurs or corporate workers. They do not understand how contribution and value addition are different from profit—and the difference between profit and net profit too is not very clear to a good majority of them.

Interest on capital investments when contributed by entrepreneurs from their own resources, are rarely paid adequate attention. Similarly, cost of working capital, market inventory, credit supplies, and return goods, etc. is not adequately appreciated. The author has closely witnessed a medium-sized company run into financial crisis, by not fully appreciating the cost of advances which it had picked up from its dealers and distributors at the market rate of interest, and with a crisp promise to make timely supplies of their future requirements. The funds so collected were diverted to other more pressing needs, without being fully alive to the stresses that were to occur in the high demand season that followed. Most of the products that were to be supplied to the market against these advances did not have adequate profit margin to bear the inherent interest burden—plus the normal cost of operation. The cloudy concept of profitability with the senior professionals of the company brought it to a very uncomfortable situation of mismanagement. A lot of hue and cry emerged in the heavy product demand season—and the corporate management had no effective cover to take.

Doubts about the very capability and/or intentions of the company emerged not only from the involved traders—the sales and services staff too commenced voicing the same type of concerns. An atmosphere of total unease developed—and the whole marketing operation fell in non-collectable pieces.

Practice of Excessive Financial Looping

Financial looping (FL) is a funds management technique resorted to in a situation of financial stringencies. It amounts to usage of funds from one source and, after the target application, reverting the same to its origin (as goods or services) or another equivalently valuable one. It also means specific employment of customer funds to be used for payment to specifically linked creditors. In certain situations, it amounts to putting the same cap on several heads in an efficiently/well-designed manner. With untrained staff or inefficient financial systems, where its constituents do not adequately appreciate the value of timely payments, collections and transfers, intensive looping may cause situations of distress. With one company that had fallen into financial stringencies for avoidable reasons, the author had an opportunity to witness intensive looping exercises. Supplies were secured on credit with the assistance of PDCs, products formulated and supplied to one or more branches which undertook to get the said PDC instruments to be honoured. Problem arose on two fronts—one, on the part of manufacturing where actions got held up for packaging components and auxiliaries, and two, on the market front where sales staff did not fully grasp the significance of timely collection. So, two crucial links of looping acted as weak links, endangering the whole operation. Hence, when an organization is not fully trained to appreciate the time element in manufacturing, supplies, sales, and collections, intense looping can easily develop into a situation of mismanagement.

Turning Business Cycle on its Head

In production-related business activities, the business cycle consists of the following key steps:

- Procurement of raw materials,
- Production of marketable goods,
- Supply and billing of goods to interested customers, and
- Collection of payments as per agreed terms.

The above ***business cycle*** is repeated the year round, or as per the demand characteristics of products and markets. The author has seen the ***normal business cycle*** (NBC) being turned on its head in the case of some organizations. They start with collection of advances from the market, normally in advance of the season; expeditiously make purchases of raw materials, manufacture goods/formulations at breakneck speed, and complete supplies to the market. Then they either revert to the normal business cycle or use a mix of the two options in a manner that customers are kept happy and the subject company's turnover swells to a desired level.

When handled inefficiently, the above deviant activity could end up with disastrous consequences. If the funds collected from the market are diverted for any purpose other than the procurement of relevant raw materials, the ***unnaturally modified business cycle*** (UNBC) will end up disturbed in a manner that the whole business operation is crippled beyond repair. It leads to genesis of trust deficit between the customers and the company—and its employees, who are supposed to service such customers, themselves start suffering from confidence deficit. Both these areas of deficit are not conducive for the long-term health of the subject corporate. Hence, in the hands of inefficient or undisciplined managers, the whole operation tends to turn into mismanagement—of difficult to handle proportions.

Lingering on with Bottom-Line Bleeding Products

In business, products and services are produced for the express purpose of generating profits. Profit results only when contribution from a product or service (selling rate minus cost of production) is large enough to take care of all the expenses involved in its sales and marketing, and also overheads of the organization. Further, the volumes of sales too have to be large enough to permit such a situation.

Astute CEOs and finance managers are expected to keep track of contributions being offered by individual products in a company's product range. For this purpose, product costing has to be consistently updated by the finance department, and all key managers in purchase, production, sales and marketing, and any other person playing a key role in the commercial activities of the company, have to be kept updated about the same.

Observing secrecy about technology is OK, but keeping product costing wrapped up away from those who are supposed to manage the same, amounts to initiation of mismanagement. These should be transparent so as to allow all concerned to be actively conscious of contributions and profit generation. It safeguards against development of surprises and trust deficits.

Products that bleed the bottom line should quickly be referred to the R&D for cost reduction efforts and, if any cost cuttings are not possible, they should be quickly disbanded without any remorse or emotions. One should remember that products are for the company, and a company is never for bottom-line bleeding products. Any deviation on the part of the professionals from what is stated above shall tend to create situations of mismanagement.

Tolerating Accounting Confusion

In a majority of corporates suffering from mismanagement, the telltale symptoms of the malady are often visible in the form of accounting confusion. In the late 1980s, the author had an opportunity for working for a sick company belonging to a large family-run business group located at Kolkata. Its accounts were in such shambles that no one knew how much was collectable from which customer. Credit notes were not passed for years together, and its sales staff was in a state of animated confusion. By virtue of his handling the marketing department, the author had to exert pressure for performance by the accounts department. Without clearance of this mess it was not possible to make any progress in the market place.

The mis-managers in this case were so strong that they were able to persuade or push the author's boss to issue orders that he should not mess up with the accounts department. But being an action warrior, the author did not give up despite the unpleasantness so generated—and finally, the mess was substantially cleansed. Its impact immediately became visible in the form of improved market response and efficiencies of the people involved.

Years later, similar confusion was witnessed in the KIL, a large agrochemicals company, where the accounts department and sales branches rarely agreed upon the amounts collectable from individual customers. Here too credit notes were not made and/or entered for years together. There was a perpetual stream of bad blood between the sales group on one hand, and accounts and the CEO on the other. A lot of productive energy was lost in the confusion. Mismanagement of a serious nature was clearly visible in this corporate: Soon it took a turn for the worse.

Overturning the Financial Cycle

In business, there are definite financial cycles specific to individual activities. For manufacturing, corporate funds are employed to procure raw materials, packing materials, and other essentials. Further, wages/ salaries, and overhead charges, including marketing costs are met out of the working capital of the company. Goods produced, as per sales/ marketing plans, are sold to dealers/distributors, and after credit period, if any, outstandings are collected and deposited in the corporate account.

A company known as KIL heavily diverted its working capital towards creation of capital assets at two different places. Matching business plans were missing from its management shelves, and no arrangements were created for the working capital needs as augmented by the addition of extra facilities for production.

For working capital needs, large advances were picked up from distributors/dealers, with the promise of choice product supplies and attractive interest payments for the intervening periods. These pre-season collections too got diverted for payments to creditors as well as towards finishing the newly created production facilities.

When the season came, shortage of working capital, reduced confidence of suppliers, and inadequate support from banks created a crisis situation—supplies to the market got affected to the extent that dealers/distributors and also the company staff, who a few months earlier were instrumental in collection of huge advances, panicked on seeing the drying up of the supply channels.

So as to enable continuation of supplies to the trade even at a reduced scale, it was decided to loop raw material purchases and payments for the same on 45-60 days delay basis, from the dealers who picked up such stocks. Thus, the corporate financial cycle was effectively turned on its head with such unpleasant results that:

(a) The marketing staff only reluctantly agreed to work the new system, and

(b) The traders who could not be part of the system grew skeptical.

The company lost credibility in the market and the sales force got demoralized as it was neither accustomed to sell what was available but not actively demanded—nor facing the paucity of products being in active demand. They were used to supplying what was demanded by the trade: they were not skilled or accustomed to sell what was being made available by the management.

This disturbance of the corporate financial cycle was attempted without due planning and training. In the final analysis, it amounted to mismanagement, as sales dropped by 40 per cent and the company found itself not in a position to pay salaries/wages and travel bills in time. Suppliers and transporters, in face of their huge accumulated dues, became impatient. Corporate morale dropped and losses mounted.

Practising Doctored Accounting

It is common for a large percentage of companies, listed and unlisted, to play with accounts for the purpose of showing better returns on investment—and also conceal income for the purpose of tax liabilities reduction.

According to a report prepared by the Pune-based Indiaforensic Consultancy Services (ICS), at least 1,200 companies listed on Indian stock exchanges forged their financial results (as per a report in *The Times of India* of 23rd Sept., 2008). These figures included 20-25 firms on benchmark sensex and NIFTY indices. The study was titled 'Early Warning Signals of Corporate Frauds' and alleged that such improper accounting included deffered revenues and inflation of expenses.

The ICS study that commenced in early 2008 and concluded by August end, examined 4,867 companies listed on BSE and 1,288 on the NSE. The survey polled a large number of willing chartered accountants.

The motivation for such frauds primarily was exceeding expectations of investment analysts and the investors. For unlisted firms such irregularities were carried out to avoid taxes, attract foreign investments, and mobilize funds.

As per the author's experiences, balance sheet mismanagement was visible with a large percentage of corporates that he worked with: It is more of a rule than an exception. And these practices, in several cases, have been seen deteriorating into a situation of serious mismanagement.

MISCONCEPTION OF OMNIPOTENCE

The American financial system had suffered for a long time from the misplaced concept of omnipotence, which was busted so decisively by its total collapse of September 2008.

Its mighty institutions, the big ones which included Lehman Brothers, Merrill Lynch, Morgan Stanley, Goldman Sachs, AIG, etc., had a great fall in the market place. Some moved for bankruptcy—and most of them had to be rescued by the Federal Reserve and the Bush administration in a manner that was so very uncharacteristic for capitalism's greatest proponents.

In the past, there have been numerous examples of financial collapses but this was the most unique case of financial mismanagement—an unanticipated happening of the unexpected.

CHAPTER 4

Mismanagement of Physical Resources

Mismanagement (mis-utilization and non-utilization) of physical resources/assets in the corporate world occurs in numerous ways. A variety of physical assets are created (buildings, plant and machinery, laboratory equipment, etc.) tying up costly funds—and in several cases they result in genesis of NPAs, becoming a long-term financial drag, and pushing the bottom line down. Lack of ***long-term planning*** (LTP), absence of critical analysis from the angle of alternatives, and practice of ***autocratic decision-making*** (ADM), singly or in multiple-occurrences, give birth to such situations of mismanagement.

Small and medium scale companies tend to avoid formal LTP for reasons of resources or lack of vision: The practice of ADM on the part of their CEOs and/or senior professionals too contributes to this inconvenient deficiency. Some of the modes which contribute towards this development are briefly discussed in this chapter.

CREATING UNUTILIZABLE PHYSICAL ASSETS OR CAPACITIES

A Chennai based agro-chemical company (known as CAL) in the 1980s, was seen creating four production facilities located at unconnected distances in different states, by default or design (not known exactly), none of which enjoyed capacity utilization beyond 20-25 per cent. In addition to the problem of avoidable inventories, co-ordination, logistics and overheads, it ran into multifarious non-resolvable difficulties, finally collapsing in a financial mess. Further, the author saw a medium level north India based company of long standing, with two plants at the same location, add another much bigger one some 70 km away in the same state, despite the fact that the first two hardly enjoyed a capacity occupancy of 25 per cent.

A few years later, under the attraction of certain tax benefits and after a lot of dilly-dallying, it further added a plant in a hill state some 500 km away. Travel and transport costs swelled but commensurate business growth did not take place; in fact, the business suffered a serious drought of working capital—creating an unmanageable situation of financial crisis. All the four sites suffered serious under-occupation. A situation of serious mismanagement developed, despite intentions to the reverse. The absence of LTP was starkly visible in this case.

Physical NPAs becoming a Drag on Profitability

The two production facilities of the company referred to in the preceding paragraph, located at its original location turned into NPAs in the absence of work, but no decision to dispose off any one of the two could be arrived at. The two NPAs plus the additional load of part utilization of capacities at newer locations turned to be too much for the cash-starved company to carry on.

Disposal of NPAs is never an easy job; firstly, it is weighed down by an emotional load—and secondly, most of such managements lack skills of thought and action commensurate for requisite cut and dry decisions. All NPAs are part of corporate valuables—the fixed assets, from the point of view of the balance sheet—permitting depreciation benefits, and eventual reduction of income tax payables. NPAs also form part of assets offered to banks as collaterals. In case of a financially deficient corporate, NPAs act like heavy gear on a drowning man. They must be cast away as soon as possible, even at prices somewhat lower than normally thought to come from the sale of such assets under normal circumstances.

Permitting any drag of NPAs on a corporate body, particularly when the latter is passing through a financial stringency, amounts to a serious act of mismanagement.

Creating Avoidable Essentials

At the time of creation of physical facilities, movable or immovable, they are all viewed as essential, particularly by the person and/or the group that moves for such acquisitions/creations. Such essentiality, often, is a consequence of inadequate analysis from the long-term utility point of view, and also consideration of alternatives. In most of the business entities, a little glance can point to the presence of numerous physical assets which are not in current usage, have not been often put to productive usage in the past, but were viewed as essential at the time of their acquisition. This type of liability, once created, is difficult to get rid off because clean-up decisions, irrespective of their nature, are always inconvenient and hence avoided; they are unpopular and need skilful preparation. Creating such avoidable essentials and not quickly disposing them off, ends up as mismanagement of resources.

Outsourcing is an efficient way of avoiding such facilities or so called essentials, whether services or products: It is often a better and more cost effective alternative. But for a majority of the senior managers, professional or otherwise, with whom rests the authority of decision making, the idea of outsourcing has been an uncomfortable one as it does not allow expenditures on new physical facilities, which subsequently could be treated as specific turfs or areas of personal influence. For some the non-essentials too are a matter of prestige and status—and hence they tend to indulge in establishment of such facilities more by design than as a productive resource for the efficacious management of the corporate concerned. Being under the influence of the forces of mismanagement, consciously or otherwise, they don't appreciate the idea or merits of a lean and mean organization. This defective thinking underwent transformation only recently, particularly under the wave of globalization.

Physical Resources Falling into Undesirable Hands

Unutilized and/or underutilized physical assets/resources such as premises, vehicles, equipment, etc., may fall into undesirable hands; it may lead to avoidable liabilities, litigation, and sometimes even in total losses. Instances of misuse of inactive premises by bad elements for assembly, planning of their antisocial or criminal activities, and even as dumping ground of legal/incriminating materials, are not uncommon. In such an event, the whole situation may develop into a case of mismanagement.

Handling of such physical resources—either their better usage or disposal is not considered as an appreciable attention catching activity: Additionally, it might involve some inconvenient decisions or actions unpleasant to peers and/or seniors. Hence, it is viewed better or more convenient to let such physical assets remain in their present form of disuse: Their existence in the present form of neglect also offers an opportunity to place blame, whenever necessary, as a diversionary tactic. Though such an approach might initially offer a certain cover, in the final analysis it ends in magnification of impacts of mismanagement.

Inadequate Maintenance of Physical Assets

All physical assets, irrespective of their type, need regular maintenance. As and when these assets go into non-utilization or under-utilization, their maintenance tends to suffer due to attention dilution. Deterioration in quality and consequently their disposable value thus becomes unavoidable. For financially tight companies, lack of resources becomes a valid argument for inadequate maintenance of such assets. Cannibalization of such assets, by design or default, also grows into a problem. Finally, it ends up emitting the smell of mismanagement.

Physical assets like automobiles, aircraft, railways, roads, bridges, and all others when not maintained properly show strong symptoms of mismanagement. Similarly, all bio-systems including business entities do require maintenance inputs if they have to stay in their designed performing forms.

CHAPTER 5

Mismanagement of Talent and Technology

Talent and technology are the two components of a corporate body, which reflect the quality of its human composition. They are the key to its operational competitiveness and eventual profitability. Being very sensitive to handling and treatment, these vital components easily fall prey to mismanagement at the hands of incompetent and/or insensitive authorities at the corporate pyramid. Some frequently occurring situations of such mismanagement are described in the following paragraphs.

IGNORING IN-HOUSE TECHNOLOGISTS AND R&D

It is often seen in improperly managed companies that its own technical persons are ignored at the time of ***critical decision making*** (CDM), particularly towards procurement and induction of new technologies. It primarily happens due to express and/or non-express manifestations of negativity, i.e., either the presence of personal ***mis-interests*** of the senior person taking the decision or his ego to demonstrate his authority. Ignoring ideas and recommendations of in-house technologists, without adequate analysis and substantial grounds, sows the seeds of negative interactions, inappropriate decisions, and consequent multilateral damages, with the passage of time.

Another obnoxious practice, which results in even worse consequences, manifests itself when a senior manager or CEO openly claims or states that his own technical people are totally useless or incompetent. These expressions exhibit his or her frustrations and/or inability to understand their own people and take them along the new path as motivated coworkers.

Such comments or observations send the corporate image for a six. As per the author's observations, KRD and SKC were both seen passing such unbecoming remarks about their respective technical coworkers. In the first case, technocrats never stayed for long with the company—and in the second, the technical people employed therein could never contribute adequately due to directional inadequacies on the part of its CEO. Both the companies met with subsequent failures of massive magnitudes—confirming the development of situations of serious mismanagement, on account of the ***peoples' factor***.

In more than one ways, technologists and R&D are vital assets of a business organization—a sort of insurance towards future crisis management or opportunity appreciation. Only incompetent or excessively negatively charged CEOs or corporate heads ignore these vital assets.

Losing Track of New Developments in the Business Line

Corporate performance, on a long-term basis, demands that its senior management keeps track of new developments in areas of its specialization. Outdated technology means poor competitiveness, poor market realization, and eventual loss of markets. Normally, incompetent managements fall prey to such situations. Non-technical CEOs who sometimes develop an active bias against technologists, do not allow concerned people to pay adequate attention to this aspect of business. In such a situation, it becomes difficult to fight development of technology deficits. When ignored over a long time, these invariably cause a situation of mismanagement.

Sometimes, a technology deficit is allowed to develop under the guise of financial stringency. More often than not, the inability of senior management to appreciate the value of technology, from a long-term point of view, becomes the basic reason of this kind of mismanagement. Catching up becomes very difficult, costly and frustrating, once a corporate falls behind its key competitors in the field of technology, and consequent product quality attributes.

Having no System for Talent Recognition and Rewarding

During his long corporate work engagements spread over 40 years, with more than half a dozen corporate bodies, the author did not find a well-established and transparent system of ***talent recognition and rewarding*** (TRAR) at any place—MNCs included. It has been a neglected area of productive manpower management.

The HR department was conspicuous by its absence even in large companies prior to the end of the 1980s: Normally the personnel department chipped in to do the job, as best or as worst, because the main function of such outfits was to locate and recruit the desired manpower, and also to handle labour issues. Labor management and HR in the Indian context gained active currency only from the last two decades of the 20th century.

In large companies—including MNCs—groupism, regionalism, and mentorship took care of talent, wherever it existed or survived. Talent development and rewarding took place more often, through default than design, or as the insignificant component flow in an established corporate system. Often, talented people had to manage for themselves either by shifting jobs or through acquisition of superior ***boss management techniques*** (BMTs). For the latter, they ran into severe competition from their less talented colleagues. With the growth of the HR function in the past over two decades coupled with improvement in job availability, TRAR is beginning to get its relevant dues. Development of IT industry has been a boon of assistance in this direction.

In small companies, this function totally rests with the CEO or the boss—more precisely on his or her follies and fancies: Only a very few of them have the time and/or intention for this delicate activity. But, what has been fully visible is the fact that talent, whenever not treated fairly, either fades away unproductively or moves out unceremoniously. In both the cases, it forms a loss to the corporate concerned in particular—and society in general. Although very few CEOs normally see it this way, it represents a severe form of mismanagement that ends up harming its victims as well as its perpetrators.

Non-Anticipation and Blockage of Technology Leakages

Technology, whether developed in-house or outsourced, needs to be protected jealously in view of the fact that it is a valuable asset that requires effort and investments to develop or acquire. But technology is not such an item that could be kept under lock and key all the time. People involved in its implementation are likely to pick up the details; there is no foolproof security for it. Patenting is the best way to protect a technology that is developed in-house. Its maximum usage during the patent's life is one of the best ways to get the best out of it.

Confidentiality or secrecy agreements with the employees who handle it, is another way for its protection; but the best insurance against technology leakages is to keep the employees exposed to it happy and well rewarded. Well-treated employees tend not to disclose technology even when they have moved out. A careless attitude towards technology, i.e., not anticipating potential leakages or thefts—and not building adequate safeguards, surely qualifies to be viewed as an act of mismanagement.

Non-Infusion of New Blood

Some managements are scared of infusing new blood, better qualified and with superior skills, on account of the fear that new additions may initiate a wave of demands and/or expectations from the existing ones, or may cause disaffection for one or the other reason. Others fear the cost of new additions and the uncertainties involved in handling them—the latter being a crucial factor.

Incompetence of one or the other type on the part of management is the main reason for non-addition of fresh talent to an organization. It is particularly inexcusable if the subject business happens to be in a highly competitive segment. Sometimes incompetent employees find ways of convincing the management against fresh additions—particularly well qualified and talented ones. Irrespective of the cause, non-infusion of fresh blood proves costly for an organization on a long-term basis, or as soon as it runs into superior competition. In such a situation, no organization can escape earning the tag of mismanagement.

Employing Incompetent Relatives in Key Positions

Almost all first-generation entrepreneurs and some even afterwards, suffer from the temptation of employing their relatives, close or distant. Most of them prove incompetent for the positions they are put in or are able to grab by design or default. Since they are not trained for the positions that they end up occupying, they breed incompetence and mediocrity. When situations of crisis develop, they fail to measure up to the demands of the business—and the enterprise ends up bearing the cost of management incompetence.

Often, they become or at least tend to become centres for groupism and also cause of injudicious distribution of credit and discredit. In several cases, family-related negative interactions have been seen by the author severely affecting corporate functioning, leading not only to inefficiencies but disputes too. In this process, ***collective creative energies*** (CCEs) often fail to come into being, i.e., emerge and fructify. Unrelated employees too, as a reaction, end up fuelling such discordant manifestations.

Professionalism is the first casualty of this high impact ***thought and action deficiency*** (TAAD) on the part of management of new/small enterprises. These TAADs quickly frustrate the forces of initiative and innovation wherever they might exist even in minor quantities. In such organizations, as a matter of rule, righteous distribution of credit and discredit does not take place.

Attempting Opportunistic Use of Technocrats

In several small and medium enterprises, proprietors tend to attempt designed use and/or circumstantial (by default) misuse of technical persons—often initially hired with a lot of fanfare and promises. The specific objectives, more often than not, are to draw maximum technologies/technical benefits out of the persons so employed. As soon as the specific objectives of the management are fulfilled or when they come to other unfruitful conclusions, attempts are initiated to sidetrack or ease out such people. Some leave in disgust while others are pushed out.

KRD at his maiden corporate outfit, which initially tasted substantial success due to association of some good technocrats with it, was seen actively engaging in such tactics. He brought in a number of technocrats, most of them his friends and colleagues, with promises of substantial benefits—and invariably, all of them subsequently regretted their decision to join a friend. Most of them were intensely frustrated and actively bitter; the whole affair becoming a massive exercise in mismanagement.

The author, along with a friend, had a first-hand experience of a similar nature and intensity at Chennai in the middle 1990s, where they had joined to assist a local businessman known as SM, towards installation of a greenfield project for a unique agrochemical unit having substantial export potential. As soon as the plant started production and initial success on the export front was achieved, the behaviour of the entrepreneur changed under the mis-influence of his non-technical cronies. They prevailed upon him with the view that when the technology was established, operators were trained in handling the plant, and markets were identified, there was no need for retention of the costly technocrats. Actually, the main reason for this manipulation was to milk the cash cow, which was not possible in the presence of outsider technocrats.

Within months of departure of the targeted technocrats, quality as well as quantity of output dropped; attempts to reverse the trend with local help did not succeed, and soon the plant fell sick, eventually closing down as a dead property. Numerous examples of such misplaced mismanagement have been witnessed by the author, none of which was seen bringing any credit to the misguided managements.

DEVIATING FROM CORE COMPETENCE

The ***Core competence*** of an organization refers to the basic areas of its strengths in terms of technology, production, brand image, market share, etc. In other words, it is an organization's capacity to face the competition, expand and grow its market dominance. It permits the subject organization to take risks and leads in the areas of its proven competence.

The concept of core competence was initiated with C.K. Prahalad[4] and Gary Hamel's path-breaking article ***The Core Competence of the Corporation*** (*Harvard Business Review*, May-June 1990). It stressed that leadership rests on being able to do something others cannot do at all or find difficult to do even poorly.[4] This vital concept has been appreciated in India only recently—primarily after the market liberalization and globalization of its economy.

Thousands of years ago, primarily in the context of governance, **Lord Krishna** had promoted the concept of righteousness as his area of core competence:[2] He pursued it throughout his long and arduous struggle towards protection of the good and virtuous from the forces of evil and wickedness. His divine ***Song of Wisdom*** or the ***Bhagavad-Gita*** continues to illuminate millions of lives even today with the never ending sparks of righteousness—His well advocated ***Core Competence***.

For a financially and structurally strong corporate, deviation from its core business sometimes becomes essential for its diversification and growth. Special opportunities do not have to be always ignored but all such activities are to be engaged into after due diligence to ensure presence of minimal risk in so doing. Adequate preparations are necessary, including assessment and assurance of adequate endurance in the event of planned results not appearing in desired times and volumes. Deviations from core competition, without adequate preparation and resources, have often been found excessively damaging. Existing businesses have been noticed to suffer long-term damages when deviations from core areas of competence were made without adequate thoughts and/or preparation. They immediately create an image of mismanagement, which often is very difficult to shake off.

Not Benchmarking with the Best in Competition

If you want to grow in your core business segment, and have the resources to back up the needed effort, then it is necessary to benchmark with the best in the sector—and put into action a suitable strategy to achieve the same. One can't reach the top without aiming at it—so one should undertake all the POLC required for the same. Not benchmarking in the suggested manner reflects on inherent deficiencies of management—and in certain favourable circumstances, not doing so, may amount to mismanagement of opportunities.

Benchmarking is not a simple or an easy activity. Firstly, it needs an intense and detailed management exercise known as SWOT—and it requires an intense follow up with detailed POLC. It can inject new energies of confidence, initiative, and teamwork necessary to catch up with the market leader, and even to get ahead.

Mediocre managements are normally scared of benchmarking with a market leader—primarily because they suffer from ***active thought deficiency*** (ATD) that does not either allow them to think of challenging the best in the trade or create an existing inferiority complex to magnify. And even when some benchmarking plans are put through, deficiencies of thought as well as action tend to linger in regard to implementation of the plans designed to achieve the same. Such plans, primarily, are not backed up with the needed resources and the repeat attention that they demand to be effective.

CHAPTER 6

Mismanagement of Decision-making: Time, Opportunities and Action

Decision-making (DM) is the major part of business: One could say that business management is nothing but the art and science of decision-making. In the context of business, DM has a very active and determinant relationship with:

- The time and timing;
- Opportunities available; and
- The post DM actions.

The author, in his over 40 years of intense corporate work exposure has closely viewed DM in its numerous fascinating aspects, some of which are described in the following pages.

IGNORING THE TIME-DECISION LINKAGE

In business related decision-making, ***time-decision linkage*** (TDL) is of the most crucial significance. The other day a colleague of mine rued, "I should have moved out from my field headquarters 10 years ago—and, from my present job itself some 5 years earlier." I reminded him that, very akin to personal matters, timing of DM in business affairs too was equally important. It prompted a discussion on time correctness of the DM of the company of our present engagement, in relation to one of its new plant locations. An unduly long spell of procrastination in this matter had led, on one hand, to substantial loss of business opportunities offered on account of tax benefits, and diversion of precious working capital on the other, which together crippled the corporate working to the extent that it qualified for the tag of mismanagement.

The same company, some 20 years ago, had missed a great opportunity in regard to putting up a plant with technology from RRL-Hyderabad, for a product that proved a goldmine for whosoever made it during the 1980s and 1990s, for the same reason of not respecting the principle of TDL. One can never have all the right data answering hundred per cent queries during a pre-project decision process, and allowing a delay on this count has left many ruing their decision incapacities for years to come. In pursuit of perfect data or knowledge, one runs the risk of decision-phobia: This is the view of some experts who inform that if one has 70-80 per cent of the requisite information, have done the analysis in this range, feel over 70 per cent confident, then one should move on. Here, the logic is that a less than ideal action, swiftly executed, stands a good chance of success—whereas no action stands nil chance for any fruitful movements. A delayed decision, often, is the worst decision, and without doubt qualifies for the title of mismanagement.

Attempting JIT while Organization not Ready for it

All attempts towards improvement, in any business environment, need an exercise of POLC. If an organization lacks resources or readiness to implement the relevant change, efforts towards creating the suitable atmosphere, rather than pushing a decision down the throats of people, will bring better results.

Attempting JIT, without being fully ready, has been witnessed landing several organizations in bitter situations. One organization dealing with agro-chemicals, and being in the practice of extending long credit to dealers and distributors, one day decided to turn the business cycle on its head. It wanted the sales staff to commit, in advance, to bring back payments within a specified period if they wanted to have any supplies. Market servicing warehouses were put on a very lean inventory; the sales staff did make relevant commitments but the purchase and manufacturing could never deliver the goods in time—because they were not geared to honour the basic requirements of the JIT operation. It led to disruption of the ongoing business process, amounting to a form of mismanagement.

Ego Interference with Decision-making

Ego is a very undesirable interference in effective decision-making: It comes in the way of wider consultations and attainment of U/A, an essential requirement of efficient and easy to implement decisions. In small and medium companies, where systems of management are not well developed, ego manifestations of owner entrepreneurs, CEOs, and some other key personnel, often acquire menacing positions. Constructive discussions are blocked and expressions of ***'I, me and mine'*** assume overwhelming proportions. In such a situation, productive information flow and interactions cease to move in the right direction.

In case of KRD, success of his enterprise had gone to his head and, though he loved to discuss, decisions always steered to his way of thinking. Ego manifestations seemed to come in the way of his maintaining a rapport with his senior colleagues/employees. He had very few friends, even fewer true followers.

The author also witnessed an ex-army person spoiling the dairy industry, which he had established with some of his friends and relations, after securing large financial assistance from state industrial financial agencies. His frequent employment of expressions like **I, me and mine,** led him to spoilage of his relations with his partners to the extent that all of them actively attempted to corner as much money from sales of goods as possible. For them sales proceeds belonged to any one who happened to collect the same. Soon the enterprise collapsed with huge liabilities on the partners. Disputes developed without loss of time and as a result, some of them had to have a taste of prison life too.

Intense interplay of ego was also seen on the part of KSC who did not believe in delegation of work and the associated authority limits for the desired empowerment of people, to help them perform the expected tasks. As a result, he failed to develop a dependable organizational structure, and in the event of a crisis, there was little that he could draw upon as a source of help.

The cases of ***avoidable ego manifestation*** (AEM) witnessed by the author during his long and diverse corporate work life were so large that to do any reasonable justice towards enumeration and description of the same shall necessitate writing of a separate book on this subject. Here, it would suffice to repeat that AEM is a strong precursor of mismanagement.

Holding Meetings without Agenda

Innumerable corporate professionals, CEOs included, tend to hold meetings without any agenda or adequate homework. They call a meeting at the drop of a hat, thus wasting their own and others' valuable time. Since the participants are not ready with their inputs, such meetings do not achieve very much, except listening to the frequently repeated monologue of the chief.

When results don't emerge as per expectation of the chief, he or she starts grumbling—making aimless unproductive noises. Over and above, proceedings of such meetings are rarely recorded for any concerted follow-up action. Often for high-level meetings, especially the board meetings, the agenda reaches the participants just in time for them to pack and carry it without even glancing at it. Sometimes, it is so attempted through a well considered design—so as not to allow the participants any time to go through it—as avoidance of a meaningful dialogue is the main objective. Most of the readers of this work, the author is sure, must have experienced or known such situations. And younger readers will definitely encounter such situations as soon as they become part of a corporate work environment.

Undoubtedly, such activities are an integral part of the massive corporate mismanagement that unfolds itself in innumerable meetings and boardroom discussions. For meaningful corporate efficiency such wastage of costly professional time and energy must be avoided, if superior results are desired.

Ignoring Employees' Convenience in Search of Extra Output

The author, in his long corporate work exposure, encountered two bosses who often held planned or unplanned meetings in a manner that the participants' departure on expiry of office hours was delayed. They tried to pass on this unprofessional practice as a symptom of one being extra hard-working and duty conscious; the facts however were different. It was, in fact, an expression of their intense negativity towards their juniors—a desire to cause inconvenience. One of them tried to pass on this practice of his, as a genuine effort to bring in greater work efficiency amongst the people he supervised, while the facts were otherwise. Additionally, he was not smart enough to effectively hide his factual motives.

All corporate workers, at one or the other point of his or her career, experience situations where the boss attempts to extend work hours beyond the official limit, on one pretext or the other. All such efforts are symptoms of mismanagement and, without fail, prove to be counter-productive. They generate a negative thought flow, mild or not so mild, among the affected people, erasing any chance of additional productivity.

ABSENCE OF TIME-VALUE CONSCIOUSNESS

Most corporate executives, despite pretensions to the contrary, are very poor in time management. It is more so when they are dealing with others' time. This attribute of theirs, is most brightly visible when they handle or conduct meetings, often called without adequate homework and precise agenda. The more astonishing expression of this managerial deficiency manifests brilliantly when they do not attempt or are not able to guide discussions during a meeting towards its specific objectives.

Discussions go on a tangent, totally unhelpful or even damaging to the planned or unplanned objectives. It is not infrequent to witness situations when the pitch of discussions becomes unprofessional—even utterly damaging to a conducive work environment—planned or existing. The whole show ends up in a massive exhibition of mismanagement.

Such situations exhibit lack of **time-value consciousness** on the part of pseudo-professionals who form an important class of the active mis-managers in a corporate work environment.

ENGAGING IN EXCESSIVE NITTY-GRITTY EXERCISE

Some managers have been seen getting into avoidable details, particularly if the work belongs to one of their juniors. Details are never enough for them: They always attempt to punch holes howsoever perfect the proposal is or the document.

KNS and KSC were two such managers who had a specifically rich accumulation of this annoying characteristic. The former, despite his multinational exposure, was master at hole-punching in whatsoever his juniors did, prepared or presented. He could never decide what details he wanted: The author had devised an effective way of solving the problem—by saying that what had been done was final and that no improvements were feasible in any manner. This invariably foxed the indecisive boss, as he was unable to initiate or undertake any changes in any document or presentation, fearing possibility of a mistake on his account. He ruined several bright careers, but finally he met his nemesis; he was demoted and finally forced into a corner.

Another fellow, a CMD of a medium-sized multiple location company, suffered from serious inability of effectively delegating anything, a deficiency probably emanating from his specific background that left him with multifarious trust and confidence deficits. He attempted to go through every detail, every voucher, and take every decision, right or wrong, without involving the appropriate levels of the organization.

It left him with no time for constructive work, for long range planning, or any thing else that a CEO should be doing. Routine work took all of his time and energy—organization structure got fully pulverized to the extent that nothing happened or was got done without his interference. As a result of this cumulative mismanagement, a potentially healthy and once profit-making company acquired multiple sicknesses.

Practising A Damaging Open-Access

Practice of open-access for a mature and self-disciplined senior professional is a mark of distinction. It is also good for a public relations manager or a HR professional, but not for a CEO. When, from a peon to a visiting dignitary walked straight into a CEO's cabin, or if the cabin door was never employed for its rightful purpose, and its occupant did not effectively use the services of a secretary to intelligently apportion his or her time, the inefficiencies of such an operative are bound to be starkly visible to one and all.

In such a situation, dilution of attention is bound to happen; discussions shall never be complete and conclusive, and unfinished work on the table will definitely assume a form of garbage dump. Such an open-access approach easily qualifies, without competition, to be entitled as mismanagement.

Allowing A CEO to Become Sole Performer

Successful corporate work is a shared activity. Once an entrepreneur or CEO becomes one-in-all or the sole-performer, taking all decisions, passing all bills, issuing all appointments, giving increments, sanctioning all types of leaves, just to enumerate a few of the activities, then the organization is unlikely to take long in falling apart or becoming an ICU case.

Excessive multitasking is dangerous; it brings down the quality of performance. A feeling of omnipotence too is an undesirable attribute for a senior professional to possess; it gives birth to the unhealthy manifestations of ego. In such a situation, juniors are likely to turn first ineffective and then non-cooperative. Initiative and innovations will become happenings of the past. A corporate on such a slope is bound to tumble with multilateral wounds and bleeding.

Allowing Absence of Weekend to Emerge

Some proprietors or CEOs of small and medium enterprises tend to think that pushing juniors into work on a weekend or on holidays will be more productive—that seriousness towards work output could be drilled into their heads in this manner. Despite having some idea of human nature, they elect to push against it in the false hope of output acceleration.

Others' inconvenience has no value for such people—and they seem to live with the illusion that the juniors have no life or requirements beyond official work.

Such perceptions or pretensions of this nature emerge from the basic concentrations of their negativity or pure selfishness. Some of them seem to draw active pleasure by putting juniors in a tight corner: They lack empathy of any type. Such activities perused beyond occasional criticalities create situations of gross mismanagement.

In the hands of senior executives with adequate energies of head and heart, empathy can become an efficient tool of people management. **Lord Krishna**[2] was a master applicator of the tool of empathy: He employed it with matchless results during his long struggle against the forces of evil and wickedness. More recently, ***Mahatma Gandhi***[5] employed this technique to corner the sympathies and cooperation of one and all during the long struggle for independence that he led so efficiently.

Allowing Frequent Shifting of Deadlines

The author has witnessed shifting of project commissioning deadlines in a number of cases. In most situations, it is a result of inadequate working of relevant POLCs, and/or absence of contingency plans. Even smooth acceptance of delays has been seen as a cause for more delays. In seasonal businesses like agrochemicals, fertilizers or anything related, a delay of a month or two often leads to loss of a full season, and consequent revenues. Expenses planned or even when not planned, continue to mount—knocking off the planned profitability.

A greenfield agrochemical project near Chennai, in which the author was intensely involved, got delayed for over six months; and being a seasonal product it was a loss of a full season. Customers were ready to take advantage of supplies in the kharif season; they were ready with their investments well in time. Since they had to wait for over six months, keeping them in operational mode became difficult; explanations had to be given by all involved. The loss of a season turned into a situation of mismanagement.

Following the Safe Route of Indecision

Like any aspect of life, indecision in a business environment too often proves costly: It assumes greater significance in business—neither because your customers are unlikely to wait—nor would your competitors like to allow you the pleasure of leisure or competing as per your choice and will. But, the convenience of indecision is too tempting for many executives to resist: Additionally, they enjoy the multiple excuses available in any event of responsibility fixation. They are also expert on deflection of blame if the situation so demands.

Making decisions in an expeditious manner needs inner strength of righteous thought process that is rich in positive balance.

It equips one with strengths of conviction, and in such a situation, even deficiency of data does not bother you—and decisions spring out quick and correct. Thus, the executive tendency towards indecision sprouts from his/her basic incompetence and richness of negative thoughts. Pushing inconvenient matters under the carpet does not help; they continue to accumulate and may even generate corporate heat that often becomes inconvenient. A somewhat not so good decision taken expeditiously is always better than not taking one or pushing it under the carpet for someone else to find at a later date.

Procrastinating—For Too Long

Procrastination too is related to decision-making. In fact, it is a form of decision toxin—it does not fully kill the idea waiting for decision but does not allow the same to materialize. It creates a condition of, '***to go or not to go, to do or not to do***.' Fear of failure seems to cripple the process of decision-making: The risk taking capability, in such a situation, assumes dominance by its total absence.

A north based company of significant size and resources debated for long whether or not to open branches to service southern and eastern states. Years passed by but its areas of confidence deficit could not be wiped out—and, as a consequence, it got typed as a north-based outfit in the eyes of competition as well as potential collaborators. The long range business growth of the company suffered a great deal.

One very effective way to handle the malady of procrastination is to actively apply peer pressure for speeding up the laggards.

For this an efficient management should train its key workers in the art of application of peer pressure—as it permits a colleague to help set another's output objectives—demand timely action as output of one tends to determine the output of others in collective work environments. Output pressure is a sure remedy to cure the disease of putting off action for another day or time.

Procrastination is bad for all businesses and a sure candidate to pin the tag of mismanagement on whosoever is found engaged in this decidedly harmful pastime.

Letting a Failure Grow into a Whirlpool of Indecision

Failures are part of the business process—a certain percentage of projects and businesses do always fail. It is the possibility of failure that raises the value of success. But, an overwhelmingly high percentage of managements—particularly first-generation entrepreneurs and the professionally deficient family-based businesses are not able to effectively handle failures. The decision-making capabilities of such people, in situations of failure, get adversely impacted to the extent that logical decisions become very difficult to come by; indecisiveness lingers on assuming a form of a ***whirlpool of indecision.*** The habit of seeing possibilities of disaster in any new proposal or suggestion allows the situation of mismanagement to tighten its grip. Confidence and trust deficits take hold of the mental faculties of the decision maker or non-decision giver.

The author witnessed the forces of indecision taking hold of RNS to the extent that he was not able to come out with any constructive or attractive proposal to revive the business unit that had fallen sick while under his supervision. KSC of the KIL was even in a worse situation; despite suggestions and proposals he could not make up his mind whether or not to close down a non-viable business unit. Lingering sickness of KIL, as a business unit, represented a classic situation of continued mismanagement. It pushed hundreds of its workers and employees into a dark whirlpool of uncertainties: Some of them were adversely affected by the unbearable uncertainties—and active symptoms of depression started showing up on their persona. Families of some of them were in no better situation.

Attempts on out-of-box thinking or on collective consultations and planning were conscious by their total absence. The management had abdicated its responsibility to guide its subordinates or dependents in a crisis situation. The weaknesses of the management became starkly visible to one and all as its unconcern spread on the not-so-friendly horizons.

Landing in a Situation of Monkey Management

When delegation is deficient or incomplete—and the manager is not able to create understanding of required depth, subordinates tend to come back for clarifications and/or with incomplete reporting. It over-burdens the manager to the extent that he or she is not left with any energy or time to do any constructive work. Subordinates either crowd around him or his cabin door is opened so often that he is reduced to the level of a confused/indecisive manager unable to direct/manage his people to any acceptable level of productivity. All of them tend to run away with whatsoever decision any one is able to extract or snatch from such a manager. A situation of monkey management develops with characteristics of lot of noise without matching output.

Here, the manager's role becomes akin to that of a person distributing peanuts to a group of monkeys—who pick up and quickly return for more: Such a person has no control on his time and/or actions.

MNCs are normally free from possibilities of development of such a chaotic scenario—but many small and medium enterprises with indecisive management—suffering from confidence and trust deficit, land themselves in such situations of mismanagement. KRD was an efficient manager of his monkeys while the KSC of KIL was not.

CHAPTER 7

Mismanagement of Corporate Structure

Stability, longevity, as well as the long-term utility of a physical structure, a building or a dam, depends on the quality of its design specifications and construction. Similarly, performance of a corporate depends on its structure—the design and the inputs that go into its assembly and maintenance, particularly the human element part of it. Depending upon their capabilities, experience and intentions, senior management professionals, particularly owner entrepreneurs, tend to mismanage various aspects of corporate structure. Some prominent aspects of such mismanagement of corporate structure, as witnessed by the author in his long and intense corporate work life, are discussed below for the benefit of the reader.

OPERATING TOO FLAT AN ORGANIZATION

In highly developed societies, where people are conscious of their duties and responsibilities, a ***flat organization*** (FO) that allows direct contact of the boss or CEO with all or most of its knowledge workers can be successful. Here, the ***large span of contact*** (LSC) is not likely to be misunderstood or misappropriated, as the very nature of society permits easy comprehension of each other's point of view.

In backward and/or developing societies like India and many others, a FO has its own limitations, as low-level workers are likely to misunderstand or exploit any frequent contact with the super boss. Further, frequent exposure of a super boss to lower levels of operation shall make him ineffective on account of ***multiple diversionary stresses*** (MDS); and both sides are likely to misinterpret such situations from their point of view. ***The gap of perception and***

comprehension capabilities here becomes too great to permit any effective benefits from such an arrangement.

First-generation entrepreneurs, technocrats-turned-businessmen, and in family-managed businesses, some CEOs attempt to create and operate a flat organization: Often, they face difficulties as absence of organizational structure forces them to intense multitasking, and overburdening with what is non-essential and releasable. Most of them, through such an approach, sow the seeds of eventual mismanagement.

The author has personally seen some CEOs attempting to run too flat an organization— almost invariably without much success and with numerous intractable problems. Once habituated to operate in this way, it is not easy for such mis-managers to change in any substantial manner. Knowledge workers in such FOs lose the capacity to work and be effective without the direct intervention of the super boss, and the latter tends to incapacitate himself or herself on account of time, energy and capability constraints. And the situations of mismanagement so created continue to compound and multiply.

KRD and KSC both suffered from an intense desire to practise a FO in the organizations that they headed. And in both the cases, workable corporate structure failed to develop to the utmost detriment of the victim companies.

Following System of Diffused Responsibilities

When an organization's structure is not well defined, responsibilities are bound to seem diffused—as if no one is responsible for certain arenas of action. In such circumstances—for jobs not done, or done improperly, and resultant failure to meet deadlines, accountability assignment will be almost impossible.

It will allow a lot of loose space for avoidable blame apportioning and spread of disaffection. The scope for improvements too will remain limited—as only voluntary acceptance of responsibilities never lead to quick correctional initiatives. Wastage of productive energies too is substantial in such a directionless situation. Situations when different people attempt the same job, and inversely, an important work is not attended to, are often likely to emerge. Forces of dis-coordination shall emerge and a lot of time of the CEO or COO shall be occupied with unconstructive problem solving, i.e., being busy with what is not important but ends up becoming important for simple reasons of non-development or presence of suitable multi-layered corporate structure..

In one corporate that suffered more than its share of mismanagement generated problems, its high level management committee once made a proposal to the effect that a purchase committee be formed in order to make purchases more efficient and transparent: Its CEO, who was a part of the decision, ignored the same by conscious design. He doggedly avoided issuing a office notification to this effect despite repeated reminders from his senior colleagues. The subject CEO desired that the senior professionals of the company should help the overburdened purchase officer in getting the job done more efficiently. He wanted an informal and voluntary arrangement wherein people assisted without any power for directing or even influencing the decision-making. From the standpoint of human psychology, it was a totally untenable desire: Its fruitful implementation was never feasible. And beyond feeble attempts, nothing could come out of it. The mess continued to stagnate and emit foul smell.

Clear responsibility assignment (CRA), with matching authority limits, and an unbiased valuation system brings out the best of people in all types of corporate situations. The lure of operating through a ***system of diffused responsibilities*** (SDR), allowing uninterrupted disturbing assesses to one-self is a sure recipe for mismanagement and resultant failures.

Creating No Clear Understanding of Role of People

It is very much related to operation of a SDR: In the loose system, where no one knows his or her real role or responsibilities, desired outputs can never emerge. Productive people will continue to grope in directionless labyrinths. Frustrations are likely to set in and productivity will touch new depths.

Accumulation of disaffection (AOD) will give rise to frustration—and then to delusion. People will indulge more in meaningless talk than work in absence of a set direction, as it remains conspicuous by its non-existence. Compounded chaos that results from such mismanagement is not easy to remedy; even through sustained corrective efforts desired results do not emerge easily. A firm reorganization becomes a necessity; and retraining of people about their role, responsibilities, and authority limits is the only effective way of reversal of the malaise. Mismanagement takes time to exhibit its impact—and, any remedial measures towards correcting the resultant situation always consume more efforts in terms of time and energy.

Consistent Undermining of Section or Department Heads

In a field, irrigation water will never spread evenly if it is devoid of some dividing lines or bunds to give it proper direction. It is likely to accumulate in one corner and than overflow to adjoining fields, creating loss of valuable resource and possibly, even conflict. Similarly, no organization can work effectively without well-formed sections or departments, each headed by a person experienced and competent enough to give right directions. Some CEOs tend to act as road rollers—smothering dividing lines, if any, into non-existence or weakening them beyond effective operation. A few of them even attempt to take pride in such actions of mismanagement and are vocal about it. KSC was such a mismanaging personality.

Like the irrigation water that gets wasted in a field without flow guiding structures, ***productive corporate energies*** (PCEs) get unevenly distributed, producing only uneven and or inadequate results in the absence of sensible work division or creation of effective sections or departments; and allowing them to function with requisite freedom and accountability is an absolute necessity. Collective work environments, including that of a corporate, in developing economies, shall always be insufficiently productive in the absence of a well-defined structure.

Open Access to CEO or Open-Door Management

Where people value their time or when they are well trained in effective time management, there is no harm in practising an open-door management: They will not misuse it to the detriment of corporate interests. But such ideal work environments where people would automatically assume productive responsibilities hardly exist; and even when such a work climate might prevail, it would need minimal operation of negative forces at all levels so as to allow every one to be effective without creating any problem or mischief.

With the prevalence of a little negativity, or a little deficiency on the part of even a fraction of the work force, an open-door policy will end up in chaos: Too much back-biting, internal politicking, and overt and covert attempts to grab credit for what one has not done will effectively ruin everything.

An efficient management shall open or close as much of the door that effective communication continues to take place in view of corporate objectives, without creating any roadblocks.

The onus for employing such a disciplinary approach is on the management—for adjusting or operating controls as the work force, white or blue collared, is always incapable of such self-adjustments or discipline.

Many senior professionals who attempt to follow an open-door policy have been found ruing for being overworked and short of time. That his or her second-in-command is not shouldering adequate responsibilities is often seen as their frequent complaint. Almost in all such cases, the complaints are found to be mismanaging; not knowing how much to talk on which subject and with whom. Some of them tend to become professors instead of managers, talking endlessly even on subjects with which their capabilities have no substantial relevance. The three great mis-managers, rich with this peculiarity, encountered by the author included KNS, KRD and KSC.

PRACTISING AVOIDABLE EAR-LENDING

The greatest cause or say the effect of mismanagement is the practice of ***avoidable ear-lending*** (AEL). You lend your ears—and they are filled with garbage of the variety selected by the person to whom you have assigned your sound perception facility.

Afterwards, your capacity not to believe the person, or cut him short, or ask him to concentrate on his work is compromised. You land yourself in a situation of confusion—to believe him or not to believe him—and both the situations are not good for you because you have become dependent on a non-official source of information or designed misinformation. Barring a small minority, managers, professionals or non-professionals, tend to fall prey to this obnoxious practice of AEL; and those who do not are the true professionals.

In fact, AEL is the most destructive input of mismanagement. It is omnipresent and omnipotent, and the only effective antidote against it is its total avoidance. Only professionals with great discipline—and those with even greater fabric of merit are able to practise the desired self-controls.

Excessive Authority Concentration

Power corrupts and absolute power corrupts absolutely, is an old saying. It seems to be true in all situations of governance and/or management: Corporate management too is fully susceptible to this malaise as its ill-effects do manifest here too equally easily.

Many CEOs attempt to concentrate disproportionate power or authority in themselves: Some do succeed while others continue to struggle with their attempts and the consequences of the same.

Such a concentration of power or authority is toxic to the executive decision making capacity. It creates in them a false feeling of being powerful, and with such a feeling, their capacity for logical decision-making is irrevocably compromised. Their ego starts clouding their vision, as well as the logical thought process—and the flow of wrong decisions overtakes the situation. It is like monsoon floods overtaking the plains of Bihar.

Negative energies of such CEOs swell beyond comprehension: They fail to disconnect the process of erroneous decisions even when they realize that such errors are taking place. They, to an extent, lose the comprehension of consequences of their actions. They become like a young newly initiated Haryana truck driver, who while pushing the pedal too hard, begins to believe and feel that the truck is running with his energy, not with that of the diesel that it burns. For him the smaller vehicles and beings on the road seem inconsequential—not able to stop him or challenge him. The author has been witness for activities of such drivers in practical conditions.

A manager with a disproportionately high concentration of power or authority also feels and behaves in a similar manner. For him the acts of mismanagement come naturally and effortlessly. GRV was a master of such power concentrate behaviour—and he had to pay for it fairly dearly.

Assigning Responsibility Without Authority

Some CEOs attempt to pin responsibility on others without either officially assigning a job, and/or not delegating the authority required for fulfilling the same. They either lack a sense of organizational requisites for efficiency, or by design attempt to keep the strings of control in their hands. Such attempts don't produce satisfactory results as they are inadequately understood or misunderstood by the people who are involved on the action front.

One CEO, with whom the author had the opportunity to interact significantly intensively, desired to reorganize his corporate empire into well defined and profit making sub-entities or profit centres, but could not gather sufficient strength to make an official announcement to this effect. He wanted this to happen simply by saying and talking: He was quite possibly afraid of a strong structure eating into the operations of his own authority. He wanted people to shoulder responsibilities, produce results and be accountable without having any authority. He ended up creating adequate confusion and non-performance. It was a case of significant mismanagement.

Ignoring or Weakening the HR-function

For a large majority of CEOs, HR is non-productive; in their view it does not produce and/or market anything. It does not do any value addition. It is a **shortsighted** view that often lands managements in precarious situations, such as those enumerated below.

- Employees missing a listening and/or sounding post,
- Inadequate understanding of corporate policies, value systems, missions and objectives,
- Build-up of negative interactions/energies in absence of suitable mechanism for grievances redressing,
- Development of skills deficits,
- Excessive staff turnover,
- Absence of performance standards awareness, and, among others,
- Unrighteous credit and discredit apportioning.

Organizations normally resist to grow beyond a level in the absence of an active and assertive HR function, and in the event of sharpening of competition and a weakening bottom-line, they are bound to be found not ready to measure up to any challenging situation. For encountering such situations of mismanagement inefficient managements attempt various methods of unrighteous blame apportioning.

Doing without Formal Appraisals

Work output evaluation or performance evaluation is an important HR-function for keeping employees satisfied and well contributing. It is, however, unpleasant jobs for all normal managers who are either not blessed with necessary skills for this function, or are not trained in this delicate human interaction. It becomes more delicate or even embracing when the person being evaluated has superior skills or attributes—tending to give the evaluator a sort of inferiority complex or feeling. Hence, in the majority of organizations it is avoided or performed in a nontransparent manner. For effective appraisals, performance evaluation interview with the person involved is mandatory, and his point of view to the evaluator's report is to be truthfully noted—and in the event of substantial differences, the matter has to be escalated to the next level of management. In order to escape all these events of unpleasantness, a vast majority of managers—both professionals and non-professionals, in practice, tend to do without this vital necessity. Irrespective of the intricacies involved, doing without formal evaluation amounts to gross mismanagement.

During his over 40 years long work span in organizations of national and international repute, the author was only once confronted with a performance evaluation report—and it was so full of inconsistencies that the matter had to be resolved at a very high level. The evaluator was termed as significantly biased and was forced to reverse his notations. He lost face and also all capabilities to effectively deal with the evaluated: On his part, it was an instance of crude mismanagement.

In fact, any manager who cannot conduct an unbiased factual evaluation, and its post evaluation interview, adequately well accepted by the subject candidate, cannot be viewed as a manager, leave aside a professional one. He is only a mis-manager or damager, and must be sent for necessary training or re-training. Any management that desires to have a well motivated and high performance work force must effectively handle the challenge of righteous performance evaluation of all its white-collar employees.

Perpetration of Non-judicious Credit Apportioning

In the absence of a systematic and bias-free evaluation of employees, non-judicious credit apportioning is bound to happen. Different bosses will follow different methods to push their favourite candidates for better increments, promotions, and placements. In such a situation discredit will get automatically apportioned to where it did not belong. Consequently, the negative interactions of disaffection, jealousy, non-cooperation, and backbiting will rob the organization of initiative and innovation. In the absence of fairness or righteousness, productivity and competitive performance shall suffer; and the symptoms of mismanagement shall not take too long to manifest in an inconvenient and visible manner. It is one of the most pernicious forms of mismanagement of substantially long adverse consequences.

Lord Krishna, the most efficient CEO that the world ever had or heard of, right from the inception of the collective work practices—ancient or modern, was a great perpetrator of righteousness. His credit and discredit apportioning was so efficient or flawless that even without being a direct ruler, He managed the vast kingdom of Dwarka—and also the massive event of the *Mahabharata*, most efficiently.

Creation of Employee Groupings other than Performing Teams

In most organizations, groupings based on region, state, and/or religion or caste are seen developing by default as well as by design. One multinational, for which the author had an opportunity to work for, had strong groupings delineated as South Indians, Bengalis, Maharastrians, and Punjabis, just to name the major ones. Another organization, an Indian family business house of substantial standing, had well developed groupings of Marwaris, Bengalis and others. When this type of groupings prevail, action needs to be taken when forming performing teams, to see that any negative effect of the same does not affect the working of the organization. A truly professional CEO shall initiate efforts, at the time of new recruitments, to see that such groupings do not get unnecessarily strong, due to an unprofessional approach towards organization development. But the skills requirement for minimizing the ill-effects of the undesirable groupings, and the resultant mismanagement, is substantially significant and not easy to acquire.

Not Allowing or Practising Job-rotation

The practice of job rotation is beneficial to an organization as well as the employee concerned. For the former, it helps avoid situations where employees staying for too long in one position or at one location develop unprofessional roots and consequent vested interests. Unethical practices and efficiency drop are some of the most commonly visible symptoms of job rotation not being in practice.

From the angle of the employees, job rotation helps provide opportunities for skills upgradation and widening of experience. It can help a technocrat turn into a well-grounded multipurpose manager, free from vested interests and non-professional groupings. Effective job rotations, thus, can help develop performing multipurpose managers capable of producing planned results.

Promotions and salary upgradations can be better justified when the same are accompanied with purposeful job rotations. Physical location rotation too helps in widening of exposure as well as capabilities. Hence, the absence of the practice of location or job rotation may create situations for growth of mismanagement. The concept of '**Bonsai Managers**', as discussed by Gopalakrishnan[6] in his recent book, is a magnification of these types of manpower mismanagement.

Offering no Opportunities for Skills Upgradation

Employees, particularly technical ones, do not work for salary alone. They look forward for better career prospects that emerge from skills upgradation.

In-house and/or professional institutional training and retraining can meet this objective. Hence, a work environment rich in this type of planning and opportunities works as a magnet for attraction as well as retention of high performance employees. It creates a work environment of positive and productive energies and initiatives. Absence of such skills upgradation opportunities sets in a process of decay of skills and capabilities, encouraging anti-productivity negative forces into action or substandard action. These are definite symptoms of mismanagement of productive human resources.

Skills upgradation programmes, whether internal or external, should never be viewed as costs or unproductive and avoidable expenses. They are investments into the future of the company. No cost cutting exercise or austerity campaign should affect them adversely.

CHAPTER 8

Mismanagement of Markets and Customers

Markets are dynamic phenomenon; they remain in perpetual motion—changing without notice or pause. Like time and tide, markets too do not wait for any supplier—they wait only for valued customers. Products and services are easily replaced—normally by better or more efficient ones. Constant supply or let us say an upgraded and ***efficient time-bound supply*** (ETBS) is essential for market share retention of any product. Markets have another important characteristic that many marketing professionals fail to appreciate:

They sell what is available at critical demand time; and customers too, after initial reluctance, adjust to what is available.

If a product is reasonably satisfying, and when there is no severe competition from a vastly superior one, market response becomes a function of supply. Fast after-sales services help product movement to sustain itself. Yet, markets often get mismanaged for one or the other errors of omission and commission. Some important ways or occurrences, which lead to mismanagement of markets and customers, are discussed herein.

EXPECTING CUSTOMERS TO WAIT

Making a customer wait in any manner goes against the interest of a business entity; a dissatisfied customer is bad publicity. His word-of-mouth needs no further confirmation for any one who hears him. Hence, he needs to be handled with utmost care, whether for supplies or after-sales services, keeping commitments as per terms of sales and supply, and/or in regard to complaints servicing.

Despite such a vital position of the customer in the business chain, several companies end up mishandling him on account of either the lack of professionalism on the part of constituent employees, or for the outright lack of understanding of ***customer-corporate interactions*** (CCI).

Several instances of making customers wait were witnessed by the author: The most incomprehendible one was the attitude of the public sector bodies handling the telephone services in India, during the last three decades of the past century. They took deposits for connections under schemes such as **OYT** or ***tatkal***, and made people wait endlessly. Getting a non-functional telephone line to work again was a nightmare. Out of utter frustration, once the author had told a senior functionary of the MTNL in the early 1990s that the time was not far when they would beg the public for having or retaining their tele-connections. The customers were totally fed up of their obnoxious attitude. The conditions of long monopoly had spoiled their heads. Further arrogance and corruption had fully clouded their judiciousness.

And with the opening up of the telecom sector from the middle 1990s, a situation developed where the offending monopolists were forced to offer incentives and improve their services just to retain their customers. In this reluctant exercise they succeeded only partly as for many customers it was difficult to forget the mistreatment received a few years earlier. Their customer base shrank a great deal. It was a serious case of matchless mismanagement.

Additionally, one should not expect a market to tolerate your inaction: It will react by replacing you and then forgetting about you.

Once, an agro-inputs supply company was seen expecting that the market will wait for its supplies irrespective of the same being illogically late. It had collected huge advances from its dealers and distributors for supply of products, which were fully seasonal in nature. On account of its mismanagement of finances, neither supplies were made to the market in time nor were the customers informed to the effect that they should make alternative arrangements. It created a huge surge of disaffection in the market inflicting long-term damage to the company's business interests. Mismanagements of more serious nature than the one detailed above, for a competitive market based company, are hard to locate.

ALLOWING UN-SERVICED ORDERS ACCUMULATION

Un-serviced orders accumulation is a double-edged weapon, depending upon who is handling it. For an efficient and responsive management it offers an excellent opportunity to gear up its production, meet supply deadlines and thus swell its market share. It could be a stepping-stone towards market leadership.

On the other hand, if not handled intelligently, it can become a stone around one's neck. Market confidence does not take much time in slumping—reversal of which is a painful and time and cost intensive exercise. The best alternative to any huge order accumulation is to tell the truth to the parties concerned—about the time the supplies are likely to take, allowing them a situation that on a latter date they do not tend to apportion blame on your door. In such a situation, the company's sales force needs to be very clearly instructed—because it has a lot of undesirable capacity to misguide the trade, as well as, the subject corporate.

NON-REMEDYING PERSISTENT CUSTOMER COMPLAINTS

Market always attempts to talk to you, whether you listen to it or not: Its signals are often feeble, and it gets loud only under conditions of extreme neglect.

Customer complaints, neglected for long take a cancerous form—very difficult to cure or correct at a latter date. Market reputation once damaged through such actions takes a lot of time and effort to repair—and often, full recovery is very rare.

Companies, when under the spell of mismanagement, either by default or design, fail to read the market or the signals emitting from it: They avoid or are unable to react to the market, its components, i.e., the trade as well as consumers; and, per force, have to bear the cost of resultant mismanagement. The author encountered a variety of instances of non-attention to problems/complaints of markets and customers enumerating which might add no further value towards stressing the point: Here, what is more valuable is the fact that readers shall be able to recollect their own experiences in the field—in regard to market and customers' neglect, and consequent complaints genesis, and how the same were handled.

DISRESPECTING PRODUCT PRICE AND QUALITY BALANCE

Product quality and pricing has a direct correlation: In fact, a delicate balance needs to be maintained between the two. Increasing the product price without increasing product quality, either of its content or packing and, in total absence of competition move in the same direction, without doubts, shall affect its volume movements. The only exception to this rule is feasible when brand image and consequent customer loyalty is very strong or say price insensitive, which normally is very rare.

This type of market mismanagement should not be attempted, until and unless, it is planned to replace the subject product with some more remunerative or better performing one. Under arguments of cost acceleration, correct or manipulated, some MNCs and large local companies have been seen escalating prices disproportionate to value advantage to consumers. Such price escalation moves were often seen in the protected markets prior to the process of market liberalization that took place for over a decade. Active competition is the only effective antidote for this type of market mismanagement.

Non-differentiation Between Supply, Sales and Marketing

Supply to market, and selling and marketing are two different things: Many marketing people are not able to differentiate between the two, and consequently end up mismanaging the situation to the disadvantage of the company. The following differences are important to note if such mismanagement is to be avoided.

Efficient marketing organizations always avoid mismanagement by actively differentiating between supplying, on the one hand, and selling and marketing, on the other.

1.	In this case one is responding to trade needs/demands.	While selling we respond to corporate needs and requirements.
2.	One is giving them what suits their business needs/ opportunities/profits.	We are attempting to give/ liquidate what we have or can supply.
3.	There is little or no effort on our part to alter things/ situation in our favour.	There is an effort involved to alter the trade working as per our situation.
4.	It amounts to our functioning by default.	It amounts to our functioning by design.
5.	We end up working in the interest of customer or the trade.	We end up working for our/ company's interest.
6.	Since we may not have in our pipeline all that the trade requires at that moment, we end up creating the impression of inefficiency.	Since we supply what we have in our depots or in production, we give the impression of efficiency or marketing objectivity.
7.	Our skills and energies don't improve because no efforts are made to alter the situation in our favour.	Our skills and energy our used in altering the working of trade in our favour—thus we become efficient.
8.	Our bottom-line is likely to remain very thin or red.	Since we operate by design, our bottom line is likely to be green.
9.	We are likely to suffer from falling of non-performance.	We will have satisfaction of performance—and it will give us confidence to do new things in the market in the future.
10.	We will always have cash flow problems if we are engaged in supplying only market needs.	We will have robust cash flow and salaries and travel expenses of sales and marketing staff will come in time.
11.	Supplying will lead us to stagnation.	Active selling will lead us to growth and development.

CHAPTER 9

Mismanagement of Associations and Alliances

Handling of associations and alliances is one such area of corporate functioning that suffers very frequent mismanagement: Some common instances of such mismanagement in the corporate world, amongst others, could be:

- Outsourcing arrangements between two business entities,
- Arrangements between a company and its distributors,
- Arrangements between a company and its contractors,
- Franchise agreements,
- Product sales and service arrangements,
- Technology supply and usage arrangements, and
- Any arrangement or agreement for mutual benefit.

All arrangements and agreements between two business entities need to be handled with utmost care. Normally in all such agreements, in light of stresses operative on the two partners being different, and there always being some dissatisfied (or otherwise interested) elements, chances of conflict of opinion or conflict of interest do always exist, in active and/or potential form.

Delicate situations also develop when one of the two parties loses the status of equality, one becoming dominant or more demanding—and not honouring a minor or major part of the agreement. A little out of the way behaviour or over-stretching of a position may lead to mismanagement of an alliance.

When righteousness is replaced by negativity, in any of its damaging manifestations, all arrangements and agreements tend to wilt.

The author once had a first-hand experience of an outsourcing alliance going the wrong way. His business unit named CIPL had entered into an agreement to manufacture and supply certain products to the KIL, wherein raw materials for this purpose had to be supplied by the latter or the same were to be procured by the former on the latter's behalf. After six months of smooth operation, deviations started from KIL's side as the agreed materials were not supplied and payments for the goods supplied were delayed. The situation took an undesirable turn when such blockage of funds started affecting the CIPL's own business. Soon, the latter had no option but to withdraw from the agreement. It led to the mismanagement of an excellent business opportunity.

In brief, mismanagement of associations and alliances takes place when (a) one of the parties attempts to shift the goal posts and persists with the attempt, and (b) normal sensitivities of communications are compromised by design, for the purpose of gaining an upper hand. These undesirable efforts should be consciously avoided if the subject arrangement is to be allowed a chance to be protected towards bestowing mutual benefits on both the parties involved, on a long-term basis.

Misunderstanding Pleasantries for Realities

Often there is a danger of expressions of pleasantries being misunderstood as realities when business associations or alliances occur among unequal partners: More often, the junior partner runs the risk of such misunderstandings.

And when reality exhibits itself, often after lapse of a significant span of time, acceptance of the same by the affected partner becomes substantially painful. The author has been witness to several such inconvenient situations, and to describe one of these, here in brief, will serve well for the purpose of adequately stressing the point.

A medium-sized agro-inputs company named KIL did substantial outsourced production work for some MNCs and large Indian corporates during the 1990s. Its CMD hobnobbed with the senior officials of the outsourcers, and the pleasantries offered by them were taken literally. A few years later, when the outsourcee fell on bad times due to some mismanaged investments and expansions, the reality of the situation dawned to the extent that substantial psychic damage and consequent personality changes on its chief became visible. It turned out to be a serious case of mismanagement of perceptions.

Accumulating Costs and Losses for False Association Values

In unequal associations and alliances, the dominant partner often tends to squeeze the junior partner in terms of costs, cost sharing, etc. It pushes the economy of scale to work to its own benefit, and the junior partner often being less skilled in cost accounting and cost appreciations, is pushed to a situation of disadvantage.

Sometimes, such disadvantaged partners assign disproportionately high value to such associations, which in their view seem to boost the social and/or business standing of the subject party. A false perception of benefit of association arises to cloud the understanding of the affected party. Soon, the accumulated disadvantage begins to assume uncomfortable financial forms; the perception of loss becoming clear and painful. Often, admitting such situations of reality becomes difficult for the chief of the affected party; and the auditor's report becomes an unwanted document. Even consultants pointing towards this reality are not welcomed by some perturbed parties.

The smart ones, on the other hand, proceed to renegotiate such arrangements, or give up the same if the dominant party makes the subject renegotiations infeasible. For some the malaise of indecisions continues to compound the situation of mismanagement. KIL and its CMD fell in the latter category.

Allowing Un-remunerative Alliances to be Operative

The author has known some CEOs who suffered from love for unproductive alliances: they kept some alliances going despite the fact that they were losing propositions. RNS, who headed a loss-making concern of a large family business house, was master of sustaining unproductive alliances. He had outsourced the total sales and marketing rights of the products manufactured by the company that he managed or mismanaged, to a multinational on terms which were one-sided—and obviously damaging to the outsourcer.

The arrangement did not work as payments for the goods supplied were to come only when the supplied stocks were liquidated in the market. The outsourcer, in an unrighteous manner, had taken part of the responsibility for the stock liquidation too, for which it was neither equipped nor was financially capable. Within two years of commencement of the agreement, the situation deteriorated to the extent that the outsourcer's senior management (the proprietors of the company) forced RNS to rethink the arrangement. It was decided that the company should have its own sales and marketing infrastructure. This is when the author came into the picture for the purpose of cleaning up the mess. In the process of remedying the situation, it was found that the outsourcer company's interests were mishandled for a consideration.

Many companies have tie-up warriors or so called experienced hands, who could arrange alliances and associations at the drop of a hat. They all need to be looked at with a strong magnifying glass—as to find out the hidden avenues for loss-making situations in their folders, on the one hand, and the arrangements for their own unrighteous enrichments, on the other. They are the master mis-managers with a purpose.

Cultivating a Dog-bone Syndrome

Some CEOs who forge un-remunerative associations and alliances, suffer from the ***dog-bone syndrome*** (DBS). Despite a clear absence of benefit inflow they seem to believe and propagate, though unconvincingly, to most of their associates and coworkers that the subject arrangements are beneficial to the company: That they add to its prestige and standing.

Here, two types of situations can exist: One that the subject CEO might genuinely not have a clear idea of contributions from such alliances, and two, he might be hand-in-glove for arranging and perpetrating a messy arrangement. When he or she is seen defending such a faulty alliance, doubts do genuinely arise about the sincerity, as well as the integrity of the person concerned. And there are cases where such mis-managers refuse to act even when specific information is made available: It leaves no doubt about such so-called professionals being high-grade experts of mismanagement.

Over-valuing or Undervaluing an Association

Over- and undervaluing an alliance, both ways, is a matter of mismanagement: Often it is done in a conscious manner, i.e., with a design. In both the situations, corporate interests invariably go through a downward thrashing.

Correcting such situations of mismanagement is normally very difficult, for reasons of the levels of people involved. The factors of bias, unrighteousness, and/or vested interests are often involved. It is not easy for people to admit that unrighteous alliances were being perpetrated: Hence, there is very little antidote available for improving such people once they fall prey to such selfish acts of mismanagement.

Assigning the right value to an alliance or association has to be a conscious, unbiased and well-designed effort: Valuation expertise too will need to be cultivated without resorting to short cuts and or bias.

CHAPTER 10

Mismanagement of Products and Performance

Products and services are the revenue earners in the corporate world. In most of the companies suffering a bleeding bottom-line, an in-depth analysis often leads to revealing of mismanagement of these revenue-earning entities. They are mismanaged on several counts, some of which could be as under:

- Having passed the prime time in the product life cycle,
- Quality parameters not being adhered to,
- Defective price quality perception in the market,
- Persistent packaging deficiencies,
- Demand supply position mismatched,
- Demand generation and sales support significantly inadequate,
- Product performance complaints not being attended to with requisite speed,
- Sales and marketing channel not allowed to make/retain adequate profits,
- Permitting competition to occupy shelf space,
- Failure to develop a compact product mix,
- Inadequate R&D support for need-based up-gradation, and many more.

Some instances of mismanagement of products and performance noticed by the author with great frequency are described in the following paragraphs.

WORKING WITH PRODUCT COST-RETURN ILLITERACY

The author has witnessed some corporates working with total ***cost-***

return illiteracy (CRI) or unconcern. It is often a consequence of (a) weak finance department in reference to cost accounting and individual product profitability concerns, (b) an over-busy senior management, and (c) where purchase department is over-indulgent in regard to its own cuts and considerations.

Normally, it is not the job of the sales and marketing department to exhibit individual product profitability concerns. Their primary job is to sell what is made available by the management—and also to highlight what is required or demanded by the market or the trade—say what is easier to sell on account of active demand.

Financial analysis, i.e., cost return of individual products, territory operations, and consolidated corporate operation is the responsibility of a commercial manager and/or finance manager. When these functions are ignored, by default or design, then the conditions of the CRI overtake the operations—and its consequences do not take much time to manifest in relevant severity. It is a serious form of mismanagement—one of the prime causes of corporate sickness.

It is not uncommon, in the corporate world, to encounter situations of CRI of various magnitudes—and it does not requires one to be a financial wizard to see such situations of mismanagement or potential mismanagement in their various stages of development and/or emergence: Simple commonsense and an unbiased approach is good enough to smell and detect the same.

Ignoring Individual Product Contribution

More often than not, corporates fail to analyze and compare inter-product contributions: It happens more often by default than design.

Normally, corporate profitability is the responsibility of the CEO, moving down to the finance department and/or the commercial manager. Since at the top level it is often difficult to apportion time for intensive tracking of various financial contributors, some companies now incorporate the position of CFO, who is made fully responsible to keep track of the finances and profitability of the subject corporate. It is his job to see and answer the following questions.

- Which product is making a loss and which is contributing very little?
- Which products are cash cows of the company?
- Which product needs to be dropped from the company's product mix?

- At what stage of the life cycle should each contributing product be placed to day?

Once these and related questions are answered, and debated with marketing and production, then effective decisions for inter-product production upgradation/adjustment, and also relative after sales support could be taken up more rationally.

Such an objective analysis, the author has not seen happening even in MNCs leave apart medium and large local companies, during his over 40 years of intense business work environment exposure. More often than not, such an effort is conspicuous by its absence.

Sales and marketing people, in a business operation, are often unaware of relative contributions being made by different products in the product mix handled by them. They are expected to sell what the market demands or what is manufactured and supplied by the company. But, when finance and top management people in a corporate exhibit a serious degree of illiteracy in this regard, then it becomes a serious matter demanding immediate retribution.

When a corporate's very existence is threatened due to financial mismanagement, any senior member of the business entity is fully in his or her rights to attempt such an analysis and confront the management with its findings. In KIL, a similar situation was detected by the author and it turned out as the main causative for the bleeding bottom line of the company.

What surprised the author most was the studied unwillingness of the purchase department and senior management to take any substantial remedial measure. Products, which contributed directly to loss, continued to be procured, manufactured and marketed with total abandon. Whispers to the effect that vested interests were at work continued to float: A situation of gross mismanagement continued to persist.

Having Unreal/Arbitrary Profitability Syndrome

It is all right to work with thin margins, but one should not let the same grow so thin that the distinction between such margins and the loss disappears into thin air.

In tie-up businesses, the producer/supplier is often so squeezed that he or she loses track of costs involved in servicing the business contract; and when someone highlights the discrepancy, acceptance of the same becomes embarrassing. Details of such dealings are not provided even when demanded, and attempts are made to employ double standards in assessing the profitability of such businesses. When personal interests of some one senior involved in such a deal are threatened by an in-depth inquest, uncomfortable situations tend to arise. But raised tones and tempers fail to hide the elements of arbitrary behaviour that gives clear smell of the mismanagement involved.

Keeping the Sales Register Open Even on Loss

In the absence of alternatives, it will be understandable if the sales of a product or product mix are continued despite awareness of loss having dawned on the management. But in a situation of multiple choices, at significant and superior profitability, such a behaviour will easily earn the designation of designed mismanagement.

For instance, a deal to supply 1,000 MT of a product by KIL to an MNC during 2007, at a rate that left such a thin margin that the cost of production, shipment and handling, transport, and various communications, leave apart depreciation, interest, etc., was not feasible to be apportioned from it, continued to be actively operated. Supplies to its own market that allowed 5-6 times higher margin of gross profit were denied, creating substantial bad blood with the traders who had either advanced the money well in time or were ready with funds. It was difficult to understand the economics of this mismanagement, through any lens of analytical impartiality.

Having Inefficient Inventory Systems and Unorganized Stores

Inventory management, i.e., keeping stores in good form, is one of the simplest parts of business management. The author knew a businessman in Abohar town of Punjab, during the difficult business years of the 1970s and 1990s, whose record and store keeping was so spot free that the state supervisory agencies never wanted to visit his shop or godown until and unless a local official wanted to impress his boss or a visitor from headquarters.

His financial dealings too were equally spotless and transparent. On the other hand, several small and medium companies are seen struggling with this simple function. Stocks of finished goods and raw materials do not tally even when computerization has been introduced. A list of outstanding collectables is never final: It is not acceptable to the field people who are required to collect such dues. It creates a situation of perpetual feud between the accounts and the sales departments; and for obvious reasons the CEOs often tend to side with the former.

Developing Negative Return Attachment

Some CEOs or unit heads are expert at ***loss perpetuation*** (LP): They develop a vested interest in loss-making performance of business units managed or mismanaged by them.

It is done by design, as it suits them to have a low profile. The corporate head or head of the subject business group pays little or no attention to the happenings in such a loss-making unit. These foxy characters want to lie low and continue with their activities of mismanagement. Whenever confronted by the super boss, they come up with a series of excuses, and escape punishment or transfer.

RNS was a master in loss perpetration. He enjoyed an unambiguously clean record as all units handled by him lingered with loss-making and then died a unnatural death. He was known not to allow any senior manager working under him to succeed in making any business unit profitable. He maintained a subdued presence, never pushing bosses for new projects or new ideas. The author had accepted the challenge of proving this foxy character wrong. From the subdued activities of a loss-making unit under his supervision, he continued to extract his pound of flesh. Whenever he visited Ankaleswar or Baroda, his normal quota of tur dal (a popular variety of pulses), peanuts and papads (a snack preparation) were always neatly packed well in advance by the local mini-bosses. After a little shouting and display of anger, he was his normal self; happy as a cat after a nice meal of milk. Indeed, he had a magnificent attachment to loss-making or negative returns.

Getting too Ambitious with Product Campaign

Campaigns for product promotion, in terms of sales, shelf-space, godown inventories, etc., may become too ambitious, incur huge expenses, and finally achieve only a fraction of the planned objectives. VKM, a senior business manager of an MNC, in the early 1980s launched 'Aswamedha yagna' for achieving a breath-taking expansion of sales of an agrochemical named Sevin, in the rice belt of Tamil Nadu. Planning for the campaign was not done thoroughly: Opinions of yes-men and sweet talkers prevailed. Huge stocks were placed with dealers and distributors and disproportionate funds were spent on market development activities, which included demonstrations, farmer meetings, dealer meetings and point-of-purchase advertisements. Emphasis was on expenditure—not on results.

A major part of the stocks remained unsold and hence payments from the trade were tardy: Huge stocks had to be taken back in battered and non-sellable form. The whole operation turned into a massive exercise of mismanagement. VKM was kicked up and posted to Singapore.

Starving the Potential Cash Cows

It is not uncommon in the corporate world when companies practise, by default or design, an emphasis and resources assignment imbalance—because of which potential profits are lost in an injudicious manner. The profit opportunity so lost often assumes the form of mismanagement. The author has witnessed numerous examples of such happenings during his long corporate engagements. The following one will illustrate the matter beyond all doubt.

In the mid-1990s, KIL started a biological products division since products of biological origin were being eulogized out of proportion in view of active realization of the undesirability of creating an excessive load of pesticides on various food, fruits and vegetable crops.

The company hired a competent technocrat and a facility to produce small quantities of fungus-based agrochemicals, was put in place. The product was launched with some fanfare but its financial contribution was never worked out: The corporate management was too busy with its large range of products, some of which moved in large volumes but contributed little to corporate profitability.

As the years passed, a large market of several thousand tonnes for the biological products developed, and the subject company remained almost totally unconcerned about it. Some companies, which wisely centered their strategies on biological products, not only made good profits but also secured positions of strength for their future growth. By the time KIL woke up to the reality of the situation in the middle of the first decade of the 21st century, a genuine case of mismanagement of products and profits opportunity had developed.

CHAPTER 11

Mismanagement of Communication

Management, as per the author, is nothing but communication—in a variety of forms and manifestations; verbal or non-verbal, written or unwritten, physical or non-physical, moral or immoral, ethical or unethical, and/or whatsoever form one can assign to it.

Hence, competitiveness of a corporate, in the long or short terms, shall always depend upon the quality of communication that emerges from it, particularly from its senior elevations.

Most acts of mismanagement, visible and non-visible, and serious and non-serious, are products of faulty communication.

If communication somehow gets mismanaged, no quality management of any type shall ever be feasible. In view of its pivotal significance, special treatment is assigned to communication in this work.

NON-DIFFERENTIATING BETWEEN RELATIVE AND ABSOLUTE

While making comments and observations, most present-day corporate professionals—including CEOs—do not differentiate between what is relative and what is absolute. Since they themselves do not know the difference, each statement and/or observation is attempted to be passed as absolute, leaving no room for themselves or those so affected or targeted, to manoeuvre out of it, if the situation so demands. As per a beautiful saying of Jainism known as ***Syat Vaada***, everything is relative—and nothing is absolute.

As per understanding of the ***Syat Vaada,*** if we say that Mr. X is not honest, then it should mean and be understood in a relative sense—not as an absolute fact. The opinion that we form or convey should always be relative.

Recently, **Swami Sukhabodhananda**[4] beautifully elaborated this concept in the *Times of India*. He stressed that when an opinion is formed about a person or subject, particularly before it is conveyed, one should raise a question: Is it absolute or relative? And if the answer from one's inner self is "relative", then its communication should be accordingly effected.

In the corporate world, in order to keep employee motivation at a desired level, keeping our perceptions/communications relative will mean to keep them open—for any future amendment. It is always better to say, ***As far as I know***, before making any firm assessment or opinion about a person or a matter of criticality. It saves avoidable creation of negative energies in the work environment.

This small precaution saves us from becoming a prisoner of our knowledge or information base. We should never treat our knowledge as absolute –and by implication, our opinions and comments too should be relative only.

In this process we do set ourselves free by not labelling others—and by implication, from tying our hands for future corrections and improvements. We should, particularly the educated and informed ones, refrain from seeing people and things not as per the labels that they carry—we should look deeper. This simple wisdom is bound to enhance happiness in inter-personal relations—and productivity in the corporate work environment.

It will not be out of place here to repeat what the learned Swami said, ***We suffer in life for we make absolute statements about others and ourselves. We can set ourselves and others free by practising this principle, which says 'may be', for things are relative. When we operate on a relative plane, we are open to other possibilities. Creativity happens in the space of openness.***

Going a little beyond—one could say that creativity sprouts in an environment of non-labelling; or in the environment wherein things are said and done relatively; or where no absolute positions are taken. It leads to avoidance of development of situations of mismanagement.

The significance of relative and absolute again comes to the fore when we examine the tendency of management professionals uttering words ***'Right and Wrong'*** in corporate communications. These two words are perhaps the most vigilant sentries in the lives of the wise and the learned. They are the two words, which the wise employ with great care while the naïve attempts a liberal sprinkling of the same. In today's corporate world, there is substantial unwise usage of these words—which not only complicates situations—but turn them into mismanagement.

EXHIBITING MISPLACED ARROGANCE

Expressing arrogance, misplaced in reference to time, place and audience, is one communication malaise that a large number of senior managers are afflicted with: It is particularly serious when it emerges from CEOs and other senior professionals.

One particular instance that has persistently refused to vacate my mental screen pertains to one VKM. About a week after having taken over as General Manager of the agro-division of UCIL, one evening he landed up unannounced at my residence, in the company of two assistants. VKM was an extrovert who loved talking—and as per expression of self appreciation he said, "I am coming straight from Palam: I wanted to interact with you before arriving at a sound understanding of the business of this division."

I welcomed him, as informality was part of our work culture. After a few drinks and an hour of discussion on various aspects of the business, its intricacies and why it was not doing well, etc., he remarked, **In a few weeks I will know all the technicalities and intricacies of the agrochemicals business.** His statement smelt of misplaced arrogance: He seemed to belittle, though not by design, the skills and the long experience of the technocrats and professionals.

Since I myself have never been a bright star of tolerance and diplomacy, I retorted, "VK, you are grossly mistaken: I have spent 20 years in this business and despite that I don't understand except a part of it: I am sure you shall take much longer than that, and you don't have that much time." It cooled his spirit: We had dinner together, but there was no chance for evaporation of the fumes of the misplaced arrogance that he had exhibited. He never forgot the lesson that he learnt—and I lost the goodwill of a boss who had never learnt to be forgiving.

BEING CRITICAL BUT NON-PERSUASIVE

It is easy to be critical, particularly when one is dealing with juniors and subordinates. It becomes particularly damaging to corporate interests when such a behaviour emerges from a CEO or a senior professional. Some of these people tend to be brusque and dismissive of what is being proposed: They attempt to show their authority, knowledge, and decisiveness in the presence of juniors who do not like to actively defend themselves or their proposals. The objective of such seniors is neither to persuade nor to guide the people concerned towards betterment. For them the right to criticize seems sacrosanct, and their sole objective. To give opportunity to the other party to put forward its position is not part of their management style.

Such a communication behaviour is a pure and clear act of mismanagement: They are running away from their managerial responsibility to guide and persuade their juniors and coworkers to take the initiative and be innovative. Unnecessary or avoidable criticality acts as chronic poisoning that kills initiative and innovation slowly but surely. KNS, KSC, AK, and ASP, just to name a few, were masters at the game of misplaced criticality and non-persuasiveness; all of them, consequently, turned out to be great mis-managers.

Speaking Without Saying Anything

Speaking for long hours without saying anything is a very useful art, particularly for politicians. It is, however, not a desirable trait for a professional manager to possess. And when any manager exhibits richness of this attribute, then he does not merit to be called a manager, least a professional one.

KNS was an expert in talking for hours without saying anything. In business meetings, often, he had to be reminded of the fact that an agenda existed and that it had to be finished. He often complained that he was not allowed an opportunity to make a point. Sometimes, we had to ask him the subject on which he was deliberating so intensely. And, though too weak a personality to retort, he did not relish any interruption of his little meaning monologues.

In due course, his mismanagement of communication was fully exposed; no one took him seriously. His bosses avoided assigning him any meaningful job; they knew that no progress would ever be made. His juniors or subordinates struggled with whatsoever assignment they had, because understandable guidance never came. All of them showed willingness to be assigned to other departments as, with this unprofessional boss, they could not make any headway.

Exhibiting a Know-all Approach

The ***know-all approach*** (KAA) of a CEO or a boss is very undesirable situation to be encountered. By implication, he or she loses the value for experienced and technically sound people.

Such mis-managers dismiss suggestions and expect to be followed blindly; and, when something goes wrong, then they hurry to blame the very people whom they earlier neglected. The KAA people ride the waves as long as things go right, i.e., in the growth phase of a business or in the high product demand season.

VKM, KRD and KSC were such typical characters—and all of them did not take time to land in situations of acute mismanagement. The first one managed to escape the punishment of mismanagement through an out-of-country transfer: The second one paid with his own life—and the third one substantially crippled his own business as well as his reputation as a professional businessman.

Stringency in Regard to Performance Appreciation

The practice of ***stringency towards performance appreciation*** (STPA) is a very common malady amongst managers at all levels—and both types, the professionals and nonprofessionals, suffer equally intensely.

The basic psychology behind such a tendency is the concentration of negative energies in such people: They don't like anyone benefiting in any manner, least through their own actions. Their own thought process propels them to such reactions; they think that some thing will go away from them if any word or act of appreciation escapes from their verbal apparatus. They are not the righteous type: They are the people of **tamsic prakriti,** basically unsuitable for management positions.

Motivation germinates out of ***righteous performance appreciation*** (RPA): It generates flow of positive energies, at thought as well as action level. The obnoxious tendency of STPA kills initiative as well as innovation. It is an attribute completely incompatible with the requirements of competitive performance. Out of the instances of acute mismanagement cited in this work, KNS ran away with top honours in regards to his richness of the STPA, RNS and KSC being good runners up. All the three succeeded in growing the seeds of incompetence and mediocrity in the corporate work environments that they happened to manage.

Having a Holy Cow Approach

- Technical production is my area; please don't touch it.
- Tie-up business is looked after by XYZ; let us not discuss it.
- Sardarji (a KIL branch manager located in Punjab) reports to me; please don't talk to him.
- Purchases are AK's exclusive domain; please don't look at that.

The above and other statements of this variety, from a CEO, smell of a '***holy cow approach*** (HCA)' which is never conducive for professional management: It creates doubts. In corporate activities transparency is an absolute necessity: It becomes yet more important, if as a CEO, one is often heard complaining of lack of transparency in another's areas of operation.

The HCA or the holy cow approach always emits signals of distrust and avoidable exclusivity. The inherent duplicity of approach does not go well if you are not a king—and in the latter case too, it can be allowed more as an exception than as a rule; otherwise it becomes a danger to the kingdom itself.

From all considerations of fairness and impartiality, and for requirements of efficiency and productivity, it is an undesirable practice to follow or perpetrate. It has all the colours and smells of serious mismanagement.

Expecting Performance without Delegating Authority

A mis-managing CEO, with ***power concentration attributes*** (PCA), normally does not like to delegate anything that is important or smells of authority.

This approach goes well as long as the company so mismanaged does well, as he can pat his own back for all the results and progress. As soon as competition heats up or the business environment gets tough for any reason, such a person starts finding scapegoats for discredit apportioning.

On further deterioration of finance, production or market conditions, nervousness overtakes such a mis-manager, and he suddenly wants people to take greater responsibilities, be proactive, put peer pressure, and help improve the situation even in areas which do not belong to them.

Though he himself was never a team man, now suddenly he wants his next in line to group into high performance teams. He may want a marketing head to look into finance and improve its MIS delivery. Also it might be suggested that the senior people should lend a helping hand in purchases too as he finds that this function is faltering. But he does not assign any responsibility in writing; the question of delegating authority does not cross his mind.

Despite immense problems, he deals directly with every level of employees, from peons to the executive directors. Since his exhortations do not inspire confidence amongst the target people to the effect that decisions taken by them will be backed, if and when the need arises for such an eventuality.

He wants performance from people without the slightest devolving of authority. It is an expectation of mismanagement that invariably ends up into disastrous consequences. The author had an opportunity of working directly with a CEO of such a work prakriti or nature.

Perpetuating the Disease of Doublespeak

The practice of doublespeak is one of the commonest maladies of corporate work environment. All levels of the corporate pyramid, professionals as well as non-professionals, are seen practising it with a high level of impunity.

It assumes a particularly damaging form when practised by senior professionals, CEOs and proprietors. On a subject, a good number of them say one thing to one person and give an entirely different input or impression to the other.

They scatter the seeds of conflict, distrust and inefficiency in the organization.

Sometimes, it is akin to telling a thief to commit a crime and alerting the police at the same time.

For some practitioners of doublespeak, it is a game of power play—for others, it is an unavoidable form of intra-organization survival effort. Often, it also amounts to avoiding accountability or currying favours.

In our list of mis-managers, KNS, RNS and KSC were masters of this game—and they invariably caused irreparable damage to the corporate work environment. Maximum play of the disease of double-speak was notices at KIL, the master players being two at the top. For one, self-interest was the definite cause for indulgence in this undesirable activity. The entrepreneur CEO, on the other hand, felt it difficult to cure the disease possibly for his inability to understand the manifestation of its dire consequences. He did not seem to appreciate that the disease of doublespeak is difficult to hide—and its consequences waste no time to emerge and scatter its malicious impact on productivity and morale in the affected organization.

The practice of doublespeak normally is a manifestation of weakness in the personality perpetrating it. It has been observed that most of the practitioners of doublespeak tend to exhibit foxy personalities with little content of dependable leadership. Such people make poor bosses incapable of effective and long-term motivation of their team components.

In the interest of a positive work environment and consequent superior productivity, it is necessary that senior professionals and entrepreneurs minimize genesis and spread of the disease of doublespeak.

Gaps between Preaching and Practice

The author has seen a number of senior corporate functionaries suffering from the disease of '***gaps between preaching and practice*** or the GBPP,' and because of it they invariably tend to lose effectiveness. Such gaps, even if essential or unavoidable, should be minimal and executives practising the same must be endowed with skills to keep them invisible to a large extent; because as soon as their visibility comes to the fore, the executive concerned invariably loses effectiveness. There is no antidote of any type for preventing such consequences.

The visibility of GBPP adversely affects the productive thought process of junior functionaries: Further, it gives birth to gossip that consumes precious corporate time and energies. In the final analysis, the GBPP produces negative interactions and productivity deficient work environments: The subject functionary loses the esteem with which, he or she was earlier held by the juniors. His or her moral authority suffers a setback, and conditions of mismanagement start becoming active in the subject work environment.

Active Urge to Prove Oneself Right

Many senior executives and/or CEOs have the habit of parroting their own views, on any subject under the sun—as if they are experts on everything.

Often, this obnoxious habit is coupled with their inherent urge to prove themselves right. As a consequence, juniors are denied time and opportunity to express themselves and put across their point of view. Thus, emergence of a participative decision is denied. Further, the active urge on the part of senior executives to prove oneself right tends to foreclose any opportunity for such senior persons to benefit from the expertise available at the actual task execution level.

A wise senior manager or CEO should listen more, speak less, and give his decision after due deliberations.

He or she has to control the active urge to speak on preference and/or to control the urge to prove oneself. For correct decision making, it is necessary to listen to diverse points of view, and then come to a comprehensive/participative conclusion. It is necessary to give juniors an impression that they have been heard. The author had seen and worked with a number of CEOs who often were in a hurry, either to impose their own views or monopolize the dialogue process: And most of them were great mis-managers of the business communication process, not as per the views of the author alone, but as per the undesirable consequences that they helped generate.

Exhibiting Work Stress on your Face

Well, business management may create some situations of stress, and it is a professional manager's responsibility not only to handle such situations but to turn them to the advantage of the business entity.

Conditions of emerging failures and crisis test maturity of senior management, and if the concerned manager or CEO exhibits such stresses on his or her face or carries them home in the evening, then he or she is not competent to hold such a position of responsibility.

Any ***visual stress manifestation*** (VSM) suffered by the chief sends wrong signals to subordinates or the middle management, often the backbone of any commercial enterprise. It becomes an admittance of failure or intractability of a situation: It creates a situation of gross mismanagement—as the whole collective work environment gets polluted by such a VSM.

A leader's job is to lead—not to get overwhelmed by development of a challenging or crisis situation: When a commander buckles under adversities on the front, soldiers don't fight any more: They lose the justification for fighting for a win.

Inadequate Written Communication

Most of the corporate workers, particularly those who are not sure of themselves or who have not put in adequate ground work, tend to avoid written communication, such as tour reports, inspection reports, suggestions for improvement, deficiencies in a program, etc. It is primarily a safety device for some, an escape route for others, and commitment avoidance for most of those so involved. Tolerating this kind of habit or practice once takes deep roots, and subsequent improvements become difficult: Escapism takes birth undermining performance and credit and discredits apportioning.

A good management should be precise, responsive, and totally committal about what is said and done. It promotes transparency, which is one of the essentialities to do well in a competitive work environment. I never said it: I did not mean it: I am not responsible for it, and many more such situations of uncertainties are nipped in the bud when a desired degree of written communication is practised or insisted upon. It prevents development of embarrassing situations of mismanagement.

Expecting others to Read your Mind

Many CEOs do that: They think that it is the job of the subordinates to read their mind. It is, indeed, an erroneous approach because right communication is a tedious process —and it is more so in a corporate work environment where commercial results have to be achieved.

Here, the communication has to be direct and crystal clear, and there should be a confirmation that it has been received and understood in right details—an express U/A must result for smooth culmination of communication.

CEOs or senior professionals who expect their minds to be read represent a situation of confusion, a type of deficiency or gap that they are unable to bridge: They end up creating a further gap of understanding, in currency of which productive business activities can not be sustained. In such an event, mismanagement becomes a consequence by default. Sometimes, this kind of approach is adopted by design too—and it is indeed bad in both the cases.

Deprecating your Own Knowledge Workers

Many senior managers and, even CEOs, engage in the harmful pastime of running down their own knowledge workers. For them it becomes an escape route to avoid accountability and/or to apportion discredit for failure or inadequate performance on people who are not present, or because of their positions, cannot defend themselves.

It is like fighting with one's own tools or blaming them for not working efficiently enough.

It, however, does not earn any credit as one who does not assume responsibility of all acts of omission and commission of his or her subordinates does not qualify to be called a manager, leave aside the CEO.

Deprecation of your own knowledge workers, particularly in their absence, is an expression of crude negativity: It is escapism of the highest order and there could be only very few examples which could qualify for a more serious act of mismanagement.

In our list of mis-managers, from this angle of mismanagement, KNS won hands down: He branded his well-qualified and experienced subordinates as incompetent in front of super bosses. These juniors, no doubt, suffered loss of promotional opportunities, but this master of mismanagement too did not escape the attention of his wise bosses. He suffered demotion and substantial humiliation, to which the author was a witness.

To a varying extent RNS, KRD, KSC and several others were seen engaging in this activity of mismanagement: It gave them relief at the thought level—a tool to befool themselves—and give them a false satisfaction to the effect that the situations of mismanagement, which they encountered were not their doing. But, despite these and many other efforts in this direction, none of them really escaped the consequence that cascaded from the fountains of mismanagement created and/or supported by them.

Talking Often of Unpleasant Past

Some mis-managers who could not do something right in the past continued to think that no one could do anything right in that area, now or at any time in the future.

They tend to employ the past failures as a shield for not initiating any productive action in the present. They want a guarantee for success in the future, well in advance. It is an escapist or diversionary tactic that many mis-managers employ in meetings to shoot down good project proposals, which have not been proposed by them or their favourites. They neither want to take the initiative, nor appreciate any one doing so: They are the great nay-sayers.

The author experienced several encounters of this nature with such mis-managers. Once a senior management meeting was assessing a project prepared by the author, in which a senior finance director of the business group participated along with the CEO of the company. After substantial discussions and probing, the finance director attempting to exhibit his seniority and authority, unwisely blurted out whether I was willing to personally guarantee the profits as shown in the project report. I said, "Yes, You guarantee that 50 per cent of the profits will accrue to me." I further added that he could proceed to prepare the commitments from both the sides on stamp paper. This prompted the Sethji to admonish the said mis-manager in no uncertain words. Finally, the project was approved—and successfully implemented.

Such nay-sayers or proposal killers abound in almost all corporate work environments; and many good projects do not see light of the day on account of the acute mismanagement practised by them. Further, they tend to assign incompetence at will to their subordinates and colleagues: They retreat only in the face of stiff resistance arising from elaborate explanations and spotless competence.

Encouraging Motivated Feedback from Juniors

Senior managers and CEOs who like to break an established corporate structure and planned line-working, just to engage in the politics of one-upmanship, engage in this type of mismanagement.

It is harmful for corporate health through genesis of negative forces. They prompt juniors to say and do things, which for certain reasons, they are not able to do themselves: It is a form of axe-grinding or the urge to prove wrong the people who do not fall in with their line of thinking and mismanaging.

In a way, it is a retaliatory measure or revenge action that they want to take while keeping themselves at a safe distance. In both the situations, such actions fall in the category of mismanagement. GRV, KNS, HCP, RNS, KSC and many more were found engaging themselves in encouraging motivated feedback from juniors. Some did it in a sophisticated and subtle manner while others practised a degree of crudeness.

Being Bullheaded in Your Expressions

***Bullheadedness* characterizes excessive concentration of arrogance and adamancy.**

Many CEOs and senior managers suffer from this non-managerial attribute; it stimulates them to fall into the trap of mismanagement, more by default than design. The author for two short years encountered a ***bullheaded boss*** (BHB) suffering with additional negatives of illiteracy, adamancy, and idiocy.

He had progressed to an all India sales manager's job through the defaults of regionalism and nepotism coupled with several other non-professional HR practices. Unfortunately for him, all the regional managers who reported to him by force of his position were superior to him in qualifications and experience.

On account of his bullheadedness, he always fought with the very people who he was supposed to manage and supervise. Conferences and meetings became interesting events for the juniors to excite his bullheadedness on some count or the other: Often, the senior management had to pitch in to rescue him from delicate situations. The management also did not take time in realizing its own folly of foisting him in a critical position. In large companies manpower placement and transfers do take time, and when a decision starts smelling foul, retracting too is not easy—as the seniors, who are supposed to decide, start taking positions—primarily for discredit avoidance.

Within two years, his bullheadedness coupled with the lack of behavioural experience, resulted in his two-step demotion. Since his qualifications and skills did not support his bullheadedness and feasibility of alternatives, he continued to suffer the humiliation of demotion, and eventual termination. We called him GRV; he realized his foolishness when it was a little too late.

Though the one dealt with earlier was in a MNC, instances of bullheadedness are more often seen in proprietary enterprises, particularly those started by technocrats. Limited success, if it comes early, has been seen to pump their ego to such an extent that they fail to assemble, develop and retain an effective team, often furiously multitasking, and finally pushing themselves into situations of crisis where they find not many people, subordinates or friends, ready to help them out. KRD and KSC were only partly bullheaded, and even this minor defect had put them into severe situations of mismanagement.

JUMPING TO OFFER WAGERS ON SLIGHT PROVOCATION

Accepting an alternative point of view, or at least to allow the

other person to put across his or her point, is an absolute necessity for a successful manager.

To expect your opinion to be accepted without deliberations—simply because you are a CEO or proprietor of the company, is a strong signal of high concentration of ***non-inclusiveness*** in your management style. It is poisonous for long-term corporate growth—and a strong indicator of the eventual growth of mismanagement.

The author has worked with some mis-managers who had no patience to hear another participant's point of view if it differed from what had already set in their non-receptive or clogged head. GRV, KSC, AK, VKM, and SCP, just to indicate a few, were typical of this breed.

GRV and KSC were often seen offering bets if what they said was not true or was not likely to emerge as correct. Both attempted to use it as a tool to steamroll their point of view: GRV did not succeed with the approach because people knew deeply his intellectual limitations, but KSC on account of his corporate ownership received only a subdued opposition. Both were, however, very successful in mismanaging what they were attempting to do.

Jumping to offer a wager, in fact, is a reflection of excessive concentration of negative energy within the person. It propels him or her to attempt to cut short a discussion through this non-professional technique. In a way, it is an attempt to browbeat the person daring to disagree. In whatsoever way or reference this technique is attempted, it does not leave a residue of cooperative or inclusiveness in the work environment: The very purpose of deliberations is lost.

Exhibiting Directional Confusion

The primary job of a senior manager or CEO is to give direction, correct and precise, for the subordinates and line managers to follow and achieve planned results.

In comfortable times when business is growing, competition is manageable, and the bottom line is healthy, directional capabilities of such biggies are not challenged, and they continue to enjoy disproportionably higher fruits of whatever they do.

But when a crisis develops, whether on account of a labour strike, an accident, loss of competitiveness, just to name a few causes, most of the senior managers or CEOs, particularly the mis-managing types, tend to lose direction.

When the great gas leak occurred in the Bhopal plant of Union Carbide, a directional confusion took hold of the senior management to the extent that, despite requests from local authorities, no one responded to tell the antidote for the poisonous gas. It happened despite the fact that its managerial manpower prided itself in professionalism, including delegation and leading by example. The so-called senior management lost its nerve—and a situation of total directional confusion prevailed for the first few days of the accident. It was a situation of total mismanagement—its employees at the middle and lower levels were not told how to react in the social environments that they were living in.

On a smaller scale, hundreds of instances of directional confusion have been seen by the author, and in most cases it is the failure at the higher level to give appropriate guidance.

Raids by sales tax, income tax, central excise or CBI authorities, whenever and wherever they might happen, invariably tend to cause conditions of directional confusion. This event of mismanagement, though innocuous to initially look upon, leaves long-term scars of mismanagement.

Passing Sweeping Remarks

Very few corporate managers, including CEOs, practise controlled communication. Often they end up making statements, which at best could have been avoided in collective corporate interest. Most of them do that by default or lack of training—only a few do indulge in such activities by design. And invariably, most of them regret making sweeping statements, subsequently in private. Public admission needs a high level of righteous thought warriorisn, which most of them lack.

KNS, RNS, KRS, CKS, and several more were habituated of indulging in this pastime. In fact, often it is an expression of directionless negative stress on the part of the indulgent managers. Their own deficiencies and failures invariably lead them to such injudicious behaviour.

Sweeping remarks travel a great deal—particularly in directions not desired by their emitters. They do not serve any purpose except reducing the productive management or performance energy in the system. Undoubtedly, they are a highly damaging form of mismanagement—and must be curbed in a relentless manner.

Chapter 12

Mismanagement and Professionalism

Professionalism is difficult to come by, hard to imbibe, and still more difficult to perpetrate through everyday activities. It is easy to say, 'Adopt a professional approach,' than actually doing so.

Preaching has always been easy than its self-practice. Why does it happen this way? An analysis of this perplexing issue lies in human psychology—its thought process that is a product of its early development as a social species. When the concept of collective living, urban or rural, got initiated, the uncontrolled human beings (monkey-habited) always found it much easier to pursue unorganized and spontaneous responses to situations—challenging or non-challenging. Whatsoever discipline human beings learned was under the ever-unfolding dangers and challenges, primarily personal and/or for group safety. Hence, professionalism never comes easy and smooth to them, irrespective of the activities that they are engaged in.

This characteristic continues to manifest itself in numerous forms even in corporate work environments, generating most of the mismanagement that is witnessed in this sphere of economic activity. It may happen by design and/or default: The first form of it is correctable only through intense training and a suitable system of rewards and punishments. Some manifestations of un-professionalism often witnessed by the author—and not dealt with elsewhere in this work, are described in the following pages.

Expecting Oneself to be Beyond the View of Normality

Normally, moral standards, ethicality and hard work flow from top to bottom, particularly in collective work environments: They follow the ***aqua flow principle*** (AFP). Standards are always set by seniors: Followers, normally, do not take the initiative to deviate.

In view of the above, a good boss should not follow the beaten track of double standards of doing numerous wrongs himself and frowning upon juniors even for minor deviations. The juniors might tolerate your unrighteous and/or disproportionately inconvenient and expensive acts, in your presence—but they shall always crib about the same in your absence.

For most bosses, the situations as detailed below seem normal—but for the juniors, they set visuals from where mismanagement does not reside too far: It soon catches up with the situations of double standards or wrongdoings. The boss thinks that you and him are two different animals—and that he is licensed to do what suits him—and further, he expects that his discrepancies or acts of mismanagement shall not be noticed or should not bother any one. He wants to remain out of the bracket—as far as the righteousness of actions is concerned.

There is always a multitude of such reactions, comments, and observations in every work environment—as bosses carry a set of two lenses—for two different purposes. It is a sincere manifestation of the double standards that they attempt to follow or perpetrate.

Fumbling with Change Management

In the corporate world, much alike the daily grind of life, challenges for handling changing situations are encountered at frequent intervals. And, it is primarily the job of senior managers and the CEO of a corporate to manage the challenge of change.

An effective and experienced management knows ***how not to react but to meaningfully respond*** to events and incidents, expected or unexpected, in the wider and long-term interests of the organization. If one starts to react and continues to do so, then reaction becomes a habit—and reactions, often being devoid of logic, end up implicating one's ego in the whole process, which leads to undesirable consequences. Several senior managers and even CEOs wear their ego fairly loosely: They prove themselves incapable of constructively responding to demanding change events, whether a union strike, an excise or sales tax raid, and/or any significant incident or accident.

In the event of change of ownership or a hostile takeover, senior managers are often seen fumbling with the demands of change: Most of them react than respond intelligently. Situations of mismanagement do not take time to manifest in such conditions.

Boss and his own action perceptions	*Boss's perception of actions or behaviour of subordinates*
When boss takes a long time—he is being thorough.	When a subordinate takes a long time—he is slow or inefficient.
When the boss does not attend to a job—he is busy with more important ones.	When a junior keeps a job pending—he is being lazy.
When your boss makes a mistake—he is just human	And when a mistake is made or detected at your end—you are an idiot.
When the boss does something—without anyone knowing it—then he is taking an initiative—or being proactive.	When you do something without being told—you are overstepping your authority.
When the boss takes a stand—then he is being firm.	When you take a stand—then you are being bull-headed or adamant.
When the boss skips a few rules—then he is being original.	When you overlook a rule—then you are being rude or insubordinate.
When your boss pleases his boss—then he is being co-operative.	When you attempt to please your boss—then you are attempting apple-polishing.
When the boss is out of the office—then he is on business or networking.	When you are out of the office—then you are wasting corporate time.
When your boss is sick and takes a day off—then he is truly ill.	When you take a sick day off—then you are always sick.
When your boss takes any leave—then he is only recovering from over work.	When you apply for leave or do not report for work—then you must be appearing for an interview.

Effective management of change is an art for which one needs to acquire true qualities of leadership. Here, training and counseling can only be of partial assistance: the major contribution has to come from within.

Putting the Cart before the Horse

Unreasonable conditions, if and when attempted in collective work environments, act like putting a cart before the horse. Even if the horse attempts to pull it, no movement is likely to emerge.

Some senior managers were noticed by the author engaging in putting such unreasonable conditions which discerning line managers either shall not accept, or if acceptance is somehow pushed through, there shall be no performing movement of any type.

Once in a project evaluation meeting, in a large family-based group located at Kolkata, a senior director of the group asked the author whether he could give a written personal guarantee in regard to the projected profits of the project. He made this point to impress his masters who were present in the meeting. It was a totally unprofessional approach on the part of a senior director who had spent over 40 years with the group. When he insisted on the point the author agreed to do the needful provided the company agreed to give him a good share of the profits. He did not relish the counter remark but the author proceeded to elaborate that it was the job of the entrepreneur to bear the risk related to a new project, as profits were to accrue to him. The Sethji appreciated the righteous point of view and chided the director for putting the cart before the horse.

During another assignment with a company that had fallen on bad times, the author witnessed its CEO demanding that the sales staff first underwrite payments to suppliers of raw materials through DDs or at par cheques, for purchases related to the products required for servicing the market. For the sales staff it looked as if the horse was being put before the cart. Since due to the precarious finances of the company there was no other way out, the proposal was grudgingly accepted: However, it did not work in practice. Both the above instances, despite their merits and demerits, represented a degree of mismanagement.

Non-alteration of Tools of Management

As one grows from a line supervisor to assistant manager and onwards to the position of general management—and then to the position of a top dog, the tools and skills of the subject manager must alter as per the demands of the position.

Maximum alteration is required in one's method and skills of communication, information collection and their effective application.

Upgrading your skills of time management, i.e., delegating—what could be done by others, and attending directly to only what is crucial —is most vital.

Areas of your previous responsibilities should now engage your minimal attention while the new components of your assignment should attract priority attention. You should do little or nil technical work as management work becomes more important as you climb the corporate ladder. Your technology to take work—and skills to motivate people to become ***self-motivated performers*** (SMPs) needs to undergo a sea change.

The corporate world is full of CEOs who doggedly refuse to dissociate from areas of their previous responsibilities: It is easier for them to continue to use their old skills then mastering new ones. They lack a mechanism of quick change-over or suffer from fear of incapability, which might be uncovered in new assignments.

They resist growing to their new responsibilities/positions—and in the process seeds of mismanagement are sown. In fact, they promote ***double directional mismanagement*** (DDM)—downwards the work is disturbed due to their unwanted or unwelcome interference, and the neglect upwards too causes undesirable situations.

NOT THINKING THE UNTHINKABLE

It is widely said and accepted that nothing is impossible. Often, this basic wisdom is given a go by in corporate activities too, encompassing almost all components of the POLC necessary for this purpose.

'Not to think of an unthinkable or unexpected event or happening,' leaves dangerous gaps in business planning. Similar deficiencies are left unattended at the second stage—namely organizing (inputs and resources). The other two stages of the business process, i.e., leading and control too do not remain free from such gaps.

If one is travelling, whether by road, rail or air, an accident is always possible—hence the need for insurance. When one adopts a new technology, the chances of competitors acquiring by copying or other means is always there. Hence the need for exclusivity agreements, confidentiality undertakings from employees exposed to it, and patent protection, if the technology is indigenously developed, becomes a necessity.

When **Union Carbide**, the US multinational, established its Bhopal agrochemicals plant based on MIC, the possibility of an accident was thought of, but whether someone will deliberately switch off its refrigeration system of the gas storage facility or whether water could be mischievously let into the gas storage tank, was not duly factored or thought of—and now the consequences of not thinking the unthinkable are well known to every one. It became one of the clearest cases of mismanagement known to mankind.

Delving a little into mythology will help further clarify this point of mismanagement. When Duryodhana, the evil prince of Hastinapura, outraged the modesty of Draupadi in full view of the royal court, despite the presence of Bhishma and Vidura, the sworn advocates of righteousness, the thoughts of unthinkable consequences escaped his mind. The whole Kaurava clan, including a large part of the then warrior class, paid the price of this act of gross mismanagement.

From an earlier era, the kidnapping of Sita by Ravana—and the consequences that he and his whole clan had to face, is another mythological instance of not thinking the unthinkable.

However, it is important to note that in both of these mythological examples, the key perpetrators of the evil acts faced the consequences with great courage and fortitude. Hence, if an act of mismanagement occurs in a corporate work environment, either by design or default, the key manager or professional should face the situation with necessary courage.

NOT HAVING A CONTINGENCY PLAN

More often than not, absence of a contingency plan is a fact of life in the corporate world—and some of them pay dearly for this act of mismanagement.

One company for which the author had an opportunity for working during the late 1980s and early 1990s, had put up a plant for manufacture of a fungicide employing the technology provided by the NRDC, a public sector unit marketing the technologies developed by CSIR laboratories. The product had to compete with a well-known MNC brand enjoying a monopoly. In its planning the new entrant company did not factor the possibility of its failure to effectively and profitably market the product in face of formidable competition. It had made the mistake of not thinking the unthinkable—that the MNC could always make it fail in the market place through ingenious usage of a variety of marketing tools. And the unthinkable happened: The new entrant could not find a foothold in the market—and every year almost as much of its product, in battered and expired non-sellable form, was coming back to its factory and godowns. The company became sick.

Soon afterwards, the author took the responsibility of streamlining its market, which was achieved fairly successfully. Further, action was taken in order to widen the company's product offering so as to avoid any reappearance of the mistake committed earlier.

Normally, contingency plans are difficult to develop as people lack the capacity to think beyond normal parameters. Most planners/ entrepreneurs don't like the idea of contingency plans because it involves (a) a prima facie possibility of failure of the planned activity, and (b) answering of numerous difficult questions right in the early stage: They find it easier to avoid both.

Ploughing a Lonely Furrow

Ploughing a lonely furrow—not becoming part of the pack, is a dangerous attribute. There is safety in a group or in doing an activity the way others are doing it.

By so doing one, however, does not distinguish or differentiate oneself: The benefit of exclusivity does not accrue. But survival and safety are ensured, which is very important for new entrants in a business. One can plough a lonely furrow if one is very strong or if there exists a strong backup of resources, technology, and a dependable team of knowledge workers.

The author had personal experience of drawing a lonely furrow while running his own entrepreneurship venture. Being strictly opposed to acts of corruption, overt or covert, he consistently refused to grease the palms of government officials who, after a initial wait, ganged up like hungry wolves for reclaiming what they thought was theirs as per the established trade practice.

A lot of time and energy was lost in attempting to convince them about the righteousness of the practice of maintaining high quality of products on one hand and not parting with bribes on the other. The dissatisfied government officials attempted to cause insurmountable problems. There was no feasibility of delayed correction as hard positions were adopted. As a disgusted yet uprighteous entrepreneur, he decided to divest from the subject business. Thus, the mismanagement on the part of the author, in this endeavor of entrepreneurship, was crystal clear. He had attempted to draw a lonely furrow without adequate planning and resources or without factoring the unthinkable.

Becoming A Dream Concentrate

Dreams are good to have; they set directions for future growth.

But, dreams alone are not enough. In isolation they are a delicate, rather fully perishable material. For conversion into reality, they require a rigorous exercise of POLC. They do not bear fruit without extracting an equivalently valuable price in terms of time, concentration, effort, resources, and investments.

In a corporate work environment, some entrepreneurs tend to become a dream concentrate: Efforts to convert dreams into concrete thoughts, then projects and subsequently to put them into the mill of organized action, remain missing or does not happen in the right sequence and with adequate intensity. In other words, the thought energy does not convert into action energy of adequate magnitude so as to overcome the inertia and other initial hindrances. Some weak dreamers get paralyzed even at the thought level by the very enormity of energy required in setting the direction of implementation.

The author has seen a number of dream concentrates struggling with their valuable thought properties. Some don't allow their dreams to escape in the direction of action, while another fraction of the dream concentrates do only incomplete ground work and give up before the take off: Only a minor fraction does a reasonable job of doing the requisite POLC. In fact, the author himself was a dream concentrate—for establishing a viable manufacturing business of his own. After over half a dozen years of partially successful operation, on account of changed business environment, and alteration of priorities, the dream was given a mid-course correction.

Several other dream concentrates were seen meeting rough patches, as the adequate ground work of POLCs was not done. KRD was a great dream concentrate—and he succeeded pretty well in the first 7-8 years of his maiden enterprise. But the acute work-life style imbalance killed him prematurely.

ASP's dream of establishing a large complex of dairy products ran into trouble just after the start-up, primarily because of the wrong combination of entrepreneurial elements (inexperienced, incompatible and non-tolerant). The partners exhibited incompatibility to the extent that one of them committed suicide and another spent a few months in jail.

On the other hand, KSC who initially succeeded fairly well in his venture of agrochemicals, could not balance the pace of implementing his dream concentrations, and in the process, through over expansion and inappropriate associations, landed himself in deep trouble, financial and otherwise. Thus, the condition of being a dream concentrate is likely to turn foul if little oversight is allowed to creep into implementation of the necessary POLC: It is a very susceptible candidate for catching the disease of mismanagement.

Imbalance in Thought and Action-Warriorism

For successful business management in the competitive environment, senior managers, particularly the CEOs, require an excellent balance of thought and action warriorism. More thought and little action is no good in any situation—and a lot of action with little thought is equally fruitless. Both the situations can develop into mismanagement, with disastrous consequences.

It is not hard to find senior business managers who suffer significant imbalances of thought and action: Some are excellent thought warriors who go into the very depth of each connected matter. They create volumes of paper work and flood the board of directors with bulky reports, but when the time for action comes, they behave like hot wax.

On the other hand, action warriors too are seen to implement projects without needed thought and analysis: They too land into inconvenient situations. But, in the overall analysis, the latter are far better than the no-action advocates. The author came across a number of mis-managers who suffered from intense imbalance of thought and action energies. KNS, the ace thought warrior could analyze a project or problem for hours, or even days, without taking a direction, leave aside a conclusion. He loved to leave the process of drawing conclusions to others: There was absolutely no chance of him taking any action. He was happy if his juniors or seniors took action. RNS suffered the deficiency of thought as well as action: He needed to be pushed from top until and unless some of his self-interest was not involved. KRD was rich in thought as well as action warriorism—and he succeeded fairly well till his work-life imbalance proved his unfortunate undoing.

Accumulating Multiple Capabilities Syndrome

Success, particularly in the case of first generation entrepreneurs, is capable of producing a non-professional and unrealistic thought process.

They tend to forget that the subject success might have been contributed by a set of favourable factors, rather than any uniqueness on their part. Also, they miss the point that the initial success achieved by them might be purely temporary. Some of them, who suffer from ***maturity perception deficit*** (MPD), even start behaving like the Tata-407 drivers of Haryana, who suffer from a perception that the tempo which they are driving is running due to their energy rather than on the diesel that it burns: They claim all the credit for its furious speed.

Having been loaded with the ***perception of power of performance*** (PPP), some managers start expressing to their friends and colleagues as if they have acquired the omnipotent capabilities, technical as well as non-technical. The author has seen some art graduates, who after tasting some initial success behave as if they were endowed with the great IITian technologies. They do not realize that little knowledge could be dangerous, and that they should be humble and careful with it. My friend KRD was like that and I had to occasionally deflate him for his own benefit. When in good mood he did admit the problem of thought imbalance that sometimes overtook him.

KSC too had tasted success, though through a protracted process—yet it went to his head and consequently he started mistaking his practice of multitasking as ***multiple capability reality*** (MCR). It led him firstly to under-rate, and sometimes even to belittle his technocrats, and secondly to disrespect the departmental hierarchy in assignment and follow-up of work. Being fairly egoistic, he avoided corrective discussions in conducive environment. He ended up creating a situation of huge mismanagement.

Mistaking Information for Intelligence or Wisdom

Some senior managers, including CEOs, have been seen to mistake information for intelligence.

Information collected from some sources, dependable or undependable, are touted as their own ability to know and do things or the capability for the same. It is not intelligence, and any pretence in this direction does not leave a right impression on people targeted for the purpose.

In order to make the right impact, information should be shared in a transparent manner, including its source. Information is an input, in fact, an investigation and analytical input and must be treated as such. Any one securing information from some source and then treating it as his or her exclusive property, or himself/herself as the originator might turn up in an unacceptable direction.

Being Intelligent but not Wise

Intelligence does not automatically ensure success, except in a limited way.

An intelligent student can end up securing high marks in an examination and also get entry into a good position, but it does not automatically ensure success in the subject work environment. For its rewarding application, intelligence needs to be coupled with wisdom, to give it the right direction towards fructification. Intelligence has been seen to misguide its holder into arrogance and/or overconfidence, and in both the situations the effects of mismanagement do waste little or no time in their emergence.

Intelligence also might cause envy and the persons so affected might create significantly difficult roadblocks in the way of its holder. Intelligent people also expect success as a matter of right and hence do often ignore undertaking the requisite POLC for achieving targeted results: It results in conditions of mismanagement.

The author himself experienced such problems—as people often got intimidated by his personality, and some cunning ones did not abstain from creating roadblocks in an overt and/or covert manner. Through self-experimentation the author learnt that for harvesting maximum rewards of intelligence, it needs to be clothed in a wrapper of wisdom.

Demanding Omni-involvement from Employees

It is not uncommon to find senior managers or CEOs attempting to put or keep their fingers in everything. This phenomenon is more visible with the first generation entrepreneurs who suffer from a hidden fear of failure; losing all that they have achieved or collected so laboriously, or being deceived at any stage. It is a manifestation of confidence deficit in their continued success. They have no confidence in delegating any job of responsibility even when capable people are available to handle the tasks at hand.

In order to hide the confidence deficit and the resultant fear syndrome, they resort to intense multitasking, resulting either in delay of execution of important works or output deficiencies creeping up for lack of plural involvement or supervision input. Early burnouts and avoidable stress accumulation are some of the other consequences of this type of mismanagement.

One CEO was witnessed expecting and even demanding that key employees should get involved in all the activities of the company and ensure that everything was done well and in time. Since he was involving himself in every activity, by implication he thought that all other key employees too should do the same. He saw this as the formula for success. As it was not practical, no successful initiative in this direction could emerge.

Permitting Unauthorized Workstation Absence

The problem of unauthorized absence of white-collar workers from their workstations is endemic to public sector undertakings and government offices. In some poorly managed business entities too, the malaise of people being absent from their workstations has been noticed. On analysis, it looked primarily a response to the boss himself being out for long hours without leaving behind an authorized representative or second-in-command for maintaining work discipline. Normally, people tend to follow work ethics of a boss and any loose operation on his part is copiously copied.

Accepting excuses or showing partiality of approach in this regard, soon assumes the conditions of mismanagement. Unauthorized absence from workstations, once allowed or tolerated is difficult to correct at a later date. BPO operators and the IT industry have successfully managed to tame this not so pernicious evil of the corporate work life. Time-related performance standards—and absolute righteousness in appreciation of good work done always tend to promote people to stick to expected and accepted work schedules. Genuinely necessary and timely informed absence from workstations needs to be accommodated—provided the pending work is performed in a manner that corporate output is not compromised in any manner.

Tolerating Uncontrolled In-and-Out Movement

Some mismanaged organizations operate without entry and exit restrictions or even without a reception. It imparts an undesirable level of indiscipline among the office workers as well as visitors. Outsiders start coming without appointment and valuable time is wasted in unproductive engagements or in activities extraneous to the official work.

Organizations with uncontrolled in-and-out movements are never competitive: they can never meet deadlines and keep their customers happy. Such work practices are manifestations of multilateral mismanagement.

Conditions of uncontrolled in-and-out movements were noticed at KIL and a number of other mismanaged organizations.

PRACTICE FAIR DISTRIBUTION OF CREDIT

One of the most important aspects of un-professionalism that inflicts maximum damage to a corporate body is the ***unrighteous credit distribution*** for an achievement or a series of achievements. The degree of fairness exhibited in the activities of credit distribution brings out the balance of negative and positive forces operative within a corporate management matrix. The methodologies of credit and discredit distribution send waves of impressions which govern the long-term commitments—and consequently the outputs of the knowledge workers.

The problem of unrighteous credit distribution (UCD) has a universal presence across the corporate world; even well-managed MNCs are not free from this malaise. Small and medium enterprises are in greater grip of this malady: It restricts their growth and competitiveness.

Adoption of an unrighteous approach while dealing with family members and professionals within family run corporate bodies is more of a rule than an exception—as different yardsticks are employed in assessing performance/utility of different people. In such cases the whole corporate management structure is based on subjective assessments, which by implication become a cause for slow progress and/or deterioration of such corporate bodies.

The presence of UCD, beyond a minimum tolerable limit, causes symptoms of severe mismanagement. In fact, it is a symptom as well as cause of mismanagement. The author himself suffered several instances of UCD in his long and varied corporate work life. Corporate workers with high IQ and output quotients—and independent thinking are particularly susceptible for suffering the manifestations of this malady. As a pernicious characteristic of UCD, complaints against this practice by the wronged party are not entertained in right spirit.

TOLERATING MISLEADING WORK OUTPUT

In the corporate world it is the work output, which should in principle determine credit/reward and discredit distribution—and the consequent growth paths of knowledge workers. The quality of intra-corporate work environment, in return, should get determined by these activities. In this process, misleading work outputs do often figure either by default or design. If accepted as productive works, such outputs become a basis for UCD and the consequent disaffections that it generates.

The author has often witnessed magnification of achievements of some favoured ones, beyond all reasonable proportions. VKM's 'Asvamedha yagna' which he implemented with a lot of fanfare, and a lot of avoidable expenses, in select districts of Tamil Nadu was a typical case in point. Misleading output reports were accepted—and UCD was attempted. Suggestions for third party work evaluations were not accepted—but soon the cat was out of the bag. A situation of acute mismanagement had developed.

Year-end booking of non-existent sales, in order to inflate corporate or divisional performance is often resorted to, incurring avoidable expenses. It takes a form of more serious mismanagement when efforts are made to reward the perpetrators of such non-existent performances.

IGNORING EMERGING BUSINESS TRENDS

A proactive corporate should, in principle, contribute towards emergence of new business trends. But if being a leading trend contributor is not feasible for any reason, one should not lose sight of emerging trends. There should be no ignorance of emerging trends in a business by default or design. Lost opportunities have deadly influence on the competitiveness of a business.

In the early 1980s, synthetic pyrethroids, as an efficacious group of insecticides, were introduced in the Indian market by a number of MNCs active in the field of agrochemicals. For certain reasons UCIL had decided not only not to be part of the international trend, but to actively oppose the same. A lot of scientific data was collected and presented in favour of its arguments, but the Government of India, through its Central Insecticides Board, decided to ignore the same.

It became a classic example of mismanagement by ignoring a powerful trend. The corporate world is full of such instances—and readers, the author is sure, shall be able to identify a number of them from their own corporate work lives.

FOLLOWING THE OSTRICH APPROACH

Keeping track of challenges and/or threats from a market and/or the competition operative therein—local or international, is the job of the management.

Emerging market trends, in short or long-term, need to be actively tracked in order to protect an ongoing corporate activity, and also to ensure its continued profitability in the future. As and when dangers are identified, protective steps need to be initiated without delay.

Procrastination or an ostrich approach is bad for future corporate health. Markets do have a silent but dynamic system that continuously tells us about the new/emerging trends, in terms of products and services likely to emerge—and an active management invariably receives feedback in a substantially conscious manner.

Some managements ignore it for one or the other reason, often by default and sometimes even by design—and, in both the cases, it assumes, after lapse of some time, a harmful form of mismanagement. The author has seen numerous examples where corporate bodies have not reacted timely to active danger signals emitted by the market and/or the concerned business environment. Readers, without difficulty, shall be able to isolate several relevant examples from their own specific business environments where such activities of mismanagement took place.

ABANDONING THE POST IN A CRISIS SITUATION

Abandoning the post in a crisis situation, i.e., not attending to one's assigned duties by absenting from a workstation or otherwise is an extreme form of mismanagement.

The captain of a ship is not expected to abandon it in a situation of crisis or distress, until and unless, all involved are safely away from the impending danger. Any action contrary to it becomes an act of indiscipline, and by consequence, a form of mismanagement.

As discussed elsewhere too, KIL ran into financial troubles on account of certain investments, supplies to market diminished—and as a result its sales and marketing staff moved out, substantially diminishing its market coverage. Desperate attempts from the trade to get in touch with the senior management were not properly responded to. Senior managers in key departments of purchase, finance, and manufacturing turned inactive: Suppliers' calls too remained unattended. No one, in fact, knew how to remedy the situation, as this organization had never worked with delegated responsibilities. The total work environment presented a desolate look; a situation of acute mismanagement had developed.

Forgetting to Smile—Practice of Furrowed Forehead

Problems do not disappear or diminish by wishing them away. They are not influenced in any manner by excessively worrying about them, least by displaying them on your face or forehead.

Forgetting to smile and letting them furrow your forehead is in fact a way of magnifying them. Since any solution shall emerge only from effective actions and communications, for both of which the presence of a third party, coworkers and collaborators, is required. The furrowed forehead approach ends up intimidating the subject person or persons: Their capacity to act or be helpful too is compromised.

Problems and challenges fade only when they are in encounter with a bold persistent person: They don't respect the weak or the feeble-hearted.

There is no point in publicly displaying your problems—your own supporters and subordinates tend to lose confidence. Hence, a professional manager, least a CEO, should not commit this act of mismanagement.

Expressing Misplaced Anger or Failing to Manage it

Poorly trained professionals or CEOs tend to believe that raising the tone of their speech or conversation is an effective replacement for logic: For some of them anger expression seems to be a solution to all problems.

The author came across a failing CEO who seemed to believe that suppressing juniors with his temper or sharp cutting down of what they attempted to say, was the way of convincing them. He continued to compound his failures, which finally assumed a severe form of mismanagement.

Anger can be an effective tool of management if employed at the right time, in the right quantity, and in the right manner. But, it is not easy to master the technology of productive anger management.

There are some mis-managers who blow hot and cold; with little resistance from their anger recipients, they buckle down in a manner that conveys a message of inbuilt weakness. If you become angry with or without valid reason, be sure where and how to stop: Don't let the victim of your anger be the decider in this situation, otherwise more damaging consequences are likely to follow.

The objective of anger manifestation should be very clear in your mind: You should use its right dosage to generate necessary positive or cooperative feelings in the mind of the target person. In fact, the best way is to achieve with *madhura* what was targeted through anger manifestation.

Lord Krishna[2] was a master of this ever-effective technology. He could effectively disarm his opponents with an irresistible smile—and reluctant supporters too were dealt with the same tool of *madhura*.

Offering Unimplementable Threats

Statements such as: "I will close down this department" or "I will close down this plant," are often made by non-performing business heads or CEOs while, in fact, they are not in a position to do any thing like that.

Their target audience knows the facts, yet the mis-managers end up making mismanaging comments. They should know that threats rarely improve performance—particularly in a collective work environment they are totally ineffective. Further, utterance of any non-implementable threats only weakens the threatening authority.

The psychology of threat is not easy to understand; it is effective only when the threat originator is in a position to implement it, in terms of power and determination—and simultaneously, if the targeted person is in a position to understand and appreciate the consequences of the same.

Practising a Wide Arena of Action Spectrum

Some CEOs believe in having a very wide arena of action: They

attempt to do or attempt to exhibit that they are capable of doing every component of the job spectrum from MD down to peon.

The problem does not end here—as some of them attempt to justify this mismanaging habit as part of professionalism, and expect other managers, senior or junior, to emulate this unprofessional approach.

In fact, it does not impress anybody—and instead of bringing in efficiency, it damages corporate structure, dilutes responsibilities, and sometimes invites ridicule from one and all.

The diseased practice of ***wide arena of action spectrum*** (WAAS) has been noticed infecting primarily the non-professional managers, more specifically the first or second-generation entrepreneurs. In more cases than not, it becomes a roadblock in progress and growth of the organizations headed by such people. It brings in a galaxy of mismanagement in the affected organizations.

Becoming a Power Concentrate

It is said that power corrupts—and absolute power corrupts absolutely. The disease of power concentration is not confined only to political dictators: The corporate world is full of power concentrates—and as political dictators spoil the economic and social fabric of victimized countries, ***corporate power concentrates*** (CPCs) mismanage the present as well as the future of the companies that they head.

The CPCs make sure that there are no truly independent directors in the board of directors of the subject companies. They accumulate their handpicked yes-men for whom a mention on the visiting card and the sitting fees are the main concern. Such managers or CEOs, more often than not, engage in or encourage unethical practices against the interests of all involved. And when symptoms of acute mismanagement appear, then they do not know where to look. Power concentration is toxic to quality maintenance, initiative and innovation, and to the overall competing performance. It is one of the most undesirable attributes for a corporate to possess.

Observing Zero Delegation of Authority

Non-delegation of authority and power concentration are mutually causative, i.e., one gives birth and sustains the other. It is difficult to see and decide which one emerges first. The results are equally bad for the victim company in both the situations. Power concentrates and practitioners of non-delegation, both seem equally inefficient in terms of corporate performance, and for all other requirements for a company to be deemed as an efficient performer.

Normally, delegation is a difficult practice for any manager to get efficient with: It needs a degree of positivity on the part of the manager to effectively adopt it. Incompetent and self-centered executives, who suffer from insecurity, can not adopt it effectively.

Efficient managers, who do not attempt to directly collect brownie points, can do an excellent job of delegation. Companies headed by non-delegating CEOs continue to suffer inefficiencies, as the true potential of white-collar workers in such organizations, to take initiative is never fully activated.

Only a capable manager, who is also a righteous human being, can do a good job of delegation. Through achievement of good results, an efficient delegator can benefit the junior involved as well as himself, as the credit for getting a good job done shall always remain with him or her.

Lord Krishna[2] was the most efficient delegator that mankind has ever known. He delegated difficult jobs to his people and associates as per their capability and aptitude, enabled them and provided timely assistance, if needed, through his unique ***supervised system of delegation*** (SSD). He ruled the kingdoms of Mathura and Dwaraka without himself being the head or the king. Further, he eliminated a huge concentration of evil forces, friends and relatives of Duryodhana, without directly being part of the fighting in the great battle of Kurukshetra. He had effectively delegated the job to **Arjuna** and the other Pandava warriors.

The author himself experimented with almost 90 percent of the available work delegation to juniors through needed guidance and totally righteous credit distribution. In case of anything going wrong he assumed the full responsibility for the same—and, as expected, no part of failure or discredit struck to him.

Create Non-professional Centres of Power

In the case of most of the power concentrates, whether in the political or corporate fields, non-official centres of power always tend to emerge. It is a consequence of either granting or acceptance of favours.

In family-managed companies, one or more close relatives of the owners tend to assume powers, which as per hierarchy and position, do not belong to them. First- or second-generation entrepreneurs too are not free from this malaise: Even in professionally managed companies such centres of power have been witnessed to be operative.

In some MNCs a mere secretary to the MD or CMD, if endowed with negative intelligence, assumes this form. Wherever and in whatsoever form, all non-professional centres of power emerge either due to the consent of the CEO or on account of some weakness on his or her part. They are essentially created due to mismanagement and continue to add to the mass of mismanagement being carried by the victim corporate.

Encouraging Hangers-on or *Chamchas*

Almost all power concentrates, irrespective of their field of engagement, tend to encourage accumulation of yes-men or hangers-on around them. The former, in fact, act like honey and the latter more like flies, in terms of their behaviour: Both attempt to seek favours from each other.

The power concentrates get their ego serviced—additionally, they secure some services, which otherwise are difficult to obtain. The hangers-on do not do anything free—they extract their pound of flesh without the other side either knowing or realizing the same.

The power concentrates, on one hand, waste a lot of time, in the company of hangers-on, and end up doing several undesirable favours to the latter despite the same not being in the interest of the corporate body. Such power concentrates as well as the company that they manage end up in undesirable actions, as well as the consequences of such acts of mismanagement.

Allowing Power Centres to Grow into NPAs

Most of the non-professional power centres, from all cost-return considerations, become non-performing assets—in other words they do not actively contribute to the bottom line of the corporate body.

In practice, they become ***active damaging assets*** (ADAs) for the company—persistently drawing upon the vital resources on one hand, and creating an environment of mismanagement on the other. These ADAs or NPAs ruin the productive work environment of the company and the system of righteous distribution of credit or discredit does not work in such a situation.

Most of the financially sick companies are very rich in

concentration of such people. Top management with the consent or active indulgence of whom such NPAs or ADAs accumulate, does not find itself either willing or capable of getting rid of these obnoxious corporate appendices. Only a change of management, preferably a change of ownership, does create the right environment of getting rid of these mis-managers and/or the products of mismanagement.

Permitting Inadequate IT Utilization

Information technology systems are the modern tools for competitive efficiencies in any well-performing corporate; not to push for their intensive usage is tantamount to acceptance of inefficiencies. In recent years, the author has had experience with corporates passing through all variable stages of IT usage. For instance:

- The corporates which had no IT facilities at all.
- The ones that had IT facilities but hardly used them.
- There were those, which made only moderate use of the facilities.
- Some which used IT to push up productivity and competitiveness.

In the present competitive work environment, not creating adequate IT facilities or creating but not using them effectively amounts to a form of mismanagement. The responsibility for such occurrences rests entirely on the senior management of the subject company.

Letting the Corporate Mission be Invisible

Corporate mission is an important component of the performance psychology/strategy of a company—as employees can be successfully steered to perform in light of the same.

Some CEOs have the habit of keeping the corporate mission just close to their chest—not letting the white-collar workers to share or appreciate the same. They do not push the HR department to do a good job of educating the members of the subject corporate in this regard. A corporate mission comes alive only through intense discussions and debate with all involved: It can turn the company working as all-inclusive.

The author has seen CEOs who have little or no understanding in relation to the vital requirements of this highly productive symbolism.

They do not make efforts to learn about its utility; their professional illiteracy in this regard continues to cloud their mind—and, by implication, the very future of the subject corporate. They should not be allowed to mismanage this intangible asset of the companies that they head. Progress towards the corporate mission should be reviewed with rigorous regularity, through internal as well as external efforts. Need-based modifications and/or upgradations should be made through wide interaction and consent.

LETTING TURNOVER MISGUIDE YOU

Turnover often misguides a majority of corporate workers, especially those not directly exposed to the intricacies of accounting.

Particularly, sales and marketing people fall prey to the illusionary nature of turnover. They relate higher sales to higher profitability: They do not understand the contribution of individual products in their product mix, and the cost of selling and marketing too is often alien to them. Their eagerness to reduce prices by offering a variety of discounts and incentives reflects the deficit of understanding on their part. In fact, it is not their fault; the senior management responsible for the bottom line of the company often fails to do the requisite groundwork and measure up to its responsibilities educating such crucial people.

Some wise people in marketing do stress that one could lose money by selling more: It becomes a reality if discounts and incentives are not kept in strict check.

Additionally, a majority of production people too fall prey to the illusion that is often created by the figures of sales and turnover: They do not keep track of the value addition that they effect. It is only value addition, or more appropriately the contribution, that pushes a corporate towards its eventual profitability.

CREATING OR ALLOWING CONFLICT OF INTEREST TO DEVELOP

***Conflict of interest* (COI) does not develop by itself; it develops either through negligence of management, and not so infrequently with its active connivance or involvement.**

The author has often seen the COI germinating and then taking deep roots in a good number of corporates, large and small, MNCs and/or non-MNCs that he worked with in his over 40 years of active work exposure.

Purchases and materials departments are rarely free from it—and so are advertising and public relations.

Despite the COI having a tendency to remain below the visible surface, some smell of its existence and/or growth does always emerge in varying intensities. It remains up to the management either to continue to ignore it or go after it with all the available resources.

It is also not uncommon to note where CEOs or proprietors place their confidantes in juicy positions and share the spoils, unmindful of its implications, or even when the rumours of wrongdoings do travel far and wide. This type of mismanagement directly hits the bottom line as well as the corporate image of the company involved.

Practise an Art of Decision Avoidance

***Deliberate decision avoidance* (DDA) is an often-practised art of management.**

Some managers are scared of accepting responsibility for the rightly or wrongly perceived fear of facing the music subsequently. Others gather expertise in pushing inconvenient decisions under the carpet, on the plates of their juniors or escalate the same to higher levels.

It is often the combination of fear, incapability, and negative thought interactions that push for decision avoidance.

Even a not-so-good decision taken with the needed speed is always better than a good decision taken in a belated manner.

The former encourages the involved workers while the latter acts as a dampener on the whole corporate work system. The author has encountered the decision non-takers or the ***decision killers*** (DKs) in all varieties of corporate work environments. No collective work place is free from such mis-managers.

The champion of indecision or decision avoidance, as encountered by the author, was KNS: He had developed it into a fine art. He kept his subordinates, about half a dozen of them—all well qualified and experienced in their own fields, on tenterhooks—for finalizing one or the other report or drafting one or the other communication. Rarely any task got finalized on account of his L&R technology. Only the author who once had to work with him for a short period, escaped the ill-effects of his pernicious technique by encountering it with a better one—namely the no-draft please or the NDP.

Expecting to be Serviced Out of the Way

Some highly egoistic managers have the habit of expecting to be serviced on priority: They consider it as a matter of right.

GRV and SCP, as per experience of the author, were two such specimens; they had truly fat egos. While working as a regional manager for the south, GRV wanted supplies, budgets, publicity materials and campaigns, all on priority. Performance of the region, as the highest sales volume contributor for UCIL products, was viewed by him as his personal performance.

When he managed to be promoted as an all-India sales manager, and was located at Delhi, his egoistic approach continued to bloom, though it put him in the trouble spot on several occasions. He wanted to speak on priority in meetings and conferences despite his bull-headedness and lack of judicious analysis. Soon, he put himself at cross purposes with the very people on whose support he had to depend for his performance: He also attempted to put his own inefficiencies and failures on the heads of his subordinates, most of whom were far superior to him in qualifications and performance. It did not go unnoticed either by his seniors.

His **me first** approach proved disastrous. Once while travelling from Chandigarh to Delhi in the author's car, he happened to see a good quality jack in the boot: He could not restrain himself from the desire of owning it. He demanded that the subject tool be given to him and that I could buy a new one—adding that he would pass the bill. The author responded that he could buy it himself from a motor parts dealer who was located just next to his Delhi office. He could not stomach the rebuff and became revengeful which hastened his downfall and eventual demotion.

Exhibiting Inability to Tolerate Competence

A good majority of managers, juniors and seniors alike, do not possess the capability to tolerate competent juniors.

The author earned rich experience in several such direct encounters, which often developed into situations of mismanagement, often for his less competent bosses, and sometimes to himself. GRV and RNS were two such cases—and they had to bear the consequences for displaying such intolerance or non-appreciation. RNS fell into the same category but exhibited better tolerance in view of his long exposure to working with a large Marwari business group. RCT, on the other hand, was fully non-tolerant but cunning, and hence suffered delayed consequences. SC, despite non-comparable qualifications and experience, did not suffer from such deficiencies: He managed well even when he had a bunch of superior subordinates. His MNC work background, coupled with his special personality, enabled him to effectively discharge this difficult function.

Thus, a good boss should not feel envious or threatened by a more competent junior—at least not in an apparent manner: He or she should know or learn how to make best use of such a situation—and thus escape mismanagement. Subordinates, of whatsoever calibre or competence, are a type of work tool for a good manager; instead of fighting with them, they should be used intelligently and productively.

Letting Two Stones Pulverize Corporate Profits

A CEO has the moral responsibility to generate profits for shareholders: He should not instal two stones, even with his own self-interests, to pulverize the profits of the company that he happens to head.

RNS had two assistants, one looking after purchases and marketing, and another all the plant work, including production, quality assurance, and despatches, etc. Between the two, the corporate profitability was fully pulverized and blown away—and it was, most apparently, being done with the consent and involvement of the boss.

The situation of full-blown mismanagement did not take any time to manifest. The author had landed in the delicate position of rescuing the profitability of the company while reporting to the boss who seemed knee-deep in the mess. Despite the odds, the job was done: One of the two stones that was grinding the profits away was removed through a skillful usage of the boss himself. The situation of severe mismanagement was ameliorated to a considerable extent.

Letting too many Men of the Boss Crowd the Corporate

In every organization, unauthorized power centres tend to develop, with or without the consent and collaboration of the boss: They become the main cause of emergence of situations of mismanagement.

In the mid 1970s, the author worked as northern region in-charge of a MNC: In response to his demand for recruitment of more sales staff for effective coverage of the huge region, the divisional general manager sent four persons who were deemed as surplus at the plant. Most of them were used to cushy jobs and hence did not like the tightly-supervised assignments at far-off places. One of them, who was short-named as PG, attempted to tell that he was the GM's man, to which he was told that, as a GM's man, he had greater responsibility to perform and not offer mere excuses. He understood the situation and, despite the tough demands of the job, ended up becoming a productive salesman.

But most of the so-called men of the boss are not positive workers: They play politics and tend to damage corporate interests—in fact, the interests of the very boss to whom they profess allegiance. Situations of mismanagement often develop, handling of which is often neither easy nor pleasant. KRD had employed a number of his relatives in the plant; most of them persistently created problems—some selling scrap and others setting commissions if any responsible job was ever assigned to them. KIL too suffered from this malady and the consequences could not be prevented.

Going by Person and not by Performance

Most of the senior managers and CEOs, who are not endowed with or have not acquired merits of true professionalism, tend to mess up distribution of credit and discredit in corporate work environments.

They tend to go, more often than not, by the person that he or she is—his/her attitude and personality rather than performance.

It becomes the root cause of disaffection—and consequent loss of initiative and innovation. The unrighteousness of this flawed approach often ends up creating situations of mismanagement; yes-men and hangers-on absorb most of the benefits at the cost of true performers.

Lord Krishna,[2] the most righteous manager and leader of people known to the mankind, ancient or modern, always valued merit and performance. A non-performing person, howsoever close to him did not draw his appreciation. He appreciated merit even when the same was reposed in people inclined to actively oppose him. He appreciated the merits and strengths of the great warrior Bhishma and also the wise Vidura, the two seniors in the court of Hastinapura. A little emulation of Lord Krishna's merit-based appreciation and credit distribution can rid the present corporate community of the massive ills that it has accumulated in this regard.

Surrounded by Files and Papers

Being surrounded by papers and files is a strong symptom of inefficiency of a manager—his or her incompetence to understand and handle the jobs at hand or inability to delegate some of the work unnecessarily kept hanging around, distinctly smells out of the pile on the table.

Normally, it is the incapacity to delegate arising among others, from fear of losing authority that causes this paralysis against depending upon any one. A senior corporate worker's love for getting into every detail, i.e., the nitty-gritty of all that is at hand, robs such a mis-manager of whatsoever productive time he or she could afford to extract from the 24 hour-day.

In the Western corporate environment, accumulation of unattended papers on the work table is not considered very healthy for a manager's reputation. The situation in India, particularly in the public sector and family-managed companies, is different. Often, managers' tables in old family-run businesses, and first/second generation entrepreneurs, present a clustered and confused state of affairs.

Procrastination, either by default or design, is bad for business: A not so good decision, taken promptly, is definitely better than a good decision taken by delaying it so much that the whole or most of its goodness evaporates well before the event of decision making.

All situations of excessive paper accumulation on an executive's table top, irrespective of reasons, represent a situation of serious mismanagement. In the case of the majority of such mis-managers, it is a pathological situation—as a number of them have been seen by the author struggling to locate a paper or file when any further delay in its handling becomes severely inconvenient. KNS, RNS, KRD and CKS often resembled such a grim business; of these the first two behaved in this manner despite being under-occupied.

Subverting the Organizational Structure

Subverting organizational structure is akin to the fool who was seen cutting the very branch on which he was sitting.

On finer analysis one could, however, always notice the vital difference—the fool did it out of ignorance while the mis-managers do so out of a well considered design. Most of the mis-managers encountered by the author often attempted to go several steps down the reporting line, in order to extract information while denying the same to the immediate supervisors of the levels so contacted: It invariably killed corporate discipline—inducing a breakdown, and avoidable tensions in the reporting line.

It is indeed surprising when owner-entrepreneurs resort to this non-professional practice—finally ending up damaging their own organization: It is like striking an axe on your own feet.

Not so long ago, an owner-entrepreneur CEO was seen indulging in a similar activity just after finishing a meeting with all the branch managers of the company. The mis-managing CEO signalled one of the branch managers into a corner and whispered something into the junior's ears—and soon, the affected junior stopped reporting through the normal channel. The disturbed system led to severe mismanagement of the business in the affected areas. This kind of un-professional behaviour seems to be a consequence of some pathological psychology of the concerned mis-managers.

Severe confidence deficit, trust deficit, and intense accumulation of insecurity seems to be at the bottom of such self-damaging behaviour.

Developing a Tunnel Vision

As discussed earlier, mis-managers who destroy organizational structure or are unable to delegate effectively, often suffer from tunnel vision: They are able to see only one side of the story or a fraction of what is needed to be seen. In their cases, the tunnel vision, to be more precise, is the ***preferentially-selected vision*** (PSV). They see what is convenient for them to see.

The inability of such mis-managers to grasp, deliberately or otherwise, the wider implications of the situations that they create, is not easy to be corrected: Most of them invariably attempt to defend themselves and assert that they did not suffer from any such deficiency. They are, in fact, ever ready to point fingers in the direction of others—and on account of their seniority or authority, they tend to escape being held accountable for all the mismanagement that they create. But they invariably lose the esteem and appreciation of the people who work for them—and the resultant consequences are never too difficult to see.

Noticing People only when they make Mistakes

The holders of tunnel vision or the various other attributes of mismanagement are normally very poor in appreciating good work done: They are always scared that the person involved might ask for some benefits or a promotion, if any of his or her good acts were appreciated.

They tend to notice people only when they have made some mistakes: They don't want to lose an opportunity to effect a dressing down—they are good at it. The irony of the situation, however, is that such mis-managers end up thinking that they are doing a good job of management. They are blind to their own deficiencies; in fact, deeply blinded by the power or the authority that they wield. They represent negativity and the consequent incompetence, at best.

Non-creation of your Own Redundancy

All good professional managers are supposed to delegate, train juniors, and create and strengthen systems, which are self-propelled—wherein, as a matter of principle, an individual's presence does not matter (not be of critical or decisive value)—the system works in a manner that human beings become a substitutable input.

Hence, systems and processes should be organized for reusability of learning and performance skills—individuals should evolve from doing to managing, in the truest sense of work efficiency. As soon as a professional manager achieves it, he or she is ready for higher responsibilities—to move up or move out.

Well-set systems and processes allow a good professional to create his/her own redundancy: In my view, it is a state of readiness for one to be ready for assuming higher responsibilities—and also to send a message to the organization that one has grown beyond his/her present responsibilities—and was ready for something bigger or more challenging.

Unfortunately, a majority of the so-called professionals do not attempt such an approach: They often suffer from confidence deficit—which finally pushes them to initiative deficit—making them averse to courting risks—or sticking out their necks for more/higher responsibilities. Afflicted by these deficits, they avoid delegation—and the major part of their energy is spent on preserving their current positions—guarding the turf that is not worth any protection. And when they fail to grow in their existing positions, frustrations take over—leading to situations of confusion and delusion. Their deficiencies of 'Thought Warriorism' lead to genesis of work stress in an undesirable manner.

The usefulness of systems and processes in an organization comes handy when things go wrong or during transition. It becomes easier, in such a situation, for key people to go on leave or on short-term out-of-station assignments. It also helps in consistency of products and services delivery.

Incompetent and or insecure managers, or those afflicted with **tamsic** nature, avoid development of systems for re-usability of knowledge or capabilities, and empowering of subordinates—and finally, towards creation of a conducive work environment of cooperation or collective action. The positive approach of creating dependable systems helps in propagating righteousness and inclusiveness: It helps in avoidance of situations of mismanagement.

ADVERTISING YOUR OWN INCOMPETENCE

Some incompetent managers/CEOs have the art of advertising their incompetence—rather than camouflaging it. Perhaps, their ego coupled with the long practice of non-restraint, pushes them into this self-destructive act. An intense urge to exhibit self-importance (I am the boss type) or self-righteousness does them in—pushing them into self-damaging acts. Yet, they continue to live with an illusion and believe:

- That they are doing a great job;
- That they are on the right path; and
- That they have a right to do whatever they were doing.

GRV and KSC were two such distinguished mis-managers whom the author had the opportunity to know and observe very closely. The former was in the habit of putting his foot in the mouth—right formation of comments and statements was not his forte. Since his juniors, most of them being superior to him in all requisite faculties of management, did not bear his stupidities of communication—formal meetings often turned into chaos. Finally, he killed his own career through persistent advertising of his own incompetence.

On the other hand, KSC suffered a persistent urge to state and re-stress that he was the boss or the CMD. He did not know how to coordinate his statements and outbursts as per composition of a meeting or its audience. From a salesman he expected a manager's job and vice-versa—and from a non-accountant, an accountant's work. His own failures, he attempted to see as others' incompetencies. The following actual instance, witnessed by the author, illustrates it magnificently.

It was 27 December, 2007: Sales staff from Rajasthan were gathered in the KIL conference room and next year's sales plans were being discussed in detail. Most of the discussions were completed by mid-day and NT had done a good job of coordinating the same. All the salesmen had completed their customer-wise accounts settlement with the designated accounts' personnel at the regional office.

KSC joined the meeting in the afternoon and, in the presence of the junior staff, could not restrain himself from saying that it was only he who could settle the customers' accounts; thus all the efforts made by the staff looked null and void. Since the accounts department of the regional office was part of the HO accounts and since this department was directly under KSC himself, his assertion smelt simply of ego and negativity manifestations or being incompetent of not knowing his own accountability. It only exhibited his naivety that further made people to doubt his competence. The staff clearly told him that he should get the matter settled with the accounts department and satisfy himself.

Through avoidable statements he ended up advertising his own incompetence—and he was, at least publicly, not regretful of his activities of mismanagement.

Allowing the Disease of Management Dieback to take Root

Discipline, hard work, honesty, and transparency flows from top to bottom.

A little slip on the part of the people manning the top has a quick and profound impact on the whole organization. When your own juniors and/or employees view you as unrighteous and/or dishonest or a person of doubtful integrity, then you can't expect them to be different, i.e., they are unlikely to hesitate from indulging in the same or similar type of activities.

In one corporate, with which the author had an opportunity to be associated, the undercurrents or whispers were that its CMD and a cousin of his were often receiving a cut in whatsoever they procured: Ample evidences of the same was cited. And they exercised a monopoly for this activity without creating verifiable and trust-generating systems.

As the financial position of the company deteriorated progressively and it faltered in regard to payments to suppliers, transporters, C&F agents, statutory payments to state authorities, these whispers turned into loud talk. Work flow, in terms of production and supplies to the market, dried up and salary and wages payments turned irregular—and, along side, the expression of employees' disaffection started taking more virulent forms.

Soon the top management started exhibiting symptoms of total directional confusion: Its strategies to procure, produce and supply failed repeatedly under demands from numerous directions and insufficient contributions that its operations generated. The top management showed signs of directional confusion, depression and delusion—and this impact started percolating to the second line of management. On a considered analysis the author called it ***Management Dieback.*** And in absence of support the victim corporate's middle and the lower parts too were affected creating a situation of total ***Management Wilt***.

It was a situation of gross/inept mismanagement.

Opening Files Against your Key People

Business organizations, irrespective of what they produce and market, need key performing professionals in order to meet their long-range objectives.

And long-term business operations, particularly in non-professional work environments, do allow generation of some unrighteous personal interests on the part of the entrepreneur and/or his or her key people. It might lead to performance inefficiencies, conflicts of operation and interests—and finally, when either losses occur or a perception of eventual losses emerges, feelings of insecurity, failures, and eventual business cessation creates active conflict out of responsibility assignment efforts.

When signs of eventual business failure become visible for one and all to see and be concerned, like in a patient of kidney failure, and when it is time for bold 360 degree correctional orientation, more often than not, the mismanaging CEO and seniors tend to engage in blame apportioning instead of taking the right corrective measures.

Instead of refilling the key people with confidence and encouragement some mis-managers attempt to open files against the very people who are expected or have the skills and capacity for a turnaround. Though it is not the time for fault finding, discredit apportioning, investigating the acts of commission and omission on the part of the key people or openly launching investigations against them, some mismanaging CEOs have been seen by the author doing exactly the same.

Eventually, by so doing, they turn even neutral people against them as an output of the environment of fear and uncertainties that effortlessly emerges out of such actions. An efficient and righteous CEO firstly should not allow such a situation to arise—but if for any reason emergence of such a situation could not be avoided, then he or she should willingly assume and accept full responsibility of the development: In any case all juniors are supposed to work for and on behalf of the chief or the CEO only. A good general rarely blames his soldiers for failures on the front.

Implementing Design Through Default

Many managers, or more rightly, the mis-managers, see action in inaction. They tend to implement a plan or design through default, i.e., without any overt action. It ends up confusing the target persons or the people involved, with or without the planned results.

KSC of KIL exhibited expertise in this art of mismanagement. He closed a business operation without overtly saying so or without taking the affected people, seniors or juniors, into confidence. Consequent conditions of total confusion emerged at most of its production/business sites—an utter display of mismanagement. People had no work for months together, salaries and wages were not paid for months together—and the involved or affected people did not know what to do, though all of them talked about the eventual worst. Each one was free to do what he or she wanted—and come and go at will. Idle discussions and gossip were at their peak—pushing the level of negativity in the deteriorated corporate environment to its peak. Truly dreadful conditions of mismanagement had emerged.

The sales staff posted on field locations, were not paid their salaries and travel expenses for months together: Further, they were forbidden from collection of any cash from dealers/distributors, for meeting their day-to-day expenses. The traders were instructed to this effect through circulars from the HO. Thus, the affected employees were effectively made redundant: They were left to see for themselves the writing on the wall; no guidance or counselling of any type was attempted. It seemed as if the dieback of management and the consequent wilting of the whole corporate structure were deliberate or wilful.

Resorting to Public Washing of Dirty Linen

In situations of intense intolerance and conflict (behaviour and/or interests) in corporate work environments, particularly between stakeholders, bosses and subordinates, and/or competing mis-managers, instances of open spats are not uncommon.

Division of business amongst siblings and/or partners often spills out of board rooms: Family-run businesses and partnership based enterprises are more prone to this kind of mismanagement. Amongst large Indian family-run business houses, a majority tends to run into such situations of mismanagement, which primarily are caused by:

- Unrighteous approach towards assets distribution and controls,
- Deficiencies in communications, and
- Intense negativity interplays.

Attempts on the part of the conflict-engaged parties to resort to public washing of dirty linen arise from their inherent incapacities for effective communication and unrighteousness fuelled intolerance. Some of them visualize the initiative to convert a conflict into a crisis and blow it out of proportion, as a tool of speeding up the resolution of the same.

It is primarily a consequence of defective thought process nurtured over a long time, which after a certain incubation sprouts into incompatible actions and behaviour. The wounds caused by public washing of dirty linen, an act of the highest category of mismanagement, do not heal easily. Through such actions, conflict resolution gets complicated, and competitiveness of the warring groups or personnel takes a severe dip.

Employees, seniors as well as juniors, in almost all types of CWEs too have been seen resorting to this defective method of conflict resolution—and, in the process, all of them end up creating situations of intense mismanagement. Employers and employees too sometimes resort to the ugly practice of dirty linen washing in public: Exit interviews, account settlements, post-appraisal interviews, etc., form some of the fertile situations for development of such gross mismanagement. All acts and attempts to put conflicts and differences in the public domain smell of incompetence and un-professionalism, and must be resisted.

CHAPTER 13

Mismanagement of a Crisis

Several situations of mismanagement tend to grow into crises of varying intensities—and mis-managers, through their incompetence and ineptitudes, further complicate the same.

An efficient crisis management needs a cool but interactive mind full of initiatives and innovations—and all such attributes are conspicuous by total absence in case of mis-managers. As a result, crises transcend from bad to worse by the time they seek or are able to obtain help from the right quarters. Some forms of crisis mismanagement, as witnessed by the author in his long and intense corporate work life, are described in brief, in the paragraphs that follow.

BEING EXCESSIVELY BOTHERED BY SETBACKS

For good professional managers who are able to respond intelligently, instead of being reactive to challenging situations, setbacks represent only commas and semicolons—never as full-stops—not even long pauses.

They are not excessively bothered by setbacks—never allowing their discerning mental balance to be disturbed. Allowing setbacks or crises to excessively impact the thought process has numerous incapacitating impacts on one's effective and corrective actions, and on their capabilities for initiatives and innovations. Efficient professionals don't allow setbacks to create this type of impact; their normal thinking, working and relaxing systems are never allowed to be affected beyond the necessary limits.

Being excessively bothered by setbacks tends to render one more prone to make mistakes that most likely end up further intensifying the already not-so-good situation. It hinders resorting to the necessary work of POLCs towards handling the unfavourable.

Just intelligently and doggedly challenge the situations of setbacks—and things shall start to commence taking favourable turns.

Showing Excessive Anxiety on your Face

Situations of crises do have the capacity of impacting the thought and action processes of the people who have the responsibility of encountering or managing the same.

Such impacts, in case of efficient professionals, are fully controlled and decently clothed: They see no point in unnecessarily exhibiting any undesirable emotions. Troubled thoughts, if any, should not be allowed to alter the expressions on your face, lest people who are supposed to assist you in handling of inconvenient situations are affected adversely by the same.

Recently, the author witnessed an associate of his face a severe financial crisis in the corporate that he managed: Additionally, as misfortunes never come alone, a legal situation too took a turn for the worse. This led to a vivid expression of anxiety and tension on his face: It was not a very good sight to witness. Since, the situation of crisis became visible to one and all, his capacity to effectively deal with his own people, as well as outsiders, was eroding.

Often, there is only a very thin margin between a win and a defeat—and it is primarily your facial expression and associated body language that does the trick. Let the moments or thoughts of weakness be contained to the fullest possible limits—and in encountering such brave expressions, the situations of setbacks start taking a positive turn.

Abandoning your Post in Crisis

In a situation of crisis, the worst thing that one could do is to abandon the post from where all controls have to be administered.

In a war, those who hold the post under all attacks do not often get defeated. Any indication of movements on the part of the commandant to the reverse brings disastrous consequences: It unnerves your supporters and encourages adversaries. Hence, abandoning the post of command and control represents the worst type of mismanagement. It can gravely complicate a situation of crisis into a catastrophe.

In the face of development of a severe financial crisis where financial instruments issued to suppliers bounced, payments to a variety of goods and services suppliers became long outstanding, and salaries of the white-collar workers got delayed for a few months, KSC lost the nerve to face people who came to the office to demand payments or assurances and deadlines. These situations of abandonment represented instances of severe mismanagement.

Retreating into Your Shell or Becoming Incommunicado

For almost all people it is difficult to face failures—and even more difficult to digest them. Human ego comes in the way of failure acceptance; reconciling with them needs logical interaction with your own inner-self.

Management of problems in a productive and successful way requires the cool inputs of emotion free application of the inputs of POLC. It is indeed possible to handle all the problems when there are intense efforts in that direction, without allowing them to un-nerve you.

Some victims of failures or setbacks retreat into their shells—they become incommunicado. It is not only the incapacity for failure avoidance that does them in, their inability to accept the reality of the situation also pins them down.

They suffer a breakdown of logical thought process—not knowing what to say and what to hear. The whole existence tends to become a burden for them. When such a situation is allowed to develop, mismanagement of crisis comes to full bloom. Crisis situations develop as a result of certain acts of omission and commission. Any remediation of the same is not feasible without the right input of case specific communication.

Abandoning Logical Thought Process

In situations of crisis, many managers are seen giving a go-by to the ***logical thought process*** (LTP). They often feel agitated and do not give others a chance to offer corrective advice or a helping hand. For them to accept that they could do something wrong culminating into a crisis is difficult. Forces of adamancy and/or obstinacy do not leave them free to initiate a logical thought process capable of seeing them out of the mess. In the process they commit more mistakes and the crisis continues to be compounded.

GRV refused to follow a LTP even when he was demoted from his headquarters job back to a southern location with truncated territory. Finally his services were terminated—and then he retreated into a situation of depression, never resorting to the LTP.

KSC too did not easily pick up the threads of the LTP. The ego of a once successful entrepreneur pushed him to continue to avoid the right path of recovery from the financial crisis into which he had landed himself and the corporate that he managed.

Appointing a Committee and Ignoring It

For low and/or moderate intensity crises, the safest way some mis-managers find is to appoint a committee—the objective being to gain time and shift the responsibility.

As and when a report comes, it becomes easy to ignore its recommendations on one or the other pretext. Such approaches are often resorted to in public sector enterprises. Governance, democratic or otherwise, often witnesses such situations of mismanagement. With further deterioration of the crisis, it is passed on to the higher level of management for grappling with it. Compounding of crisis, or the same getting out of control, often is the consequence of such manipulations.

Not Reorganizing and Regrouping

Under the effects of mismanagement, some managers/CEOs fail to reorganize and regroup all the available human and material resources even after noticing or facing the situations of setbacks or crises. They don't follow the battlefield logic: a defeat does not have to be accepted until and unless all the methodologies and techniques of escaping the same are tried and exhausted. Management of a situation of crisis is found only in regrouping and reorganization, including handing over of the command to the most competent and committed. Any effort to ignore such a necessity is bound to lead into further complication of a crisis situation—and mis-managers often are apt at it.

Losing Sense of Direction

In a case of truly serious crisis, managements are known to lose sense of direction—as, in face of defeat incapable commanders have been seen vacating their commands. It further deepens the crisis—bringing more misery and devastation. In corporate history, the Bhopal gas tragedy decidedly was one of the gravest crisis: And the events that followed had all the ingredients of uncommonly severe mismanagement. Some of these included:

- Absence of damage avoidance/reduction advice to the public,
- Company management missing from the command,
- Hospitals not advised of antidote and curative treatments,
- Absence of regrouping and reorganization of resources,
- No crisis specific communication—not even to company's own employees,
- Absence of concerted prompt relief,
- Disturbance of logical thought process as well as communication,
- Non-coordination of media management,
- Development of massive information deficit, and amongst others,
- Letting rumours have a field day.

A complete loss of sense of direction occurred: A massive loss of human life was the consequence of this unique mismanagement of crisis. The subject company suffered a complete loss of its facilities. Government authorities too lost face as they gave massive proof of mismanagement of crisis and its follow up: Insensitivities and incompetence of the administration became uncomfortably visible.

Amongst all kinds of mismanagement, crisis mismanagement does invariably have the most serious consequences, often even beyond human comprehension. The best remedy is crisis avoidance; and if that is not feasible, then all efforts must be made to minimize its impacts even during the period of its unfolding. Fast regrouping and reorganization of available resources can limit a lot of damage and unpleasant consequences.

CHAPTER 14

Mismanagement and Bio-Lethargy

The theory of bio-lethargy, as propounded by the author, states that all bio-systems tend to sag under conditions of operational dilution.

The term bio-system, in this context, encompasses all living beings, all of their systems and sub-systems, and also the living and working environments where any act of collaboration, production, distribution, growth, self-sustenance, and/or competitiveness takes place. It extends to encompass all collective and non-collective living and working environments, irrespective of the degree or sophistication or development experienced or endured.

Management energy, in all its forms and variations (actions inactions), is normally work environment dependent. It is a response to the stresses operative therein—as the ***Law of Stress Balance*** (LSB) ***states that any action, negative or positive, is a consequence of stress balance in a work situation or stresses operative on the organism that happens to be a part of or in the centre of an active situation.***

When food supply is plentiful, all organisms—carnivorous and/or herbivorous, become relatively lethargic as efforts and/or inputs necessary for survival and reproduction reduce substantially.

The same thing happens to a regime, an army, a corporate or any group of workers—irrespective of the colour of their collar or skin.

A wrestler loses his skills and stamina if he has no challenge necessitating regular practice and/or training. Fighting forces too lose their edge as and when challenge diminishes.

Similarly, a corporate tends to sag if there is no one to compete with or benchmark against, or if it loses the desire to grow and excel. For instance, a restaurant that gets only a thin stream of customers shall never be able to offer prompt service and good quality in the long run.

When work reduces in a corporate work environment, the speed of work as well as daily output of almost all workers takes a dip; after a lapse of some time, getting anything done there tends to become almost impossible—as no one will be spotted on his/or her work station when some work emerges. It is like a flow of water where a high input volume always tends to generate greater flow speed.

Normally, bio-lethargy sets in in a progressive manner, and swipes one and all, without any exception. It is a biological response wherein non-use of capabilities always leads to progressive degradation and/or disappearance of the same.

Cause and Effect

Bio-lethargy enjoys a complex relationship with the forces of mismanagement: It is a cause as well as effect of mismanagement; mutually they continue to catalyze genesis and spread of each other. While mismanagement enjoys a much wider effect spectrum, the bio-lethargy impact spectrum limits itself only to creation of mismanagement.

Negativity plays a vital role in genesis, spread and perpetuation of bio-lethargy. Sometimes, it can also initiate itself through negligence, and deficiencies of initiative and other output associated in capabilities.

Insensitiveness for common cause, an often manifesting form of negativity deludes a corporate worker to fall victim to bio-lethargy. Further, the forces of bio-lethargy, in a collective work environment, are highly contagious and contaminative; they spread swiftly from one worker to another—and sometimes, its victims may not initially

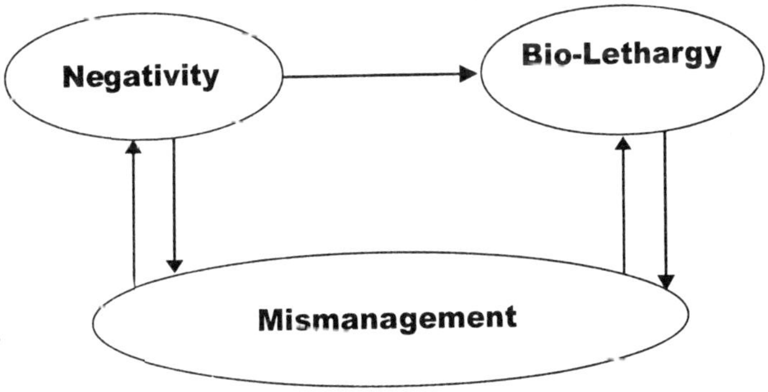

even become aware of coming in its grip. The forces of negativity, bio-lethargy and mismanagement tend to have a complex inter-relationship as depicted below.

SYMPTOMS AND EFFECTS

Bio-lethargy, by itself, is a composite symptom that is identifiable through the reading of several specific symptoms or sub-symptoms—some of the frequently visible ones are:

1. Delays and extended delays to response to a query—or non-action, the absence of which adversely impacts collective interests, corporate or otherwise.
2. Insensitivity to customer complaints and services is a very important index of operation of the forces of bio-lethargy.
3. Insensitivity to inter-departmental queries and replies speaks a lot about prevalence of this malady.
4. Peer pressure and response deficits are other definite signals for the active presence of bio-lethargy.
5. Negligence of queries, total or partial, from juniors reflects the inbuilt/deliberate operation of these anti-performance forces.
6. Desktop work accumulation, papers or otherwise, is one of the definite symptoms of bio-lethargy presence in the collective work system.
7. Non-attention or delay in response to incoming phone calls is a sure symptom of non-concern to collective corporate interests.
8. Any delay or negligence in attending to visitors could be interpreted as a sure sign of manifestation of bio-lethargy in the subject corporate work environment.
9. Late office arrivals and early departures do throw some light in this regard.
10. Extended lunch hours and uninformed/unapproved absenteeism are definite symptoms of active operation of this malaise.

There could be a lot more variety to the signs and symptoms of presence and operation of bio-lethargy in a given collective work environment. Through measurement of their intensity and frequency of occurrence, the anti-performance disease of bio-lethargy can be quantified. The author has developed a methodology for measurement of the presence and operation of bio-lethargy in any corporate and/or collective work environment.

The author encountered and experienced widespread presence and operation of bio-lethargy at the UKBM and KIL. In case of the former, its Kolkata headquarters and also the production facilities at Tarataula, presented a non-functional and morose picture. People were rarely spotted at their work stations prior to 11 a.m. and it, indeed, was very difficult to get anything done. People were interested mostly in discussions or gossip, locally called as "Katha". It was a sick company and it could not be said with any definitiveness whether the sickness was caused by bio-lethargy or the latter was the consequence of the sickness: The two seemed to be supporting each other as a beautiful symbiosis.

At KIL, the situation was no less serious or complex: Here, incoming phone calls were rarely picked up—and if and when they were, the callers more often than not, got only evasive replies. Calls and queries from over a dozen branch offices rarely evinced matching responses—the primary cause of which, as discussed elsewhere in this work, was the excessive power concentration within the hands and persona of its CMD. There was an equal and matching response from the branches too: The queries and instructions from the HO were rarely responded to. It created an environment of non-information and inaction, until and unless the CMD exerted intensively and directly. In brief, all the ten symptoms listed earlier were actively visible in this performance deficient work environment.

On deeper analysis, here, the intense play of negativity, inexperience, and incapabilities conspired to create operational and financial sickness—and one of the serious consequences, along with others, visibly manifested in the form of bio-lethargy.

Types of Bio-Lethargy

When one attempts to understand the phenomenon of bio-lethargy in a deeper sense, one comes to realize that it operates at the following two planes:

1. On the intellectual plane—it is thought inaction, and
2. On the functional plane—it is inaction oriented.

Those suffering the type: (1) bio-lethargy normally get afflicted by idea deficit; they are not able to come up with new ideas and proposals. Initiative and confidence deficits continue to hold them back or dissuade from offering any new idea or approach. It is primarily a type of individual bio-lethargy. When a number of persons suffering from this malady congregate in a collective work environment, then it starts manifesting in a collective form too.

The individual type of bio-lethargy could be intentional and/or non-intentional: It could, among others, sprout from:

(a) Intention deficit,
(b) Skills deficit,
(c) Consequences understanding and appreciation deficit, and
(d) Credit/discredit apportioning imbalance.

Individual bio-lethargy also has a tendency to be person (in reference to whom it is operative) or position specific: Its perpetrator or practitioner—his or her actions of avoidance and delay become visible in the collective work environment. Often, most of such operators do not exhibit this tendency in relation to their dealings with their direct bosses or super bosses.

In UKBM and KIL it was seen being intensely operative. This variety of bio-lethargy enjoys a huge capacity for misguiding the super bosses—and, in the absence of realization or awareness at the highest level, it continues to damage the corporate body like termites do with a wooden structure.

Action or functional bio-lethargy too operates on the individual as well as collective plane. Its victims may not be thought or idea deficient—but they are not able to take action—timely and in requisite intensity to generate appreciable results. Peer pressure, intense and persistent, seems to negate part of these effects.

Non-action as an Action

Some practitioners of individual bio-lethargy perceive 'action in non-action' as for them no action itself seems to solve the problems: For them time itself is a great doer.

They do not do anything until and unless reminded a few times. KNS, RNS, RPJ, AK and several others were seen by the author intensely practising this art of action mismanagement. They believed strongly that doing nothing, or not doing a bulk of things, saved them from chances of doing a wrong that might invite punitive attention of the boss.

Allowing the **'do-nothing approach'** to solve issues, or let issues decompose through non-attention, was seen by them as a workable strategy. KNS, RNS and KSC were true master practitioners of this technology.

For most of such mis-managers, it is a risk minimization or risk management technology. But, in the final analysis, it does not solve problems; it complicates them as a festering sore. The individual practitioner of this type of bio-lethargy or negativity might sometimes escape consequences to himself or herself—but the corporate for which such persons work never escapes the damage in the long-run.

CORRECTION METHODOLOGY

Correction methodology against the dreaded disease of bio-lethargy, in principle, has to be situation or corporate work environment specific: No single general rule shall apply. In each case, after intense study of its causes, intensity, and the damages being inflicted to the corporate body, a package of short and long-term measures has to be designed. And if the need for correction is intense, then such a corrective package needs to be discussed at the senior and middle management levels—attaining full U/A of key people is absolutely essential for obtaining any success. The vested interests that the long-term presence and operation of bio-lethargy creates are fairly difficult to counter and/or eliminate.

HR department needs to take an active part in the designing of any such package—as its long-term application and management cannot be done by any other department. Association of an outside consultant is always necessary for administering a bitter corrective pill.

While designing any effective package, major emphasis has to be laid on measures at the thought level: First, the thought level bio-lethargy needs to be corrected and/or eliminated and then only action on any other plane shall have chances of success.

Lord Krishna's 'Principle of Karma' needs to be taught intensively—to the point that individual actions are energized with soul force. People need to be turned appreciative of intense self-less action—subjugating personal interests in favour of the larger or collective good.

Once problems or rigidities on the thought level are broken or neutralized, corrections on the action plane become easier to implement: People become more receptive for the actions of collective good. Detailed POLC action steps need to be worked out—and persistence of corrective measures need to acquire a high priority.

Chapter 15

Mismanagement—Symptoms and Consequences

Mismanagement is a type of disease endemic to a business environment. Hence, on account of its basic nature, it always gives out telltale symptoms—to recognize which is the job of the management.

An organization is very much like a human body: When it suffers a disease, symptoms are invariably given out—some loud and others silent. To recognize them initially and to go to the doctor is the responsibility of the being that resides in the body.

Many living beings misuse and mistreat their bodies: Similarly several managements use and misuse the organizations that fall under their control. To recognize the symptoms of mismanagement is the responsibility of the management that is busy, by default or design, in mismanaging and/or exploiting it.

Hence, as a principle, recognition of the symptoms of mismanagement is often delayed: Admittance of a situation of mismanagement is not allowed as long as it is feasible to hide the same. So, there is no question of timely initiation of corrective measures.

Corporate sickness admittance is rigorously concealed from the statutory authorities that could take any meaningful notice of the disease. In varying proportions, it is also concealed from shareholders, employees, as well as customers of the subject corporate. Consequently, a majority of companies suffering at the hands of mismanagement continue to endure it in lack of any viable alternatives. It is violation of the basic trust with which corporate bodies are constituted.

Symptoms and consequences of corporate mismanagement are

often interlinked—in other words, often a symptom could be understood as a consequence and vice versa. Hence, the subject of symptoms as well as the consequences of the corporate disease of mismanagement is being dealt with, in an integrated manner, in the paragraphs that follow.

Subdued Waves of Discontent

Discontent or disaffection, silent or vibrating, is the primary symptom of mismanagement being practised in any corporate work environment.

The labour class, because of being organized, is the quickest to exhibit signs of dissatisfaction. Any delay in payment of wages or any other agreed benefits immediately finds reaction in the form of a threat or other suitable group action.

White-collar workers wherever organized, for instance in public sector banks, are also quick to sense the signals of mismanagement—and they respond to the same in a collective and result-producing system.

The managerial staff, in fact, is the first to come to know of acts of mismanagement but they react slowly as they are part of the process of this corporate disease generation. Often, they are not organized too—and, as such, their interests are best served through the suppression of the symptoms of the disease of mismanagement because any investigation or diagnosis is likely to impact them first.

Often, the management staff, except those directly connected to the active mis-managers, respond by moving out to equivalent or greener alternatives. They make the least noise.

Active Attrition of Productive Employees

Attrition of skilled and productive knowledge workers, beyond a certain percentage and with an inconvenient regularity that sends recruitment costs sky-rocketing, should be not only a worry to the HR department but an important cause meriting serious investigations.

No one likes to quickly leave a well paid and challenging job that offers unhindered career growth, in a righteous management environment. Major causes of attrition include:

1. Unhelpful and incompetent boss,
2. Unrighteous systems of credit and discredit distribution,

3. Poor remuneration, and
4. Visible favouritism in placements and promotions.

The author had intense experience of all the four factors being operative in almost all types of work environments, MNCs and non-MNCs, and small and large, during his over 40 years of active corporate work life.

Out of the above listed four factors, the third one that deals with money is the least consequential. Talented and self-confident knowledge workers don't tolerate discriminative behaviour and practices, which essentially form part of the other three causes. Unfairness and unrighteousness are severe forms of mismanagement, which silently weaken corporates and also seal their future growth opportunities. They don't allow development of an impressive corporate brand.

Loss of Competitiveness

Loss of competitiveness is a serious symptom of the prevalence of mismanagement in a corporate body over a long period of time. The factors or situations leading to loss or drop of competitiveness could be numerous, but the primary one always remains the mismanagement of its human resources—as it is the people who handle or manipulate all the factors of production, whether goods or services.

Unrighteous HR policies leading to disproportionate distribution of credit and discredit, along with factors such as injudicious placement, non-delegation, lack of motivation, visible and invisible favouritism, lack of training and capability upgradation, absence of corporate mission visibility, and perceptible unethicality on the part of senior management, prompt the knowledge workers to lose initiative and innovation. It finally causes the loss of competitiveness.

Almost all of these causative factors were seen to be present and actively operative in the KIL, which had lost most of its well-established and visible competitiveness during the past ten years of its operation; the last two years were truly miserable. In the case of UKBM, the absence of the basic skills deficit compounded with a variety of the factors listed in the previous paragraph.

On the other hand BOL suffered primarily due to the manifestation of multilateral incapabilities of its CEO and prevalence of a high degree of negativity and unethicality of the two inter-related members of its management.

In brief, the principle of competitiveness states that the quality of the knowledge workers of its HR component and its righteous management determines the rise or fall of its competitiveness.

Drop in Business Turnover

It is one of the most visible symptoms of mismanagement. Despite being the most investigated and talked about issue in the respective locale of its appearance, in more cases than not, it escapes a true and impartial investigation.

Corrective measures to still or reverse its downward movement are not only difficult but also painful to effect. It requires a lot of judiciousness, initiatives and the capability to take unpopular steps on the part of senior management.

Sometimes, totally out-of-the-box thinking and approach are required. This symptom of the complicated corporate disease does not disappear until and unless concerted efforts, on a requisite long time-frame, are made in a completely objectivity centered manner.

Almost every one connected with a corporate body, in such a situation, suffers inconvenience: The primary sufferers of such a situation are employees, its creditors, and to an extent, even its consumers.

Bleeding Bottom Line

When competitiveness is lost, turnover takes a downward journey, and at the same tine if costs, expenses, and liabilities are not contained and/or controlled, the bottom line is not left with any alternative but to bleed to the utter discomfort of the shareholders and/or the entrepreneur.

Like any uncontrolled bleeding of the human body, a bleeding bottom line of a corporate body poses grave concerns for its health, and even to its very survival. A corporate with a bleeding bottom line normally attempts to make appropriate noise whenever it is able to draw attention of accountants, auditors, banks and other financial institutions, and also in the meeting of its board of directors.

Any treatment of such a bleeding corporate is possible only when the causes of the disease of mismanagement are removed—and further steps are taken to avoid its reoccurrence.

Emergence of Multilateral Debts

Emergence of multilateral debts is the advanced form of the

disease caused due to mismanagement of a corporate.

It is akin to the spread of cancer to several parts of the body causing multiple organ failure. Since no effective treatment is feasible at this stage, the patient is admitted to the intensive care unit where the objective is rarely to nurse the sick body back to normalcy but to allow it to linger on for psychological benefits of those related to the subject patient.

The multilateral debts can emerge from a variety of persons and/or institutions (financial or otherwise) related with the working of such a corporate being: These are normally the symptoms of a corporate desperately fighting for its survival with its back to the wall. At this stage simple treatments don't work; multidisciplinary desperate measures need to be undertaken—including removal of a diseased portion for survival of the rest of the being.

Non-compliance of statutory requirements and non-payment of suppliers for long periods are two serious implications of the emergence of the situation of multilateral debts. Authorities for recovery of statutory dues come up with various intimidating measures, which do not make life any less miserable for the affected management or the proprietors.

Delay in Payment of Salaries and other Employees' Dues

Delay of not only days but of months in payment of salaries of white-collar workers of a company is again a grave symptom of long-term mismanagement, for correction of which adequate steps were not taken well in time.

It tends to uncover bankruptcy or potential for it, which is very unnerving for the staff. In such a situation, people tend to spend a lot of time discussing the uncertainty, and productivity takes a severe hit qualitatively as well as quantitatively. For survival and/or revival of the affected corporate, the earliest removal of this incapacitating symptom of mismanagement is the most urgent necessity.

It is not only the delay in payment of salaries that has an incapacitating effect on the morale of the staff, accumulation of their medical, LTA, and travelling dues contribute equally severely towards dislocation of the minimum required work efficiencies—and, along with the salaries, these accumulations too need to be handled expeditiously if survival of the affected corporate is of genuine concern.

NON-SETTLEMENT OF ACCOUNTS OF FORMER EMPLOYEES

When active attrition begins in a mismanaged organization even the formality of exit interview is given a go-by.

A more frustrating aspect for ex-employees of such organizations emerges when the queries in regard to settlement of their accounts are not answered satisfactorily. As months pass, the situation grows more and more frustrating: It spreads and advertises the message of mismanagement in the subject corporate in a totally devastating manner.

This entirely undesirable symptom or consequence of mismanagement does not leave even the leftover employees without severe output reduction impact. The author saw this phenomenon actively prevalent in UKBM, BOL and KIL—and, nowhere prompt actions to remedy the situation were initiated by the crippled managements. The inconveniences and the miseries, which the ex-employees and their families have to go through on account of this non-professional approach, are often substantial.

INABILITY TO PRODUCE IN TIME

The cumulative effect of the multilateral impacts of mismanagement drastically curtails an affected organization's capability to produce goods and/or services in adequate volume and deliver the same in time; quality management takes a back seat as the emphasis normally remains on getting the output out to waiting customers.

Dissatisfied customers and disheartened sales staff continue to grumble for better attention and services.

The situation of reduced production/supplies has cascading impacts on turnover—and contribution remains on slippery grounds: It does not add to the recovery process in any manner.

The condition of suspended animation continues to prevail. The inability to produce enough and in time is a cumulative consequence of the diseased organization's failure to procure requisite raw materials and other inputs in time, in the face of suppliers' disaffection.

QUALITY DETERIORATION AND MOUNTING GOODS RETURN

Mismanagement affects all aspects of a diseased corporate since the negative energy flow moves silently—crippling its vital organs. The first casualty of accumulation of negative energies within an organization afflicted with mismanagement is the quality of its output.

The chain of management for controlling the quality of production and deliveries is often broken down in the presence of active mismanagement or becomes extremely weak to exert effectively.

When products and services from such organizations are not able to meet market expectations or minimum acceptability of customers, and complaints are not promptly attended to, the highly problematic reaction of return goods raises its ugly head.

It is the ultimate symptom of active mismanagement operative at the production and quality assurance level. The problem of return goods was most acute with UKBM as its non-sellable goods were often returned in containers of its biggest competitor. The author had an opportunity to fix this type of problem in a manner that within a few months the badly battered brand of UKBM started giving a bloody nose to its mighty rival, a MNC market leader.

Loss of Customers and Markets

Inadequate and untimely supplies dry up the confidence of the market, the dealers/distributors network and, in the final analysis, the ultimate consumer starts turning to other competing products as they gain better shelf-space visibility. For the trade too, it is a painful process to effect a change of basic suppliers, as they do not immediately get favourable terms—and again they have to perform with the new suppliers, and tactfully have also to manage the final consumers by giving them some viable excuses. For sometimes, a market gets into turmoil but the ultimate sufferer of the mismanagement remains the subject company. Its troubles do not end with the loss of markets and customers: It has to find a way out of the trouble of dwindling output and shrinking markets, growing non-sellable goods, and all other associated problems.

Shrinking order books (SOB) is another manifestation of the impacts of mismanagement, and it appears not too late from the other ills of supplies and markets as discussed earlier. It is initially a symptom of the disease but as soon as remedial measures are initiated in right earnest and intensity, it undergoes a metamorphosis and converts into a cause or hindrance in slow or halting process towards the cherished objective of recovery.

Employee Indiscipline and Dissatisfaction

Accumulation of the products of mismanagement and their compounding over a period of time causes employee disaffection, which in turn tends to assume the form of indiscipline; negative gossip rather than gainful occupation becomes the norm.

Their psychology of work and communication starts showing strains in the form of unhelpful comments. As a result, even small routine actions are avoided or mismanaged; responsibility and accountability take a back seat.

Stress accumulation and its negative manifestations travel into the business and work premises; the family life of employees gets adversely affected. Efforts in the direction of alternate jobs search do not produce immediate results for everyone—and hence, all such employees tend to linger on in the seesaw game staged by cloud depression and sunshine of hope.

Un-informed Absenteeism and Non-performing Presence

When people remain unoccupied or grossly under-occupied, under conditions of growing stresses, uninformed absenteeism tends to grow unhindered: There remains no shortage of excuses in such circumstances—and often there is no one to ask. Those who remain present are able to mark only a non-performing presence, discussions of uncertainties remains the only occupation.

KIL, after years of accumulated effects of mismanagement, presented exactly this type of scene towards the end of 2007.

Once the market gets wind of mismanagement in a company, and when the same is coupled with the drying up of supplies, unexplained delays in order servicing, and non-attention to all types of customer complaints, the sales force becomes totally demoralized and ineffective; the trade, i.e., the dealers and distributors lose patience and become irritable—difficult to deal with.

Further, collection of old outstandings becomes a progressively non-remunerative process—and in this type of situation the sales force takes recourse to ***non-performing presence*** (NPP).

Excuses Galore and Last-Minute Unexpected Hitches

Under conditions of inactivity and non-performance what emerges unhindered are excuses galore. Since there is no productive activity, non-occupancy takes the form of excuses and unkept promises. Such activities add fuel to the fire; they serve no useful purposes.

Since everything takes an uncertain form and uncertainties accumulate, even renewed efforts to start some semblance of activity meets most unexpected hindrances—as people have stopped doing any POLC. The leftover structure and/or facilities tend to become inconsequential.

Absence of Formal Reporting

Formal reporting is an essentiality for any well-run corporate, and its absence—or occurrence in bits and pieces are a symptom of malfunctioning in the organization.

It is a symptom as well as a cause of mismanagement taking place in its day-to-day operations. But, cause is always more important to be attended to on priority, as symptoms normally automatically correct themselves as soon as the adequate doses of remedial measures are injected.

Non-line reporting (NLP), bypassing the boss or department head, often is an irritating disturbance in mismanaged organizations. It generates multiple interactions of negative feelings and energies, leaving visible and/or invisible disturbances in the way of effective collective working, teamwork being the biggest casualty.

Spread of misinformation—and the right quarters being kept out of the loop creates enormous unhelpful work management and HR implications. It helps scatter the seeds of non-co-operation and consequent inefficiencies: They do not take much time in germinating and eventually blocking efficient working. The author has known a number of corporate mis-managers who actively employed their avoidable expertise in this direction. KRD and SKC were two great users of this nefarious tool of mismanagement: The former did not live long enough to realize the ill-effects of his unprofessional practice, but the latter continued to suffer the bitter fruits of his own creation.

Un-authorized information flow (UAIF) is another delimitating impact of the absence of formal reporting, resulting in information travelling to wrong destinations where its non-target applications are often resorted to.

In all forms and intensities, and irrespective of levels and directions, ***absence of formal reporting*** (AOFR) is an unacceptable form of mismanagement. The tolerance of AOFR tends to further create numerous negative implications, some of which are listed below:

- Excessive office gossiping
- Loud deliberations
- Visible lack of authority and direction
- Non-response to management's directions
- Unplanned travel and fat travel bills
- Frequent crisis developments
- Unattended mails and customers
- Ignorance of non-performance
- Non-judicious credit and discredit apportioning
- Cry-baby management

Except for frequent crisis developments, the above are causes as well as symptoms of mismanagement. In viewing these from the standpoint of attempting any improvement, first the causative aspects need to be handled; the rest normally is easier to manage.

CHAPTER 16

Managing the Mismanagement

In the foregoing chapters, mismanagement has been discussed from a variety of angles. It is easy to locate surface visible manifestations of this malaise in any corporate—and also to gossip about or even discuss it in a serious manner. But it becomes a difficult subject to handle—from beginning to end, when one wants to find ways and means of either preventing or curing it to any meaningful extent.

The following seven-point programme needs to be worked through for any reasonable success against the forces of mismanagement:

- Anticipate occurrence of mismanagement,
- Identify and quantify its spread—inclusive of its key perpetrators,
- Classify its dominant forms,
- Decide appropriate control measures—preventive as well as curative,
- Undertake the necessary POLC for each of the selected measures,
- Rigorously and impartially implement each selected measure, and
- Review righteously and re-plan.

ANTICIPATING OCCURRENCE OF MISMANAGEMENT

Anticipation of occurrence of mismanagement is primarily the job of senior management. The seeds of mismanagement can sprout anywhere, at any time—with or without any warning signals.

In principle, the malaise of mismanagement is omnipotent —it can be anticipated (in some cases), prevented and controlled—but cannot be eliminated.

It is a manifestation of basic human nature and its components of negativity, which assign it almost a type of immortality in any collective work environment.

But despite the limitations of its omnipotence and near immortality, it is possible to anticipate a major part of it—because it sprouts through the energies of human thought and action—with most of which senior and experienced professional are acquainted with.

These forces of mismanagement emit certain definite recognizable symptoms (discussed in an earlier chapter) in a ceaseless manner—and it is up to the supervisory senior management to intercept and decode the same—and then respond to them. The seniors have to keep their antenna on—and themselves free from the contaminants of negativity and un-ethicality.

Identifying and Quantifying its Spread

When signals from the forces of mismanagement are intercepted and decoded, the identity of mismanaging forces can be established—and at the same time, with some planned effort, the extent of spread of the malaise could be assessed and quantified.

Such quantifications assume importance from the point of assessment—as to how easy or difficult confronting the damaging forces is going to be—and whether the cost of control measures is justifiable from the short, as well as, the long-term point of view.

Quantification of the damages inflicted to the bottom line of the victim corporate—and the likelihood of continuation of the same should, in principle, decide the management's response.

Classifying its Dominant Forms

The dominant forms of operative mismanagement—and the forces causing the damage should be classified as: (a) temporary or transitory, and (b) durable or permanent—and, in other words, whether the same were malignant or non-malignant.

Such an assessment will determine the ease with which the mismanaging forces could be confronted with—and the financial and non-financial costs of implementing the requisite measures. Without such analysis and assessment, the control efforts themselves run the risk of assuming the form of the disease at which such efforts are aimed at.

How much of the disease of mismanagement gathered by a

corporate is accumulated by default? And what share of it is caused by design, needs careful determination—since the former responds, as per its nature of origin, much faster to measures initiated against it.

Deciding Appropriate Control Measures

The intensity and spread of the disease of mismanagement, its malignant and non-malignant nature or forms—and also the intentions of the mis-managers involved, decide the control action steps—their mix and quantum.

The action steps planned, and the POLC to be undertaken in this regard, should take into account both types of the malaise—the one emerging on account of design, and also the one being caused by default or carelessness.

The mix and intensity of such action steps should be energetic enough to break the inertia and resistance that the organizational and non-organizational factors might offer. Vested interests, normally, do not give up easily.

Security of those spearheading these efforts should not be ignored—and their long-term interests too need to be safeguarded.

While designing the action steps for this purpose, persons responsible for the same, dates for completion and review of such steps, need to be specified. The steps so designed should also cover the actions needed for prevention of re-occurrence of this obnoxious corporate malaise.

Accounting for Mismanagement

One effective way of dealing with existing mismanagement in a corporate body is to actively and rigorously account for it—more precisely the damaging or revenue loss-inflicting impacts of the malady.

It is, however, feasible only when senior management, particularly the CEO, and the board of directors of the victim corporate are seriously seized of the matter.

The first step in this direction involves a precise and unbiased identification of the areas of the diseased parts of the organization, some of which, among others, could be materials and purchases, inventories and storages, transport and communication, power and utilities, production losses, travels and expense accounts, sales pricing and discounts, sales promotion, and goods return, and finance and accounting, etc. In fact, no part of an organization could be free from the in-principle possibility of occurrence of this malaise.

First, an approximation of the damages inflicted in each area needs to be made in consultation and with U/A of the respective department head; being a sensitive activity, nothing is likely to be achieved without the latter. As a second step, such estimations are to be converted into costs inflicted or avoidable costs—and then, prior to any correctional initiative, a proper and detailed POLC exercise needs to be worked out—so as to give the problem a comprehensive professional treatment.

For all the correctional action steps incorporated in the POLC plan, ***measures of performance*** (MOPs) and ***standards of performance*** (SOPs) need to be specified for effective periodical evaluation and reporting of progress.

Correcting the malady of mismanagement is not easy from any standard or imagination—and resistance and obstacles must be anticipated: Perseverance should take care of these when adequate determination for getting the planned measures through, has been factored for.

Correcting mismanagement is not for the faint-hearted; and accounting it needs yet greater guts.

Association of consultants with this activity is very useful.

Preventive Action as Part of Mismanagement Containment

The following measures when implemented actively can contribute to prevention of mismanagement and its eventual consequences.

- Active anticipation,
- Build up of preventive measures in project planning and implementation of action plans,
- Identification of employees of high negativity,
- Supervised delegation,
- Righteous distribution of credit and discredit,
- Observing a high level of ethicality on the part of senior management,
- Objective and unbiased appraisals,

- Avoidance of excessive power accumulation,
- Operating high order of transparency,
- Effective use of the forces of peer pressure,
- Have and exhibit inclusive approach in regard to work and reward,
- Training and retraining of people,
- Making people aware about occurrence of mismanagement, and
- Employing the voluntary forces of whistle-blowers.

Most of the above points have been discussed elsewhere in this work: Hence, further elaboration of the same will serve little purpose. What matters a great deal is the alertness and commitment of management not to allow germination and growth of the forces of mismanagement—and when it is done with the requisite degree of righteousness and fairness, adequate protection against this malaise could be easily afforded.

Attachment-I

Terminologies Employed

Active Thought Deficiency: It is a situation where people are habituated of being spoon-fed—they are told what to do and as such do not strain their thinking apparatus.

Avoidable Ego Manifestation: Such display of ego—where it would have been better to avoid it in the interests of collective working.

Avoidable Brusque Attitude: Some mis-managers suffer from this unhelpful attitude that does not invite co-operation.

Avoidable Ear Lending: An activity of mis-managers that drags them to listen to one and all—particularly those who work less and do more of story carrying.

Action Warriors: Corporate workers of this category actively involve themselves in doing things rather than simply talking.

Autocratic Decision Making: A non-consultative way of decision making where instead of U/A, the management attempts A/U.

Bottom line: Refers to the profit or loss figures in a balance sheet.

Bull-headedness: A characteristic of unrighteous or non-inclusively pushing of decisions.

Boss Management Technologies: Some mis-managers employ ethical as well as non-ethical measures for controlling the boss—all of which put together fall in this category.

Chalta-hai: A local replacement of the laissez faire approach.

Contribution Analysis: A methodology for measuring value addition for products and services produced/provided by a corporate.

Corporate: In this work, the term 'corporate' has been employed to describe business entities—irrespective of their nature of incorporation

Clear Responsibility Assignment: A merit of a well structured organization where responsibilities and accountabilities are clearly delineated.

Collective Cooperative Energies: Refers to the positive energies of initiative and cooperation which manifest in righteously managed CWE.

Constant Fault Finding: It is a technique of unbalancing the inexperienced juniors—and a number of mis-managers adopt it.

Core Competence: The main area of competence of a corporate where it is ahead of the competition

Cost Return Illiteracy: Business operations wherein no attempt is made or skills developed to have a correct handle on product costing and to update the same at a required frequency.

Deadwood: Refers to such employees or participants of a collective work process who are not capable of contributing towards its express objectives: They have passed the productive phase.

Destructive Delusion: A performance related delusion that prompts one to think of favourable results despite being engaged in activities of opposite consequences.

Dhritrashtra: The blind king of *Mahabharata* who was one of the greatest mis-managers known to mankind. His partialities and incapability for taking right decisions were legendary.

Double-Directional Mismanagement: It is an emphasis imbalance noted amongst in-house or departmental promotees. They normally continue to concentrate on their old job—thus mismanaging downwards as well as upwards at the same time.

Dog Bone Syndrome: Refers to relishing of a business effort where in fact nothing is added to the corporate kitty; a syndrome of false profitability perpetrated by default and/or design.

Dominant Egotism: Unmasked expressions of "I, me and ours" instead of we, us and ours.

Disaffection Accumulation: Accumulation of disaffection is a visible characteristic of a deeply mismanaged organization.

Energy-Information Impulses: This is the scientific composition of thoughts: In fact all things and beings—material and non material are derivatives of energy and information impulses.

Financial-looping: A system of financial management where payment to suppliers and service providers is linked to a time-bound performance of the marketing department.

Flat Organization: An organization where its head directly deals with a large number of employees—rather than through department heads or a conducive corporate structure.

Honest Dissent: When a person is free from thoughts of ego and negativity—and offers his/her honest opinion that goes against the views or propositions of seniors.

Hurried Branding: It refers to senior managers' defective approach of branding people good or bad, hard working or lazy—and so on—without in-depth analysis. It is injurious to the company as well as the employees so marked.

Inclusive Approach: A positive management practice that generates quick results.

Information Deficit: Refers to inadequacy of information flow—a deficiency of corporate MIS, which may lead to non-decision or wrong decision—both being the conditions of mismanagement.

Kargil: Kargil refers to a hilly terrain of J&K state of India, which Pakistan attempted to occupy and grab towards end of the last decade of the 20th century: It had to beat a hasty retreat under Indian response and international pressure.

Know-all Approach: Where a senior manager or CEO tends to convey that he or she knows everything—and in the process often belittles knowledge workers.

Laissez Faire: Represents a situation or response of unconcern.

Large Span of Contact: It is a characteristic of a flat organization where the CEO is in direct contact with a large number of employees, irrespective of their position or rank.

Logical Thought Process: The process of taking logical decisions wherein righteous thoughts do not abandon you.

Management Dieback: Dieback is a plant disease wherein a plant starts showing signs of sickness from top downwards—and it quickly affects the whole plant. Similarly in some corporates the top bosses start exhibiting symptoms of non-management or mismanagement—and consequently the whole corporate body starts suffering its consequences. Finally, very much like an infected plant, an affected corporate too wilts into non-performance and losses.

Mismanagement: It refers to various acts of omission and commission on the part of management that damages its efficiency as well as the afflicted corporate's performance and also its future growth opportunities. It is a man-made negative activity that occurs by default as well as by design.

Mis-interests: Un-righteously conceived interests of corporate workers.

Monkey Management: A situation of mismanagement wherein a chief or CEO directly deals with a large number of subordinates bypassing their bosses or section heads and attempts to keep them happy or performing by doling out concessions and goodies to those who make the maximum of noise.

Multiple Diversionary Stresses: Refers to a situation where a CEO or senior is professional Over-stressed due to excessive multitasking and his/her inability to delegate the delegatable.

Mutual Appreciation Club: It is a situation where two mis-managers engage in appreciating each other.

Negative Energies of Power: Some mis-managers draw and accumulate a lot of negative energies—to effect things which in principle should not be attempted.

Negative Thought Process: When genesis of negative thoughts or thoughts of selfishness overwhelm the thinking process.

Negativity Interplay: When in a mismanaged organization a free expression of negative thought assumes sway, in most of the official as well as non-official deliberations.

Nepotism and Extravagance: Both the components of this habit contain intense negative energies—and as such are not good for managers.

Non-acceptance of Accountability: This characteristic is common amongst a large number of mis-managers.

Non-Inclusiveness: It is a character of a mismanaged organization where decisions are taken without involving the concerned people and credit distribution is undertaken in an unrighteous manner—not including some of those who deserve the same.

Non-line Reporting: It is a situation of mismanagement where subordinates report to a senior boss or the CEO bypassing their immediate bosses or section heads.

Non-performing Presence: It refers to the presence of such employees who just mark their presence or adorn the seats that they occupy: They do not contribute much, either by default or design—and a weak or incompetent management continues to tolerate the same.

Peoples' Factor: The human element involved and its responses.

Power Concentrate: Refers to CEOs and senior professionals who tend to maximize concentration of maximum powers in their hands: They fall an easy prey to mismanagement.

Performance Dysfunction: It is a consequence of the operation of the forces of mismanagement—fall in work, products and/or services output—their volumes as well as quality are its symptoms.

Productive Corporate Energies: Refers to those assets and actions of a corporate, which lead to fruitful activities in terms of output and profits.

Rajjasic Prakriti: It is one of the three types of human nature described in the ***Bhagavad-Gita*** and refers to such people who are a mix-up of sattavic and tamasic characters: They are normally power accumulators and consequently get involved in activities of ruling or governance.

Righteous Performance Appreciation: When performance credit or appreciation is made in an unbiased manner.

Sattavic Prakriti: It is the category of human nature where merit and righteousness content is at its highest.

Self-motivated Performers: Includes the people who do not require too much of outside motivation or pushing, for achieving their targeted assignments.

Tamasic Prakriti: People of this nature possess the highest concentration of negative energies—and, as such, form the worst type of mis-managers.

Toxic Communication: The verbal or non-verbal communications that convey or help generate negative energies and/or reactions.

Target Person Pleasing Capacity: It is a unique capacity of some mis-managers to effectively please and control the boss.

Trust Deficit: It refers to a situation where senior corporate operatives are not able to create adequate trust in the minds of their subordinates—a fertile ground for doubts emergence.

Thought Warriors: In the context of the present work, this term refers to a category of corporate workers who primarily engage in talking or thinking processes. They do not seem to believe in validity of action—for them the thought—and discussion itself is equivalent to action or work done.

Ultimate Level of Incompetence: All mis-managers are expected to rise to their ultimate level of incompetence from where they are often demoted or terminated.

Unauthorized Information Flow: It is one of the numerous characteristics of a mismanaged organization: Herein, information does not follow the authourized path in its information flow system or the MIS.

Visual Stress Manifestation: When a CEO or a professional allows all work stresses to be visible on his or her face, It leads to consequences of mismanagement.

Whistle-blowers: In corporate reference, it is a category of people who dare to disclose or raise their voices against actions of mismanagement.

ATTACHMENT-II

The Key Mismanagers

Every organization, irrespective of its size and nature, is inhabited by some mis-managers who, in varying intensities, exert an anti-performance impact on its working. Normally, large organizations tend to accumulate a larger presence of them because, as size grows, implementation of performance standards too tends to grow loose.

The author, an indefatigable student of mismanagement since his early corporate days, was able to easily identify most of the mis-managers encountered by him in any collective work environment, commercial or non-commercial, with which he happened to work or interact during his over 40 years of active corporate work life.

In this work, several of the mis-managers have been referred to, at appropriate places, in reference to their key anti-performance activities and the impact that they exerted on the work-output and/or the lives of their coworkers. The main text of this work identified them only with abbreviated identifications—yet, in the interest of deeper and quicker understanding, an inquisitive reader might need to have access to their fuller identities and peculiarities: It might help him/her establish greater rapport with the mismanaging characters dealt with in this work. They were all real people—only their names have been partly altered for reasons of anonymity.

Here, an effort has been made to elaborate upon these key mismanaging characters—their mismanaging habits, practices and techniques—and also the impact that the same brought upon the work output, health of the victim corporates, and also the main associates who, per force of the situation, had to suffer them.

AK OR ARUN KUMAR

AK was part of the senior management team of the KIL or Krishi

India Ltd. Some twenty years ago, as an unqualified and raw lad, he had joined the company primarily because of being related to its CMD. He came, as learnt from his colleagues and relatives, from a family of very limited means, and initially, was short on academic qualifications as well as professional training. Subsequently, he acquired an MBA from a local institution.

He was basically a foxy character endowed with a lot of selfish and unrighteous energies. But, on account of his ***target person pleasing capabilities*** (TPPC), he influenced the CMD of the company or let us say that the latter, being a first-generation entrepreneur of very limited means –and himself with inadequate professional corporate experience, needed extra hands who could be initially trusted; or who could feed his un-satiated ego along with being useful for certain other purposes. The both served each other's purpose—and soon formed a ***mutual appreciation club*** (MAC). Without any loss of time, AK became an active carrier of information and the CMD lent his ears to an ample extent. Soon, as per the needs of his master, AK entered the purchase or materials department, ensuring a handsome cut for his benefactor, part of which he cornered right from early times. The CMD did not mind it: He seemed to have budgeted for it.

In order to ensure a trouble-free or unhindered operation, AK did not allow any functionary of his department to be either effective or to last for long. He did all the prices determination and supply terms negotiations without help or involvement of anyone else, except the CMD himself in some cases. Thus, with the consent or connivance—active or passive, from his boss he established his omnipotence as far as the revenue spending function of purchases was concerned. The suppliers, who did not service his needs, either never got in or were squeezed out unceremoniously. Soon, in the whole agro-chemicals industry, he came to be known as Mr. 10 percent of KIL.

Such a reputation did not matter to him—as he was fast accumulating a tidy balance for himself—creating substantial revenue generating assets. It helped fattening of his ego, which soon caused problems of coordination with finance, production and marketing departments. The CMD too, through his covert and overt actions and decisions, fuelled the problem. Since good times do not last for ever, continued and accelerated mismanagement landed the KIL into a pit of financial difficulties; its revenue and profitability dropped to the extent that almost all suppliers' bill settlements were delayed to the extent that further supplies fully dried up; salaries and wage payments became pending for several months, and advances secured from customers against promises of specific supplies continued to incur avoidable interest. Neither suppliers nor customers were suitably answered to or assured of eventual clearances. The two great mis-managers started hiding from both types of creditors.

Inter-personnel communication within the company assumed an unprofessional tinge as acts of mismanagement and their accumulated effect started to multiply. The weekly meeting of the ***business management committee*** (BMC) had to be discontinued due to ***analytical communication intolerances*** (ACIs). KIL's physical diversification of creating two new manufacturing locations faltered—as (a) it was not based upon sound projections and (b) substantial working capital diversions crippled the day-to-day operations of the company. His pet project of the ***tie-up business*** (TUB) faltered because while it serviced his unstated but obvious interests, generation of adequate revenues did not materialize. In the process, the cash cow of the company, i.e., the trade sales business suffered an almost unattended demise.

Despite the multilateral problems caused, the CMD's obvious dependence on this mis-manager continued to linger—and the consequences of such mismanagement engulfed the whole corporate. People, the productive ones, started leaving with a predictable frequency. The shadow of mismanagement did not leave any one uninfluenced. Very much like a skilled scavenger, he continued to extract benefits from a dying organization.

The strains of the obvious bias of the CMD in favour of AK let the latter blame the finance department for non-transparency while the facts of the situation, to an unbiased observer, led to conclude that the origin of non-transparency and un-professionalism, more often than not, emerged from the CMD and his mismanaging protégé.

ASP or Ajeet Singh Pratap

The author had known this egoistic mis-manager since 1971: A common location of postings had brought them to know each other, more as a matter of chance. He worked for the army while the author served a central banking institution. His army background coupled with family and social influences assigned him with a frank and brash expression, which initially appealed to the author as a positive manifestation of honesty.

Off-and-on meetings and communication continuity in the intervening years led to sustaining of an acquaintance that had bordered on a restrained friendship, or so was it perceived by the author. With the passage of the years, both the parties in this relationship progressed to their different posting locations, yet they stayed in contact with each other. During their Delhi postings, the families of the constituents of the association enjoyed greater contact with each other.

Towards the mid 1990s, when ASP reached near his retirement and the author too was contemplating to start some self-employment activities after expiry of his engagement with the BOL at Chennai, the relationship between the two grew further in light of their mutual perception for some fresh engagement. During the intervening years, ASP had lost his wife to a recurrent kidney problem. Despite the setback, he had managed to timely free himself from the responsibility of his two daughters by marrying them off in a manner befitting an army officer of his standing. But, the lack of interest of his son in studies or any productive activity had kept ASP worrying about the future of the family. Efforts to turn the family landholding in an isolated Haryana village into a business activity too had turned financially unsustainable. In fact, it led to the deterioration of the health of his wife, on the one hand, and inadequate attention to his son's education, on the other.

Just after retirement, ASP's efforts to set himself and his son in some business turned out as misadventures only. His retirement from a middle officer's rank in the army and its interactions with the family background and location in a semi-urban Haryanvi environment had equipped him with an uncommon tendency to take risks and, despite failures, restart with something new. Most probably, his need to settle his son, who had failed to acquire any employable qualifications, was propelling him to take new risks. In 1995, ASP and the author had planned to start some manufacturing and marketing activity for which a private limited company was registered. But in the meantime, ASP's interactions with his local acquaintances coupled with inadequacy of understanding of intricacies of a particular business, led him to start a dairy enterprise involving collection, processing and marketing of milk and its byproducts. All the four new entrepreneurs who had joined hands with him and contributed the participants' share of funds had assumed the positions of directors in a newly formed company. Funds from state financial institutions too were employed to commence the enterprise in a half-baked manner. And, right in the beginning, mismanagement of project and project funds started with considerable vigour, as expected from the highly negative and non-business attitude of the participants, and their non-professionalism and defective understanding of profit and profitability. For them every sale, irrespective of quantity, was a profit—and whosoever collected the outstanding payments or sales proceeds from the market, did not think it necessary or desirable to deposit the same in the corporate account, assuming that he or she being a director of the company had the right to retain such collections. Soon, they ran out of funds to pay to raw materials suppliers and meet other associated expenses. Conflict arising out of misplaced concept of ownership and profitability began to assume non-managing proportions. ASP's ***avoidable brusque attitude*** (ABA) towards problem solving or dismissal of views and approaches that differed from his pre-set ones further compounded the situation.

Lack of confidence and tolerance for each other amongst the directors deteriorated to the extent that an active struggle for controls erupted: Threats, veiled and not so veiled, were issued, complicating the situation to the extent that unprocessed milk suppliers and other creditors started landing in groups at the company's office, which was located at the residence of one of the directors.

The accounts of the company were in an intractable mess, and no one was ready to extend a helping hand. As operations came to a grinding halt, the struggle for wresting control of the unit became grim. In the heat of the struggle and under intolerable pressure from creditors, one of the key directors, more precisely, the managing director, committed suicide and left a note, which implicated ASP for abetting the same. The family of the deceaserd filed an FIR naming ASP for his role in the crime. With his contacts in the local police force ASP did escape being arrested but the case progressed in the local courts and after the passage of five years, the court found him guilty: He was arrested and sent to jail. The mismanagement took its toll in its fullest form.

Mismanagement of finance, project resources, and more decidedly the communication amongst those involved soiled the whole situation.

It led to closure of the project, its eventual takeover by the state financial institutions and, in the end, its auction to recover the dues. Thus, the process of mismanagement ran its full and uninterrupted course.

GRV or Gopi Rao Vasudeva

GRV was a beefy and idiotic character. He was not well qualified or trained in any specialty: Most likely he had passed only high school. Though unintelligently cunning, he was short on information and understanding. He had worked as a fuel pump assistant somewhere in the USA before returning to India, where he joined a Bhopal-based multinational with the help of some of his family connections. It happened in the early 1970s when large corporations tended to give a lot of weightage to returnees with foreign work exposure and/or recommendations from known sources.

GRV's first job with the said MNC was that of a lowly field assistant, and he knew almost nothing about the technicalities involved in the sales and marketing of agrochemicals, which the employer MNC was engaged in. But, he was a good talker and his American accent appealed to his then boss, an expatriate himself. Besides, he was master of all other ***boss management technologies*** (BMTs) available at that time. He knew the art of credit misappropriation—grabbing it without the same belonging to him.

In the initial years, the company's business grew fairly well and GRV, through his credit grabbing and boss management techniques, climbed the initial corporate ladder steps very fast. And, as luck would have it, his expatriate boss died in a plane accident. GRV filled the vacancy as he had grabbed good reports from his departed boss: And the senior bosses had no in-depth idea of what went into the making of a successful agro-chemicals sales and marketing business. By 1974, when the author happened to join the same company in its R&D wing at Bhopal, GRV had become the branch manager for the southern region. He had acquired a powerful position and the ***negative energies of power*** (NEOP) had polluted his already beefy head.

The grossly undeserved upward career movements had gone to the head of GRV: And his bullheadedness became a topic of active discussion in the whole agro-division of the company, and even beyond. The author's colleagues, who had had longer stay in the company, lost no time in briefing him about GRV and the kind of uncomfortable effect he had on other departments which, in course of the corporate work, came in touch with him. Some of them proceeded to warn the author against likely encounters with him. His acts of ***nepotism and extravagance*** (NAE) were widely known and resented.

As luck would have it, the author had to make a visit to GRV managed branch at Bangalore, soon after his joining the said MNC at Bhopal. As per his long cultivated habit, the great mis-manager attempted to exhibit his bossism by moving around in the market with the visitor (the author) from the plant, and to influence the matters related to inter-departmental issues and conflicts. The author quickly measured his intellectual depth and put him in a place that rightfully belonged to him. Being a peculiarity of his personality, he did not like any one finding faults with his working: And any support to or defence of some of the HO-based departments and personalities, particularly the R&D and product development, with which he often had professional interactions, was anathema to him. Thus, the seeds of his long intolerance towards the author were sown in his unprofessional and actively biased mind.

Soon, business reorganization and lobby effect resulted in GRV being placed in the critical position of sales manager at the corporate HO level. Little prior to it, the author himself was shifted to the sales department as head of a regional branch, in light of the express desire of the MD of the company. In this upheaval of reorganization, the bullheaded GRV became the direct boss of the author. Of the five other branch managers who reported to him, four were GRV's direct ex-colleagues: They were fully literate on his innumerable stupidities and weaknesses.

Since he was short on merit and capabilities needed for managing an all India operation, monthly corporate meetings held for business planning and review became an active battle-ground where GRV, the great mis-manager, had to often eat his own words and comments. He fought with the very tools with which he was expected to fight the war of sales and marketing in a competitive market. His utter lack of management skills that were essential for work coordination at this level became starkly visible, and the senior management started regretting the decision that had led to his being hoisted in a critical position. Through his acts of omission and commission, he confirmed that he was promoted to his ***ultimate level of incompetence*** (ULOI).

One of the branch managers had aptly described GRV as one who suffered from ***adamancy, arrogance, idiocy, illiteracy, and ignorance***. He became the centre of innumerable non-professional jokes and digs. But, as far as the vindictiveness was concerned, GRV was endowed with an elephantine memory. He had, however, substantially damaged his capacity to act decisively against any one of his subordinates with most of whom he had acquired a ***position of active intolerance*** (POAI).

Amongst the numerous gaps and deficiencies in GRV's personality, a prominent one was that he did not know when not to open his big mouth and how to frame his words. Often he talked without thinking, and his inherent inability for in-depth thinking and analysis further complicated situations for him in gatherings where seniors were present. He did not know how to avoid conflict with his own juniors and subordinates.

For GRV, it took a year of gross mismanagement, for getting himself demoted to his earlier position, with a substantially reduced territory. He, however, was not a person who could smoothly reorient either his working or his communication. He was also not capable of hiding his hurt, and continued to make mistakes. His performance fell while un-professionalism saw no decline. His former juniors and assistants either ignored him or made fun of him. Apparently, towards the premature end of his corporate career, he exhibited a lot of capacity to tolerate unfavourable comments and insulting remarks. His basic lack of formal expertise and consequent inability to find alternative work complicated his situation. He was also not picking up the management signals that were telling him that his time was up. Finally, the management gathered courage to admit its mistake and GRV was sacked in a quick operation. For a few years he remained without work. Under the accumulated stress of failures and absence of alternatives he met a premature end due to heart failure, when he was just around his mid forties.

KRD or Kirti Raju Damodaran

KRD came from a middle class rural Andhra background: He was a Kamma, a landowning community known for its resourcefulness. An engineer by training, he specialized in sugar manufacturing. In the late 1980s, a premier research laboratory in Hyderabad had made substantial progress towards development of technologies for production of agrochemicals, which were experiencing, at that time, a significant demand surge. In India, it was a time for self-reliance and import substitution: Any effort in this direction was appreciated by state agencies as well as in the corporate world.

Due to the presence of some friends and contacts in the subject laboratory, this energetic and ambitious engineer came to be aware of the emerging market opportunity in relation to this product group: He decided to expeditiously enter this field with his meagre resources. He received encouragement and support, financial and otherwise, from his previous employer—a local sugar industrialist.

A scientist from the subject laboratory, possessing hands-on experience with the new technology for Monocrotophos, a broad-spectrum insecticide of growing demand volume, too joined hands with KRD, or say that the latter was able to rope in this technologist as an insurance for his maiden business enterprise. While the two worked hard in the initial stages of project implementation, their conflicting personalities too could not manage but exhibit a high degree of incompatibility. KRD was ambitious, egoistic and brash: He could not tolerate any one other than himself getting any importance or credit in the corporate of his creation. The other collaborator was mild by nature and in expression: He was primarily an output-oriented person but carried adequate self-respect. The short period of their working together, just enough for project commissioning, led to crystallization of their incompatibilities.

Within the early years of project operation, the two were able to separate with a manageable load of acrimony: KRD assumed full control of the project and his estranged collaborator departed to establish his own enterprise, covering the same market segment, at a distance of over five hundred miles. And he met with substantial success in his maiden individual enterprise.

During the years that followed, KRD's project turned out a true cash cow, enabling him to emerge as a dependable and significant supplier of Monocrotophos. His standing and reputation in the Indian agrochemical industry grew substantially. Enthused by the success, his ego inflated substantially and, with considerable abandon, he threw himself into:

- 18-20 hours a day work schedule,
- Intense multitasking, and
- Plotting further expansion of his business.

Aware of being overworked, he attempted to entice a number of professionals from the industry, including his ex-colleagues, with good salaries and even better promises. But, being a victim of ***high ego-concentration*** (HEC), trust-deficit, and intolerance towards anyone attracting any importance in the organization, he could not retain any one of them. Further, with most of them he spoiled his acquaintance and friendship. His reputation in the industry, as an employer, suffered beyond repair. He either did not know the delicate art of delegation or his egoistic self did not permit him to trust any one for anything that was viewed or had potential for significance in the company, financial or otherwise. The fact that he was not professionally trained or experienced in the art of man-management dawned on him only when the damage was done.

On account of these and several other deficits of his personality, he was left with no option but depend upon only young and inexperienced technocrats. He was specifically incapable of working with talented and experienced persons, even when they exhibited a slight superiority over him in any segment of production, marketing or other segments of business. He did not like any one who happened to be equal or more intelligent than him except the freshers whom he could, at least for short periods, bring under the spell of his business success.

As a consequence of his personality deficits and inability to adopt the requisite level of professionalism, he overstressed and over-stretched himself. As the author had warned him, he died young without adequately enjoying the fruits of his hard work, and/or creating adequate mechanism to sustain the business in his absence. The need for a succession plan had never crossed his mind. Despite several merits and strengths, he became a great corporate mis-manager.

KNS or Krishna Narayan Sharma

KNS was a puny and foxy character: His under-endowed physicality seemed to give him an inferiority complex, though he exhibited complete avoidance of the same. His mental endowments more than compensated for his physical deficiency. Though he was sharp and intelligent, but, in front of superiors and bosses, he tended to be non-committal and foxy. Irrespective of the composition of the audience, he could talk for hours, without saying anything. He was master of commitment avoidance: Whether in the company of seniors or juniors, it did not really matter. His skills of escapism or commitment avoidance were legendary.

He was, in fact, a pure thought-warrior, and action avoidance was one of his several non-performance skills. More than action, he was scared of its consequences: He was not unhappy if anyone from within or outside of his department took action, which otherwise should have originated from him. Most probably, he had not read the works of ***Lord Krishna*** or he did not trust his teachings in regard to action and result expectation. For him thought itself was an action.

After his doctorate from Germany, and a few years of work experience, he had gravitated to a Bhopal-based MNC, where he headed a section of its R&D department. In the year 1974, when the author entered his department as a young commercial researcher, he had a group of five knowledge workers—all of them well-qualified and experienced in their individual specialties. However, without exception, all of them were terribly unhappy and insecure, almost on verge of active depression. They did not know how to deal with their crafty boss, in any successful manner. He had developed the art of keeping them imbalanced. He had, through the technique of ***constant fault finding*** (CFF), perfected a methodology of making them feel that they were good for nothing—and that the management was terribly unhappy with their performance. He seemed to possess expertise in the usage of fear of management as a tool to browbeat his juniors.

There seemed a design in his madness of human resources mismanagement. For years together, he succeeded in passing his own non-performance as a deficiency on the part of his juniors. He always gave one picture to his bosses and an entirely different one to the juniors. He skillfully avoided development of any decisive displeasure of the management.

Progressively, his mismanagement relating to inaction, decision avoidance, ***non-acceptance of accountability*** (NAA), and performance credit distribution was exposed—and the senior management started to doubt all his actions and excuses. It led to his transfer to inconsequential positions, and finally he was eased out of the company in a most unceremonious manner. His bosses insulted him in apparent and conspicuous manner: Several times, it happened in the presence of the author. It seems that, on several occasions, these insulting sessions are deliberately designed to ignite his self-respect so as to force him out. But, more often than not, he seemed to absorb all intolerable insults and humiliation. As a flow of natural justice, he had to endure and tolerate much more humiliation and indignities than what he had collectively heaped upon all of his subordinates in approximately two decades for which he was able to perpetuate his ingenious human resources mismanagement specialties.

Even on his home front he had to pay for his excessive cunning and foxy nature: His wife understood him well and she often gave him adequate punishments in terms of verbal comments and nagging. His only son too imbibed some of his unrighteousness and, despite the elder's substantial gift of riches and properties he received unexpectedly huge mistreatment at the youngster's hands. In the final analysis, the great mis-manager had mismanaged his own life to a dreadful extent.

KSC or Karam Singh Chaudhri

For all practical purposes, KSC was a first-generation entrepreneur with meagre financial resources. His professional management exposure and experience too was inadequate. Soon after graduation and a brief stint with a Delhi-based family business group, at a very low level, he started with KIL which was started as a small scale unit by his father, initially with the express purpose of doing some job work for an established Indian business house active in the field of agrochemicals. After the initial hiccups normally associated with new enterprises, the business at KIL grew well under the overall direction of KSC's father who had had substantial grounding with a MNC. Father and son while forming a performing team exhibited sharp differences of perception and style. Except a brief setback in the mid 1980s, KIL grew into a medium-scale unit employing over a hundred people.

Towards the late 1990s, with the liberalization of the Indian business scene, competitiveness in this business sector grew substantially. In the meantime, the protective umbrella in the form of his father's presence was also gone. Being aware of the high negativity content of KSC's personality, other family members had kept away from the KIL business process. In terms of growth and complexities, KIL's business had grown to the maximum level where competence limitations of KSC started to show their limiting influences.

As per peculiarities of his personality, training and exposure, KSC suffered from several deficits—of which the confidence deficit, trust deficit, technology deficit, information deficit, delegation deficit, decision speed deficit, just to enumerate only the major ones, and the same started to limit the quality of management and consequently corporate performance. Insecurity and trust deficit complexities had persuaded him to associate two of his cousins with the business. While it looked a helpful and wise decision in the beginning, it showed the seeds of non-professionalism on the one hand, and made him susceptible to ear lending, on the other. It also landed him in the unprofessional habit of inflating the purchase costs, right in the beginning, as an effort for an unearned and advance profit grabbing. Further, it also magnified his incapabilities of dealing with professionals in a professional manner. His unrealistic self, in a mysterious manner, wanted every white-collar worker to work and behave in a meek and subdued manner—and put in extra hours even when the need for the same was not justified or pressing.

KSC's management deficiencies became apparent in numerous areas—of which the following were distinctively visible.

- The habit of getting involved in everything,
- Avoidable nitty-grittying,
- Inability to prioritize for management time allotment,
- Inability to delegate even inconsequential matters,
- Lack of faith in corporate structuring and job specialization,
- Righteous credit and discredit apportioning,
- Fear of appreciating any person or his/her actions and output,
- Expecting people to assume responsibilities in an informal and unassigned manner,
- Excessive negativity concentration,
- Fear of failure—and hence, inability to trust, including his own decisions,
- Fear of delegation of any authority,
- Inability for effective crisis management,
- Inability to give and give-in gracefully,
- Excessive multitasking, and
- Commitment appreciation.

Mismanagement of a variety of types, including that of human resources, corporate finances, production facilities, products and processes, talent and technologies, opportunities for association and performance, time and timing, communication, and confidence and commitment became a hallmark of his personality.

Towards the later years of the first decade of the 21st century, cumulative effects of mismanagement began to manifest in a multilateral manner: KIL, as a corporate, exhibited strains of a chronic disease of management and systems failure, some of which manifested in form of the following.

- Substantial accumulation of suppliers' bills,
- Drastic dislocation of raw materials purchase process,
- Dislocation of production process—and drying up of supplies to market,
- Non-fulfillment of commitments to customers from whom advances for specific supplies were obtained,
- Non-payment of salaries and travel dues of employees for months together,
- Accumulation of contractors and transporters' bills,
- Internal and external communication breakdown, and all other ills, which a mismanagement afflicted corporate could possibly attract.

The process of uncontrolled mismanagement led to dislocation of the logical thinking process—and the resultant decisions and actions, which a performing management could never afford to let happen.

PG or Parvin Gaud

PG was a fashionable MBA equipped executive of a Bhopal-based MNC. He was employed with the materials department of the company. Substantially egoistic, he seemed to suffer from massive mis-assessment of his capabilities. Suppliers' favoured treatment to purchase-men of a MNC had possibly spoiled the thought and action responses of PG and also most of his other coworkers.

In the middle 1970s, the company found that it was carrying an excessive employee load in the purchase department—and, at the same time, its sales and marketing department wanted to add more hands for better market coverage.

The company's senior management thought it fit to relocate a few extra hands from materials and production to the sales and marketing department. Since the author was managing the northern region of the sales and marketing operations, which were in principle deficient in manpower, a few of the surplus hands were allotted to him. PW was one of the components of the lot.

He suffered initial adjustment pangs as sales and marketing in the agrochemical operations of the company was substantially different and possibly a more difficult work area. Reluctantly, PG saw the realities of life and adjusted to the situation. Finally, he was polished into a productive salesman.

NT or Neeraj Tomari

NT managed the sales and marketing arm of KIL: He was located at Bahtinda. As a performing ego-concentrate, he had worked hard to establish the marketing network of the company.

He took good care of his staff and thus had established good command on the operations of the company in his area of control.

The CEO of the company loved NT's performance and the benefits that accrued from the same. He was, however, uncomfortable with NT's ways of management and standards of living. But, he could not say anything on account of the lack of risk taking capabilities with which he suffered.

KSC, the CEO of the company, suspected that NT and the finance head of the company had developed some unholy alliance—but was not able to actively voice his concerns due to his personality limitations.

After a lot of dilly-dallying, NT was finally transferred to the head quarters of the company, and, in an unrighteous manner, the CEO attempted to groom an assistant of NT to step into the position of his boss. It created huge problems of coordination and performance for the company and, in a decisive manner, pushed the company down-the hill.

RNS or Ram Naresh Saroff

RNS came from the renowned Marwari community and carried some of its typical characteristics. He exhibited substantial control over what he said: Commitment avoidance thus came naturally to him. He was an engineer by training but no residue of any technicalities were visible in him, either in overt or covert manner, when the author came in contact with him.

He worked for a large family-run business house located at Kolkata: It was his first as well as last job: He seemed incapable of taking risks or separating from the roots that he had grown with the said business group. His father too had spent his lifetime in service of the same business house, and in light of it, RNS seemed to follow the tradition. In the said business group he was known as a person who ensured failure of whatsoever he managed or attempted. Further, no subordinate of his was ever known to have succeeded in doing anything substantial. In his early fifties, he looked more weather beaten than the actual length of his non-performing career. With this awesome reputation and over two decades of non-performance, he was assigned the not so glamorous job of handling a sick company of the group. It was known as UKBM and had two non-performing units—one at Kolkata and another located at Ankleswar, the industrial hub of Gujarat. The latter dealt with production of agrochemicals: It was established to commercially exploit a recently developed technology by RRL, Hyderabad. Despite good potential, it was a substantially mismanaged unit.

In 1987, the author joined this group with the express purpose of infusing some economic viability into the agrochemical unit referred to earlier. Early discussions with RNS and his key subordinates threw ample light on the precarious condition of this unit. Here, production seemed to run with halting gasps: There was no dependable system of quality control for raw materials and/or finished goods. Product packaging was deficient to the extent that unconsumed/unsold goods came back to the factory in precarious condition, often in outer containers employed by the competition for this purpose. Dealers and sales staff of the company were unhappy with the poor quality of the packaging of its products: Yet, thanks to divine providence, the company's products carried a good performance perception at the level of dealers as well as the consumer farmers.

The sales and marketing operations of the company presented a sad state of affairs. For considerations of scale of operation and physical coverage of the agro-markets, sales and distribution of its products was unintelligently outsourced to a MNC. And the terms set for this purpose were grossly in favour of the marketer: And the latter employed the assigned resources entirely to its own benefit. Sales proceeds, though very small in volume, did not reach the producer company even in a tolerably inefficient manner. Certain state-territories-wise sales and marketing arrangements smelt of unfair dealings.

The task of re-organization seemed fairly challenging, where normal methods of working or window dressing that did not unsettle the vested interests involved, did not seem to possess even remote chances of success. Purchase, production, quality control, packaging, transport and several other relevant areas of work and output were being ground to pieces between the two stones that existed there in the form of two senior employees, here referred to as Joshis. Hence, in order to discontinue the grinding pressure, one of the two stones had to be removed. There was no other viable alternative. Though unpleasant, the only available way out had to be pushed through.

Frank discussions at the MD level and the latter's desire to unshackle the company from a multitude of man-made inefficiencies, led to acceptance of the author's proposal for removal of one of the stones, and placing the same in a non-critical position. It was indeed a difficult decision to be taken in view of the vitally viewed considerations of loyalty that normally got associated with the length of service in such corporate bodies. Though apparently supportive, the mis-manager within RNS was not happy. He was, however, too meek to rise in support of his own inefficiencies.

Initiation of improvements in packaging of goods, transport, and supply coupled with the opening-up of the market, brought encouraging responses from the trade. Performance linked incentives energized the newly assembled and trained sales force. Within months of these improvement initiations, one of the company's leading products started challenging the long established MNC brand, which was based upon the same generic inputs. The company's productivity, brand image, and bottom line made positive leaps.

RNS went along these actions of improvement; he even seemed to enjoy the resultant spurt of activity. He made frequent visits to Ankleswar—and his scavenging habits continued unabated. His supplies of tur-dal, peanuts and papadam (all three were local food items) were arranged well in advance by the local plant in-charge. In my view it was a small price to bear in the interests of work harmony and non-interference.

RCD OR RAM CHAND DEWAN

RCD was the second senior most person in the newly-formed division of agrochemicals at IARI, New Delhi, when the author joined the division as a doctoral student. Despite his mediocre qualifications, intellect and personality, he was afflicted with a fat ego. He gave it ample expressions while dealing with students and junior staff of the laboratory. He attempted to assume scientific and intellectual capabilities without in fact possessing the same.

Within a few months of the author joining the department, RCD felt that his primacy was being threatened. Since the department's staff and students were scared of contacting the head of the department for their day-to-day problems and RCD did not have a helpful attitude, they started coming to the author for necessary guidance and assistance.

RCD felt challenged with this development: Fired with unnecessary insecurities he started to feed untruths to his head of the department, in regard to the day-to-day work and developments in the laboratory. The head of the department was a wise and scholarly scientist and could easily see through RCD's discomfiture. He advised RCD to perform his own work output and not to bother about matters, which did not directly concern him.

Though disheartened a little, he did not give up his habit of resorting to avoidable feedback.

RCD had a small laboratory entirely for himself: It was stocked with some rickety and out-of-service equipment. Being an ego and negativity concentrate, he did not allow any other scientific worker and/or student to touch the same. He was like a rat with a piece of cloth that had proclaimed himself as a wholesale cloth merchant.

His ego was progressively deflated in the course of some seminars and presentations, which were regularly organized in the department. Further, he was pursuing his doctoral studies as a departmental candidate and for this purpose had to attend some courses. Being an old hand at the institute, he was managing to secure reasonably good grades through his contacts and colleagues. However, he got exposed while attending a course of statistics, which was compulsory for all the doctoral students. There, the teachers conducting the course were strict and RCD did not have any favourable contacts. As such, he was a poor student and found statistics very difficult to handle. During this period, he attempted to befriend the author—and during the examinations made a point to sit next to him. When he found it impossible to tackle the questions, he gathered courage to ask the author to lend him the completed answer books to copy from. In this process, he himself punctured his own ego balloon.

In another course, he disgraced himself by arranging to obtain 'A' grade without attending classes. It became an issue of open conflict and the course in-charge had to make amendments under pressure from deserving students. His acts of mismanagement became the talk of the department. Finally, he was divested of all the powers that he had enjoyed as a second-in-command.

RCT or Ramesh Chand Tyagi

RCT was a more dangerous mis-manager than RNS. He too was an engineer and had served the same business group for long. He was a shrewd operator and had developed skills with which he did not allow failures resulting from his mismanagement to stick to his own persona in any manner.

UKMB was gaining steam of performance and its market image had improved substantially, encouraged by which expansion of its product range was planned through addition of Monocrotophos and its associated products. Preparation of project report, internal approvals, sanctions from financial institutions, pollution clearance and most other formalities were completed by the end of 1990, when RCT gate-crashed to appropriate RNS's position as head of operations of the company. He had closed down a group unit and as a reward for mismanagement, claimed this position as UKBM was now on the path of expansion. It presented a good opportunity for the mismanager in RCT to grab an unearned cut in the course of project implementation. RNS was unhappy to see control of a happening project slip through his fingers, but he was too mild a mismanager to protest loudly or walk away with dignity.

RCT attempted, as most mismanagers do have a tendency, to bring in his old team of mismanagers so that his designs on financial mismanagement were neatly implemented. In the process, he developed an active conflict of interest with the author as the latter's presence was sure to be inconvenient to him in his acts of mismanagement. The author could see the shade of things as they were to unfold under the mismanaging presence of RCT and, prior to his disassociation from the company for revival of which he had worked hard, he had predicted that the great mismanager in RCT was sure to bring the company back to a sorry state of affairs. RCT and his team did active scavenging of financial resources, as they were accustomed to from their accumulated experience, and within a year, the company fell into severe financial crisis that led to its eventual closure in a year's time.

RCT, as per his well-practised strategy, moved out after skinning the company to maximum limits. RNS came back to take charge of the company that was taking its last gasps of air, as a seasoned scavenger.

SM or Sayad Miraj

SM was a Chennai-based second-generation businessman. His father had created businesses in shipping, export and imports, and real estate. As a young man, SM had acquired several wayward and extravagant habits—and despite the active efforts of the old man, he earned no professional qualification and/or experience. He looked introvert and had expensive tastes.

When in his thirties, his father forced him to establish himself as a separate entity. He was given charge of a basic chemicals unit and a beach located five-star hotel property that was given on a long lease to a renowned hotel group. He was installed as one of the non-working directors of the subject hotel company. The senior had thought that it would give him an opportunity to interact with seasoned professionals and in the process he might pick up some basic strands of management. These legitimate expectations of a father did not seem to materialize. SM had employed two finance persons, related to each other, for managing his business. Both of them were extra cunning and truly foxy characters. SM was a poor judge of people: Further, he suffered from a chronic disease of ear lending. The foxy pair had mastered the art of saying "Yes Sir" and managing to boss to their benefit. SM misunderstood it as their loyalty. Further, his capacity to understand financial reports/balance-sheets, etc., was limited.

The duo understood SM's limitations fully well and planned accordingly to defraud him. It was observed in the course of implementation of a greenfield project for manufacture of a specialty agrochemical, for which the author and a technocrat friend of his had joined SM with specific commitments for mutual benefit. The project, including technology transfer, product quality, and production costs, etc., proceeded well. In terms of timing too, only minor overruns occurred in the process of implementation. The foxy friends of SM, despite their routine financial manipulations and cuts, did not like their boss coming under the influence of technocrats. When project operations turned fully smooth and local staff were fully trained in its operation and maintenance, the duo worked hard on the boss for the need to save expenses that were being made on the technical experts associated with the project. Intellectually SM was no match for their manipulative ear feeding—and came to understand their game only when it was too late.

Fed up with the internal politics the two technocrats, including the author, separated from the project. The duo was left with a free hand to mismanage both the businesses of the mismanaging proprietor. The two had persuaded SM to put up a textile dyes unit, despite clear advice against it from the technocrats. The pair had planned to corner a substantial part of investment through a fake consultant. With attractive presentations and a vice like hold on the thought as well as action capabilities of SM, the two succeeded in pushing him into this project with unsustainable bank financing.

As anticipated, the project failed to materialize, in terms of output and quality. In the meantime, market conditions deteriorated and the whole project turned into a bad idea. Funds from the agrochemicals unit too were diverted to save the crumbling business—and, as a result, both the units slumped into intractable red—beyond the capability of the mis-managing trio to resurrect the same. Both the units were taken over and auctioned after years of effort, by the financial institutions. SM, as an unavoidable punishment of mismanagement, had to sell off some of his old properties to settle accumulated dues. Financial stringency resulting from the development put some limits on his wayward lifestyle and extra-spending habits. The duo of his favoured financial wizards had left him high and dry.

References

1. Deepak Chopra (1999), "*Everyday Immortality*," Random House, London, SWIV 2SA.
2. U.V. Singh (2008), "*Management Wisdom of Lord Krishna*," New Century Publications, Daryaganj, New Delhi.
3. Peter F. Drucker (2000), "*The Practive of Management*," Butterworth-Heinamann, Jordan Hill, Oxford OX28DP.
4. C. K. Prahalad and Gary Hamel (1990), "*The Core Competence of Corporation*," Harvard Business School, May-June, 1990.
5. Mahatma Gandhi: Essays and Reflections on His Life and Works, edited by S. Radhakrishnan, London, 1939.
6. R. Gopalakrishnan (2007), "*The Case of Bonsai Manager*," Penguin Portfolio, India New Delhi.

Index

The Author

Dr. Udai Vir Singh is a management consultant specializing in productivity improvement acceleration (PIA) in corporate work environments.

He possesses a brilliant academic record, and a Ph.D. in 1966 from IARI, New Delhi. He has also earned a Post-Doctorate from CNRA, Versailles, France.

Early in his professional life, he entered the corporate work environment, passing through diverse fields of research, product development, marketing, market development, project planning, production, technology upgradation, technology transfer, business diversification and productivity acceleration, and garnered an indepth and varied experience over 40 years. In the latter part of his career, he concentrated on management training and consultancy work aimed at collective work output acceleration for a number of corporates.

Throughout his career, Dr. Singh attempted to sustain an active mix of thought and activism. He has been a keen student of human nature and its manifestation in collective work environments. He developed and productively employed several of his thought formulations in many intense and challenging work assignments. Of these, the theory of bio-lethargy, theory of negativity, law of stress balance, and principle of potential interaction were fruitfully employed. The HPLC system of manpower selection and deployment proved particularly effective in non-urban work environments. Some of the above concepts and formations will be converted for publication in the near future for the benefit of corporate professionals.

The fact that intelligence needs to be coupled with wisdom for sustained results in corporate working led Dr. Singh to assign priority to complete the present work. Further, the recent emergence of the great fraud of Satyam necessitated a wider study of the subject of corporate mismanagement by all those exposed to the business work environment.

His first book, the *Management Wisdom of Lord Krishna*, was published in 2008, which was widely acclaimed.

Dr. Singh's recent occupation with human nature and its interactions with practical philosophies led to another work entitled, *Gandhian Philosophy for Elimination of Terrorism*, which is scheduled for publication this year.

READERS ARE WELCOME!

Corporate readers, while going through this book, are likely to recollect various instances of mismanagement encountered and/or witnessed by them during the course of their working life. They are welcome to convey them to the author on udaivisingh@yahoo.co.in, which might be selected for inclusion/narration in the next edition with due acknowledgement.